Setting Standards in Graduate Education

Setting Standards in Graduate Education

PSYCHOLOGY'S COMMITMENT to EXCELLENCE in ACCREDITATION

EDITED BY
Elizabeth M. Altmaier

AMERICAN PSYCHOLOGICAL ASSOCIATION
WASHINGTON, DC

Copyright © 2003 by the American Psychological Association. All rights reserved. Except as permitted under the United States Copyright Act of 1976, no part of this publication may be reproduced or distributed in any form or by any means, or stored in a database or retrieval system, without the prior written permission of the publisher.

Published by
American Psychological Association
750 First Street, NE
Washington, DC 20002
www.apa.org

To order
APA Order Department
P.O. Box 92984
Washington, DC 20090-2984
Tel: (800) 374-2721; Direct: (202) 336-5510
Fax: (202) 336-5502; TDD/TTY: (202) 336-6123
Online: www.apa.org/books/
Email: order@apa.org

In the U.K., Europe, Africa, and the Middle East, copies may be ordered from
American Psychological Association
3 Henrietta Street
Covent Garden, London
WC2E 8LU England

Typeset in Goudy by Stephen McDougal, Mechanicsville, MD

Printer: Sheridan Books, Ann Arbor, MI
Cover Designer: Berg Design, Albany, NY
Technical/Production Editor: Jennifer L. Zale

The opinions and statements published are the responsibility of the authors, and such opinions and statements do not necessarily represent the policies of the American Psychological Association.

Library of Congress Cataloging-in-Publication Data

Setting standards in graduate education : psychology's commitment to excellence in accreditation / edited by Elizabeth M. Altmaier—1st ed.
    p. cm.
  Includes bibliographical references and index.
  ISBN 1-59147-009-9 (alk. paper)
  1. Psychology—Study and teaching (Graduate)—United States—History.
I. Altmaier, Elizabeth M.
BF80.7.U6S48 2003
150'.71'73—dc21
                                                                                                   2003005129

British Library Cataloguing-in-Publication Data
A CIP record is available from the British Library.

Printed in the United States of America
First Edition

CONTENTS

Contributors vii

Preface ix

    Introduction 3
              Elizabeth M. Altmaier

    Chapter 1.   Accreditation in Psychology and Public
                  Accountability 7
                  Paul D. Nelson and Laura C. Messenger

    Chapter 2.   The History of Accreditation of Doctoral
                  Programs in Psychology 39
                  Elizabeth M. Altmaier

    Chapter 3.   The History of Accreditation of Internship
                  Programs and Postdoctoral Residencies 61
                  Cynthia D. Belar and Nadine Kaslow

    Chapter 4.   The Impact of Accreditation on the Practice of
                  Professional Psychology 91
                  Tommy T. Stigall

    Chapter 5.   The Future of Accreditation 113
                  Deborah C. Beidel, Susan D. Phillips, and
                  Susan Zlotlow

    Introduction to the Appendixes 135
                  Jason Kanz

Appendix A:	Excerpt From Loyal Crane's *Plea for the Training of Psychologists,* 1925	139
Appendix B:	Excerpt From "Graduate Internship Training in Psychology," 1945	141
Appendix C:	Excerpt From "Recommended Graduate Training Program in Clinical Psychology," 1947	147
Appendix D:	Excerpt From "Criteria for Evaluating Progress in Clinical or in Counseling Psychology," 1958	149
Appendix E:	Letters From Donald Marquis to Directors of Graduate Study at the Office of Psychological Personnel, 1945; David Wolfle to Robert Sears, 1946; and Robert Sears to the Committee on Graduate and Professional Training, 1946	151
Appendix F:	Excerpt From V. C. Raimy's "Accreditation of Training Universities" in *Training in Clinical Psychology,* 1950	159
Appendix G:	*Accrediting Procedures of the American Psychological Association,* 1970	167
Appendix H:	*Report of the Joint Council on Professional Education in Psychology,* 1990	169
Appendix I:	Listed Members of the Committee on Accreditation, Past and Present	173
Appendix J:	List of Conferences on Accreditation	177
Appendix K:	James McKeen Cattell's "Retrospect: Psychology as a Profession," 1937	181
Index		185
About the Editor		191

CONTRIBUTORS

Kenneth M. Adams, PhD, Ann Arbor Veterans Affairs Health System, Ann Arbor, MI
Elizabeth M. Altmaier, PhD, Division of Psychological and Quantitative Foundations, University of Iowa, Iowa City
Deborah C. Beidel, PhD, Department of Psychology, University of Maryland, College Park
Cynthia D. Belar, PhD, Education Directorate, American Psychological Association, Washington, DC
Kathleen R. Boggs, PhD, Counseling Center, and Department of Educational and Counseling Psychology, University of Missouri—Columbia
Annette M. Brodsky, PhD, Department of Psychiatry, Harbor–UCLA Medical Center, Torrance, CA
Martha Dennis Christiansen, PhD, Counseling and Consultation, Arizona State University, Tempe
Clyde A. Crego, PhD, Counseling and Psychological Service, California State University, Long Beach, and University of Southern California, Los Angeles
Ronald E. Fox, PhD, The Consulting Group, A Division of Human Resources Consultants, Chapel Hill, NC
Dorothy E. Holmes, PhD, Department of Clinical Psychology, George Washington University, Washington, DC, and Baltimore–Washington Institute for Psychoanalysis
Jason Kanz, MA, College of Education, University of Iowa, Iowa City
Nadine Kaslow, PhD, Department of Psychiatry and Behavioral Sciences, Emory University School of Medicine, Atlanta, GA
M. Marlyne Kilbey, PhD, Department of Psychology, Wayne State University, Detroit, MI

James H. Kleiger, PsyD, Private Practice, Bethesda, MD
Arthur L. Kovacs, PhD, California School of Professional Psychology, Alliant International University, Los Angeles
Douglas H. Lamb, PhD, Department of Psychology, Illinois State University, Normal
Laura C. Messenger, MA, University of Maryland, College Park
Stanley Moldawsky, PhD, Private Practice, Chatham, NJ, and Institute for Psychoanalysis and Psychotherapy of New Jersey, South Orange
Paul D. Nelson, PhD, Education Directorate, American Psychological Association, Washington, DC
Virginia E. O'Leary, PhD, Department of Psychology, Auburn University, Auburn, AL
Sidney A. Orgel, PhD, State University of New York Upstate Medical University, Syracuse
Susan D. Phillips, PhD, Department of Educational and Counseling Psychology, State University of New York, Albany
David H. Reilly, EdD, Office of Graduate Studies, The Citadel, Charleston, SC
Helen J. Roehlke, EdD, Counseling Center, University of Missouri—Colombia
Edward P. Sheridan, PhD, Division of Academic Affairs, University of Houston, Houston, TX
Tommy T. Stigall, PhD, The Psychological Corporation, Baton Rouge, LA
Susan Zlotlow, PhD, Office of Program Consultation and Accreditation, American Psychological Association, Washington, DC

PREFACE

This book describes psychology's 50-year history of accreditation, a complex system of self-regulation and quality enhancement in doctoral and postdoctoral education and training maintained by peer evaluation. As is outlined in the chapters that follow, psychology's "experiment" with accreditation has undergone many iterations, some changes coming in response to early outcomes of the experiment, some in response to influences outside of psychology within higher education, and some in response to factors in society at large. These influences have not disappeared; indeed, some loom larger on the horizon now than at any time in the history of specialized accreditation within psychology. Thus, although this book provides a look back and brief glimpses of what may lie ahead, it cannot conclude with any degree of confidence whether this experiment has succeeded or will succeed.

The *American Heritage Dictionary* includes the following definitions of *to serve*: to be of use, to be worthy of reliance or trust, to discharge a duty or function, to furnish something desired or needed, to answer the needs of.[1] The members of the Committee on Accreditation (CoA) over the years have truly *served* psychology and the psychological community. Although opinions may vary on the effectiveness of their efforts, or even the accuracy of their judgments, there should not be any disagreement on the difficulty of their task or the effort that they devoted toward its completion. All of the members of the CoA (and its predecessor committees in the American Psychological Association) during these 50 years are listed in Appendix I. To them, and to the public members of the CoA in particular, we are indebted.

This book brings together a number of people who authored chapters and who wrote "boxes." The latter are meant to add personal voices to the

---

[1]Morris, W. (Ed.). (1998). *The American Heritage dictionary of the English language*. Boston: Houghton Mifflin.

details of history, a richness that can be overwhelmed in a recitation of dates and events. The history of accreditation is actually a history of people's interactions with ideas and ideals, with the complications of personal context, and with systems both large and small, and thus the box authors' own experiences supplement the historical record.

I wish to thank my colleagues on the CoA during my tenure as member and chair for their obvious commitment to excellence, their sense of humor in stressful times, and their manifestations of both humility and pride. I also thank Paul Nelson for the idea of this book, a project generated through his love of history, his memory, and his voluminous archives. As members of the CoA can attest, Paul's guiding hand and clear thought are evident in most of the achievements within accreditation. I also thank Gwen Le and Patricia Martin of my university department who supported this project to completion.

The title of this book denotes my belief that excellence aspired to by programs in their training, by practitioners and researchers in their work, and by those serving the profession in their varied roles, is achieved only through an intense and personal commitment of people to each other and to the task at hand. That is my challenge to current and future members of the CoA, whatever their composition and reporting structure, so that the next 50 years will be characterized by as much progress as we have attained so far.

Setting Standards in Graduate Education

INTRODUCTION

ELIZABETH M. ALTMAIER

What activities are involved in this process called *accreditation* in psychology, and why are they always so controversial? These are questions that I believe will be answered for readers after they finish this book. Psychology has experienced 50 years, and a bit more, of specialized accreditation. Most knowledgeable people would define accreditation as a voluntary process of peer review with the goal of improving the quality of one's work. For psychology, accreditation is the voluntary review of doctoral programs, internships, and postdoctoral residencies by peers with the goals of monitoring the degree to which the unit achieves its own self-set objectives and outcomes and of improving its quality. It is hard to see why reasonable people would disagree with this activity, yet disagree they have and continue to do.

The chapter authors in this book are all people who have been intimately involved during the past 50 years with the sets of events that have shaped our current system of accreditation. Thus, readers are hearing from true experts who were "there" and have relayed their experiences as well as commented on them in the context of hindsight. Further, each chapter contains boxed text that features personal reflections of specific aspects of accreditation history. The box authors were chosen to represent a wide range of perspectives on accreditation and were given great latitude in that they were asked simply to "write about your personal views and experiences related to accreditation." Last, the appendixes contain a wealth of historical information (documents, reports, letters) that will give readers a contact with the events and decisions that are repeatedly referred to in the book.

The authors of chapter 1, Paul D. Nelson and Laura C. Messenger, are both associated with the Office of Program Consultation and Accreditation at the American Psychological Association (APA), Paul as former program director. Together they thoroughly explicate psychology's development of specialized accreditation within a context that comes as a surprise to many psychologists. Psychology is only one of many specialized accrediting disciplines, and its accreditation exists in the historical development of accreditation in the United States, a history that is itself fascinating and with many ties to the 50 years of developments related to accreditation within psychology. Boxes in this chapter were written by David Reilly on the use of a joint task force to resolve accreditation questions in the specialty of school psychology, by Clyde Crego on the importance and role of self-study, and by Arthur Kovacs on his personal experiences as a practitioner educator.

I wrote chapter 2, which traces the changes in accreditation scope, criteria, and procedures within the 50-year history of accreditation activities in psychology. Many changes in accreditation came about through the experiences of psychology educators and of the members of the Committee on Accreditation (CoA) with previous sets of criteria; other changes came about as other "constituencies" (practicing psychologists, consumers, students) gained influence via national conferences and other lobbying efforts. But in spite of the changes, several core issues have remained the same over the 50 years, and these issues are also defined in the chapter. Boxes for this chapter were written by former members of the CoA regarding their personal experiences: Dorothy Holmes on accrediting a doctoral program in a faith-based institution, Marlyne Kilbey on the function of a task force to define necessary changes in accreditation, and Virginia O'Leary on the occasion of her joining the "new" CoA after it was revised in 1992.

Cynthia D. Belar and Nadine Kaslow, psychologists with significant personal involvement in issues related to internship and postdoctoral training, authored chapter 3 on accreditation of those programs. Because students occupy very different roles as intern and as postgraduate resident than they do as students, accreditation issues for internships and postdoctoral residencies are different than for doctoral training programs but no less contentious and no less important for psychology to solve. Five psychologists with lengthy personal involvement in this aspect of training wrote the boxes for this chapter. Sidney Orgel describes his personal experiences serving as a site visitor for internship programs. Kathleen Boggs and Helen Roehlke both discuss accreditation activities as they affect counseling center internships. And James Kleiger and Annette Brodsky both offer descriptions of obtaining accreditation for postdoctoral residencies.

Practitioners should have much to say about how training programs operate because programs educate future practitioners as well as future academics. One significant source of influence was a commission chaired by Tommy T. Stigall, the author of chapter 4, on how professional psychologists should be prepared at the doctoral level. This chapter discusses how this commission, and other influences from the practice community, affected accreditation activities. Boxes written by Douglas Lamb on trainee impairment, by Ronald Fox on the different cultures of education and practice, and by Stanley Moldawsky on how science and practice found common ground during his tenure on the CoA are contained in this chapter as well.

Given the interesting, and sometimes contentious, history of accreditation traced during the first four chapters, it is important to think ahead to the future of accreditation, which is what the authors of chapter 5 do. Both Deborah C. Beidel and Susan D. Phillips are former chairs of the CoA; Susan Zlotlow is program officer for accreditation at APA. These three psychologists are in an ideal position to look backward over the 50 years of accreditation and then to look forward to the next 50 years in terms of key issues to resolve. Boxes for this chapter were authored by psychologists who were also former members of the CoA and are currently serving in positions at their own institutions from which they can also have a sense of the future in light of the past. Martha Christiansen describes her personal history with accreditation activities in many roles, Kenneth Adams discusses how accreditation conflicts mirror those of our profession, and Edward Sheridan provides a provost's perspective on both the history and future of accreditation.

There are many historical documents related to the past 50 years in accreditation: reports, letters, meeting minutes, task force recommendations, and so on. The appendixes, introduced by Jason Kanz, provide only the minutest glimpse at these documents but do present a complete historical sampling of them. I wish to note that many of the historical documents related to accreditation are in my possession, and I would be happy to share them with interested readers on request.

After reading this book, readers will be more familiar with the conceptual and contextual issues that influence accreditation's criteria, scope, and procedures and also with some key figures who have made an impact on these activities. It is also to be hoped that readers will be stimulated to become involved in accreditation activities as a site visitor, a committee member, or an informed respondent on accreditation issues.

1
ACCREDITATION IN PSYCHOLOGY AND PUBLIC ACCOUNTABILITY

PAUL D. NELSON AND LAURA C. MESSENGER

In December 1945, the Board of Directors of the American Psychological Association (APA) received from the Veterans Administration (VA) a request for a list of universities whose graduate departments of psychology had the requisite capabilities to train clinical psychologists at the doctoral level of education. Within a year, the U.S. Public Health Service (PHS) made a similar request of the APA (Sears, 1947; see Appendix E, this volume). The impetus for these requests was threefold in nature. First, psychologists during World War II had demonstrated the value of their discipline to the public through applied research and clinical practice. Second, in the war's aftermath, with significant numbers of returning veterans in need of psychological services, there was a dramatic increase in the need for psychologists in the public sector of health care. Third, to increase the supply of psychologists to meet these needs for service, there were public funds available to support the training of clinical psychologists at the doctoral level.

The APA's response to these requests from public agencies was positive and as prompt as might be expected of a national professional organization, but was not without challenge (APA Committee on Training in Clinical Psychology, 1947, 1948, 1949; Sears, 1947). As chapter 2 details, the reports of the committees established to identify academic departments suitable for the task went beyond simply listing universities with appropriate graduate education facilities in clinical psychology. These reports also set forth the first set of published accreditation criteria and procedures for assessing quality among doctoral programs in clinical psychology. Within a few years, criteria and procedures would be adopted for use in evaluating doctoral programs in counseling psychology and, a decade after that, for doctoral programs in school psychology.

In the process of developing these criteria and procedures, several concerns were raised. Most notable were the following, summarized by Sheridan, Matarazzo, and Nelson (1995). First was the fear that the imposition of criteria for judging the quality of clinical training in graduate education departments would stifle the innovation and freedom of inquiry so vital to scholarly growth, a concern that remains as valid today as it was 50 years ago and one that historically has been inherent in the accreditation of postsecondary education institutions and programs. The second pertained to the question of whether and, if so, how science and professional training can be integrated, or even coexist, in academic departments. This concern reflects the nature and history of psychology's dual identity as a science and a profession.

Thus was born accreditation in professional psychology, conceived in response to public need and subsequently validated in terms of public accountability. In serving the general public, accreditation in psychology, as in other professions, must balance the value orientations and expectations of the academy (i.e., faculty and administration of higher education institutions) and those who regulate and practice the profession. Ultimately, however, accreditation must benefit the public. How that goal has been articulated and achieved in accreditation generally, and in psychology specifically, is the focus of the present chapter. The goal of public benefit, and its corollary responsibility of public accountability through self-regulation, is a value common to accreditation and the professions (Nelson, 1998; Nelson & Aletky, 1987; Peterson, 1976). It is also a value that has characterized higher education in this country from the colonial days (Bok, 1990).

PUBLIC ACCESS TO EDUCATION: THE NEED FOR STANDARDS

Higher education in America began with a sense of responsibility to the greater community, thus serving the public. Preparing teachers, clergy, others of the learned professions, and leaders of moral integrity among those relatively few citizens privileged to be so educated was clearly a part of the mission among our earliest colleges. At the same time, these early American education institutions also preserved many of the traditional values of the academy as an independent community of scholars, the primary purpose of which was to declare and advance knowledge. Although disputes over matters of curriculum began early, even among these historically select institutions, the public need for standards of higher education was not a salient issue. The higher education institutions of that day were relatively few in number and elite in terms of who they educated. By the mid-19th century, however, the relationship between institutions of higher education and the general public changed significantly.

As the American frontier moved westward, as the population grew, and as seeds of the industrial revolution took root in what remained a highly agrarian society, the public need for increased access to higher education led to the Land Grant Acts of the 1860s and 1890s, and the consequent establishment of land grant colleges and universities. During the same period, public secondary school systems grew significantly. In addition to increasing public access to education, the developments of this period resulted in increased numbers of and greater diversity among education institutions, a characteristic that defines current American higher education. Of additional consequence was the establishment of the Bureau of Education with the passage of the first Land Grant (Morrill) Act of 1862. This was the first major interjection of the federal government in American education affairs. The role of the new federal bureau was also important in the history of accreditation, its primary purpose being the collection and publication of data on schools and colleges in the United States.

The formation of regional associations of colleges and secondary schools following the Civil War sowed the seeds for accreditation activities in the United States. This process began in 1885 with the New England Association of Schools and Colleges and continued through 1962 with the formation of the Western Association of Schools and Colleges (preceded since 1948 by the Western College Association). In their earlier years, Bemis (1983) pointed out, the formal process of accreditation as it is known today was not a major objective of these associations. Rather, they developed definitions of secondary and postsecondary institutions and standards of articulation between requirements for high school graduation and admission to colleges within the various geographic regions represented by the associations (Bemis, 1983; Young, 1983). Perhaps more closely approximating the origins of accreditation at a national level was the 1906 meeting of the National Association of State Universities to establish a plan for college admission standards across regions of the country in the face of increasing numbers of students migrating from one state to another for their education (Young, 1983). By 1909, however, the North Central Association of Colleges and Secondary Schools, which had begun accrediting high schools four years earlier, had drawn up standards for the accreditation of colleges in its region, thus leading the way to institutional accreditation by regional associations. By 1913, the North Central Association published the first public list of accredited colleges (Bemis, 1983).

Thus, Young (1983) asserted, the formative years for what was to become the state of higher education in America during the 20th century were those between the Civil War and World War I, a period labeled by McConn (1935) as "the Age of Standards." Woodrow Wilson, then president of Princeton University, addressed the Middle States Association of Colleges and Schools in 1907:

> We are on the eve of a period of reconstruction. We are on the eve of a period when we are going to set up standards. We are on the eve of a period of synthesis, when, tired of this dispersion and standardless analysis, we are going to put things together into something like a connected and thought-out scheme of endeavor. It is inevitable. (cited in Young, 1983, pp. 4–5)

GROWTH OF THE PROFESSIONS: THE NEED FOR STANDARDS

During the same time period as the initiation of regional associations, another related development was under way in the professions, most notably in the medical profession, for which the quality of education was of major concern by the end of the 19th century (Glidden, 1983; Young, 1983). At that time, medicine was in the process of transformation from an apprenticeship system to science-based education integrated with clinical teaching (Starr, 1982). The earliest efforts to improve standards for medical education came from the medical schools themselves, having organized themselves first into the American Medical College Association in 1876 and subsequently into the Association of American Medical Colleges in 1890. In years that followed, the major medical practitioner organization, the American Medical Association (AMA), also became involved in medical education and, by 1904, had established the Council of Medical Education (CME). The CME subsequently developed a rating system of medical schools and a process for on-site review, both of which led to the first public classification of medical schools by 1907. In addition, the AMA collaborated with the Carnegie Foundation in a formal study of medical education and contracted educator Abraham Flexner to be the principal investigator for the project. The report, later published by Flexner (1925) in a broader context, was highly critical of medical education at the turn of the century and led to the transformation of medical schools and education in the United States. In so doing, it provided a foundation of standards for what would become the first case of specialized accreditation: that is, accreditation of professional education and training schools and programs. The report called for the elimination of proprietary medical schools. It also recommended that medical schools be an integral part of universities, where full-time faculty could teach the scientific foundations of medicine, conduct research necessary to advance clinical practice, and provide clinical supervision of medical students in university-affiliated hospitals. This thus led to the concept of teaching hospitals, which became a significant feature of medical education in the United States.

Although there were certain prescriptive qualities to the recommendations set forth in what became known as the Flexner Report, less often acknowledged from that report was a more philosophical paradigm for medical education, as follows:

> the medical school cannot expect to produce fully trained doctors; it can at most hope to equip students with a limited amount of knowledge, to train them in the method and spirit of scientific medicine and to launch them with momentum that will make them active learners–observers, readers, thinkers, and experimenters—for years to come. (Flexner, 1925, p. 176)

Law is another profession for which the roots of accreditation lie early in the 20th century. The Association of American Law Schools by 1900 had standards for membership that were related to criteria for quality of legal education (Glidden, 1983). In 1921, the American Bar Association had begun its own law school review process from which it published an annual list of schools that met "minimum standards" (Cardoza, 1975).

In the examples of medicine and law, it is significant to note that two types of associations were involved in setting education standards and developing a quality review process for education in their professions. These were the associations that represented the profession's educators (i.e., the association of their professional school deans) and the profession's practitioners (i.e., their professional membership associations). Initially, within each profession, these different associations worked independently on issues of education standards and accreditation; but over time they collaborated, with quite different structures of collaboration operative today for accreditation in these two professions.

Yet other models of specialized accreditation were to come, and by 1930 the list of professions with one form or another of accreditation practices included, in addition to law and medicine, dentistry, landscape architecture, library science, music, nursing, optometry, teacher education, and collegiate business education (Glidden, 1983). Had psychology developed professionally following World War I as it did after World War II, it might have been among these early accrediting professions.

INSTITUTIONAL AND SPECIALIZED ACCREDITATION: A STRUGGLE OVER STANDARDS

Much of the past century of accreditation has been characterized as a "struggle over standards" (Selden, 1960; Young, 1983). *Standards*, by their nature and intent, connote benchmarks or measures of quality. For some, they are aspirational in nature, whereas for others, they are requirements. Consequently, central to the struggle over standards has been the question "How is quality to be defined and assessed in education?" Historically, the variance of response to this question, and hence the source of the struggle, can be attributed to differences in value orientations and publics served through the accreditation of institutions (Bemis, 1983) and professional programs (Glidden, 1983), the roles of government (Bender, 1983; Chambers, 1983a) and nongovernment agencies (Chambers, 1983b) in the oversight of accreditation for benefit of publics served, and the needs of students as public consumers (Stark & Austin, 1983). The question about what constitutes educational quality was analyzed more recently across different public constituencies (Jones, 2002), with discussion of the implications these different perspectives might have on accreditation.

However quality has been defined, there has been general consensus over the past half century on the purpose and process of accreditation. Its purpose, stated generally, is to assess, enhance, and publicly attest to the quality of higher education institutions and programs. Its process consists of voluntary self- and peer review, guided by published procedures and standards, guidelines, or criteria appropriate to the task. Accreditation is both a simple concept and a complex system. Likewise, it is an evolving system in regard to the purpose of accreditation, definitions of quality and the nature of standards, and the processes by which accreditation is implemented. The underlying principle of accreditation in any event is that of self-regulation. The "self" in this concept refers not only to the institutions and programs of higher education but also to the accreditors of institutions and programs and to the voluntary, nongovernmental associations of higher education that bring the educators and accreditors together in a focus on common values in higher education and a common commitment to public accountability. Although many countries now experiment with the American process of accreditation, it is the principle of self-regulation that historically distinguishes our nation's quality control of higher education from systems of comparable intent in other countries, where government regulatory authority may be the principal quality control mechanism.

There is no question that both state and federal government agencies, especially the U.S. Department of Education (DoE), have had an impact on the nature of accreditation as practiced today in the United States. At no time in recent history was this impact clearer than during the 1990s, in which reenactments of the Higher Education Act had a profound impact on postsecondary accreditation. The crux of the issue was essentially public accountability of education institutions, programs, and accreditors in the context of public funding for higher education institutions and repayment of student loan debts. The impact of tighter federal regulations was that accrediting bodies were expected to be more prescriptive and regulatory themselves, if they were to be recognized by the U.S. Secretary of Education. This is an outcome antithetical to the value orientations of nongovernmental agencies of higher education accreditation that historically have placed greater value on the principle of self-regulation by academic institutions than on regulation by authorities external to the academic institution. Unlike the federal government, private nongovernmental associations of educators and accrediting bodies in the United States, through different iterations, have served as valuable forums for the debate of contested issues of accreditation and, through the process of consensus among the parties affiliated with them, have largely shaped the value orientations and concept of good practices in American accreditation over the past 50 years, the period coinciding with psychology's involvement in accreditation.

The need for oversight function in accreditation became especially apparent by the mid-20th century, by which time most of the regional accrediting bodies were well developed and professional (specialized) accrediting bodies were increasing in number and authority. In many of the licensed professions, the movement toward linking eligibility for licensure with graduation from an accredited professional program or school was of considerable consequence for academic institutions sponsoring professional degree programs (Lenn, 1987) and, among contemporary issues, in the globalization of professions and professional credentialing (Lenn & Campos, 1998). The accrediting bodies in many of these professions developed prescriptive standards for accreditation in regard to program resources and curriculum, thus exerting significant regulatory pressure in their own right on the academic institutions. Thus, self-regulation assumed a somewhat different meaning for the professions and their accrediting bodies than it did for higher education institutions and their accreditors, all of whom spoke of their intent to ensure quality of education and public accountability. The challenge that neither accreditors nor academic institutions alone would resolve was how to coherently define standards of quality and processes for assessing quality of entire academic institutions and specific professional degree programs, of which, on increasing numbers of academic campuses there were many with competing demands for resources.

OVERSIGHT OF ACCREDITATION: WHO SHOULD BE RECOGNIZED BY WHOM AS RELIABLE ACCREDITING BODIES?

In 1949, the year of the Boulder Conference and the first national endorsement of accreditation in psychology, the National Commission on Accrediting (NCA) was established to slow the growth in new specialized accrediting bodies and to reaffirm that educational institutions, through their boards and faculty governance, were the foundation for quality education. Although the American Council of Education, representing college and university presidents, had published position papers for many years on issues of higher education quality, it and other national associations representing postsecondary education institutions had been reluctant to assume a role of monitoring or regularly reviewing the practices of accrediting bodies through a formal recognition process. This role was first assumed by NCA, which became the first organization to establish criteria of good practice in accreditation for the recognition of reputable accrediting bodies. That is, the NCA defined what it is that accrediting bodies should and should not do in regard to their policies and practices, thus providing a standard frame of reference and value orientation for the development of accreditation in higher education. In another way of thinking, the NCA established standards for the public recognition of accrediting bodies, standards that addressed such issues as the need for accreditation, clarity and limits of accreditation scope, respect for the rights and responsibilities of education institutions and programs, fair procedures with due process, and accountability to the public. A major force of thought behind this development was to prevent accrediting bodies, especially the increasing number of those representing the professions, from developing highly prescriptive standards that would place undue demands for resources on university administrators and seemingly compromise the rights of faculty to exercise leadership in the development of their professional education programs.

About the same time in history, as Bemis (1983) described, the regional accrediting bodies formed the National Committee of Regional Accrediting Agencies (NCRAA) to facilitate cooperation in accreditation across regions of the country and to provide a regular forum for discussion of common problems in accreditation. Although the NCRAA achieved these goals, a decade later it was superceded by the Federation of Regional Accrediting Commissions of Higher Education (FRACHE), a larger organization formed by the regional accrediting bodies to address and influence broader national issues of higher education. Like the NCRAA, the FRACHE enjoyed approximately a decade of life and clearly established itself as the reputable national voice for the accreditation community in the United States from the mid-1960s to the mid-1970s.

Although the NCA and the FRACHE shared a concern about the proliferation of specialized accrediting bodies and sought to limit their numbers and influence, neither did much to include the specialized accrediting communities in their policy deliberations. Growing in numbers by this time, the specialized accrediting bodies organized their own national forum in 1973, the Council of Specialized Accrediting Agencies (CSAA). There existed yet no single forum, however, for university presidents, regional accreditors, and specialized accreditors to share and discuss their concerns in a common setting.

While these developments occurred in the private sector of higher education, the federal government had become increasingly involved in concerns about the quality of higher education institutions and programs. This involvement resulted from the increased investment of federal funds in student loans and other provisions of the post–World War II GI Bill that expanded higher education opportunities to new heights in America.

In 1952, with the passage of the Korean GI Bill, the new U.S. Office of Education was directed by law to publish a national list of accrediting agencies recognized to be reliable authorities of quality in higher education institutions and programs. The federal government lacked a set of criteria by which to make such judgments and so, according to Chambers (1983a), the U.S. Commissioner of Education approached the NCA to explore the possibility of using that newly formed body's recognition criteria for the discharge of the federal government's new responsibility. Although the NCA allowed the use of its criteria for the government's listing, it stipulated that the Office of Education make clear that its listing was specific to provisions of the GI Bill and did not constitute an endorsement by the government of the practices of accrediting bodies it listed. An eventual outcome of the federal government's role in recognizing accrediting bodies, however benign it may have seemed at the time, was that of linking educational institutions' eligibility for federal funds with the institutions' accreditation by a government recognized accrediting body. This outcome compromised in the minds of many the voluntary nature of accreditation for academic institutions and programs, in much the same way as was to happen in the professions when licensure eligibility was tied to an individual's graduation from an accredited program.

By 1968, the U.S. Office of Education established the first Advisory Committee on Accreditation and Institutional Eligibility. That committee, and its sequel under what eventually became the DoE, assumed an increasingly greater voice in all aspects of the accreditation process with concomitant effect on higher education institutions themselves. This change paralleled the activities of the NCA, the FRACHE, and, by the mid-1970s, the CSAA, each with their own agenda, but all purporting to serve the public interest. Moreover, if the private sector of higher education represented by the NCA, the FRACHE, and the CSAA was to have any impact on the increasing and often seemingly intrusive role of the federal government in higher education, it became clear that it needed an umbrella organization. A nongovernmental association would be needed to bring to one table all parties to the accreditation process, including the educational institutions and national associations representing their interests, the accreditors (institutional and specialized), and, most importantly, representatives of the general public, the presumed primary beneficiary of higher education and accreditation. In 1975, the Council on Postsecondary Accreditation (COPA) was formed to serve that purpose.

ACCREDITATION IN PSYCHOLOGY: INFLUENCE FROM EXTERNAL FORCES DURING THE PRE-COPA ERA

The early recorded history of accreditation in psychology, other than its genesis in response to the VA and PHS, reveals relatively little attention to, let alone influence by, governmental or nongovernmental forces external to the field of psychology. Consistent with that history, in 1952 the NCA, in its initial public listing of accrediting bodies, classified psychology among the specialized accrediting bodies that "are not legally entrenched," the likely meaning of which is that their accreditation was not linked by statute or regulation to eligibility for funding or licensure. This status of recognition implies that psychology's accrediting activities, as those of other accrediting bodies with which it had been categorized, could more readily be brought under the umbrella of institutional accreditation by regional accrediting bodies.

By 1970, the APA achieved its first national recognition as a reliable authority in accreditation by the U.S. Office of Education. Its scope of activities at the time was limited to doctoral and internship programs in clinical and counseling psychology. In the same year, APA's Education and Training Board published a new set of accrediting procedures developed by what was at that time the APA Committee of Evaluation. Approved by the Council of Representatives in 1969, the document's preamble gave attention to issues of fairness and due process, including the development of a more formal appeal process than had previously existed, thus being "in keeping with the Code of Good Practice promulgated by the National Commission on Accrediting for the guidance of accrediting bodies it recognizes." (APA Education and Training Board, 1970, p. 100; see Appendix G, this volume).

This is the first formal recognition of influence by an external body on the policies and practices of accreditation in psychology. In addition to acknowledging the NCA's role in accreditation, it is important that the principles of fairness and due process were mentioned as a context for the procedures, as these principles remain today a major guiding force in the operation of recognized accrediting bodies. Another principle first elucidated in the new procedures at this time is that of confidentiality in the accreditation process, a principle that served to protect the accreditors and the institutions or programs accredited, but one that would be challenged in the decades ahead by advocates for the general public and others external to these groups who would argue for greater disclosure of accreditation outcomes.

In 1971, the accrediting body in psychology was renamed Committee on Accreditation (CoA), an important change in that the term *accreditation* was used, thus opening the door to other policy and procedural changes that would authorize greater responsibility for the committee on matters of accreditation (e.g., final responsibility for accreditation decisions and responsibility for formulating accreditation policy). In May 1972, the CoA was advised that the U.S. Office of Education was revising its recognition criteria. Ronald Kurz, then the accreditation officer on APA staff, had participated with other accrediting agency staff in meetings of the U.S. Office of Education and NCA related to proposed changes. This opportunity for accrediting agency involvement in the recognition criteria revision process was an important precedent for such change in the future, by either governmental or nongovernmental accrediting body recognition authorities, for it signaled the recognition of the legitimacy of specialized as well as institutional accrediting agencies and others affected by the accreditation recognition process. A significant feature of the revised criteria was the requirement of representation of the general public (the term *knowledgeable laymen* being used) on accreditation decision-making bodies. The APA Board of Directors, on being advised of this requirement, expressed strong support for this change as an opportunity rather than an imposition, and directed the Education and Training Board to expedite a public representative appointment to the CoA.

To this point, the CoA and its predecessor Committee of Evaluation had fared remarkably well under the auspices of both governmental and nongovernmental reviews. There had been little if any impact on their operations by the FRACHE (the regional agencies for institutional accreditation), despite earlier intentions to the contrary, and they had enjoyed continuous recognition by the NCA and the U.S. Office of Education with contingent modifications of their policies and procedures to comply with the recognition criteria of those organizations. In 1974, however, the CoA experienced a short-term setback in that regard when it petitioned the U.S. Office of Education for recognition of an expansion in its scope of accreditation to include doctoral programs in school psychology. The petition was denied because of its conflict with the scope of the U.S. Office of Education recognized practices of the National Council of Accreditation in Teacher Education (NCATE) that included programs in school psychology. The U.S. Office of Education advised the CoA to work this issue out with the NCATE, thus relieving the U.S. Office of Education of responsibility for resolving a conflict of scope between two specialized accrediting bodies. Because the National Association of School Psychologists (NASP) was the constituency within NCATE responsible for school psychology programs, this event triggered the development of an APA/NASP interorganizational committee to clarify for the public the nature of education and training programs in school psychology as well as similarities and differences in criteria for their accreditation. Within a year of denying the petition, the U.S. Office of Education granted the expansion of scope to CoA on the basis of clarification of distinctions between the NCATE and CoA accreditation activities related to school psychology programs. The APA/NASP committee, on the other hand, has been a vehicle for communication and problem solving to this day between these two organizations on a variety of education and credentialing issues in school psychology (see Box 1.1).

ACCREDITATION IN PSYCHOLOGY: INFLUENCE FROM EXTERNAL FORCES DURING THE COPA ERA

When the senior author of this chapter assumed responsibility as APA staff officer for accreditation in 1982, perhaps the most important thing his

BOX 1.1
Joint Ventures Could Succeed

David H. Reilly, EdD, Office of Graduate Studies, The Citadel, Charleston, South Carolina

Although I have been on many site visit teams and also on several accreditation appeal panels, my most vivid memories of the accreditation process revolve around the joint American Psychological Association and National Association of School Psychologists (APA and NASP) Task Force. This task force was formed to address three issues of concern for the accreditation of school psychology training programs: (a) the entry level for school psychologists, (b) the acceptability of the term *school psychologist*, and (c) accreditation.

At the time I served on this task force I was Dean, School of Education, University of North Carolina at Greensboro. Thus, I had background serving on APA and the National Council for Accreditation of Teacher Education (NCATE) accreditation teams, as well as being administratively responsible for both school psychology and graduate programs in education accredited by NCATE.

APA accredited only doctoral programs; however, NASP, operating under the umbrella of NCATE, accredited both doctoral and nondoctoral school psychology training programs. This posed severe problems for program coordinators. NCATE/NASP accreditation was necessary to meet certification requirements, whereas APA accreditation was preferred for internship and employment opportunities. The cost of obtaining accreditation from both organizations was expensive, if not prohibitive.

The task force met repeatedly over the course of several years, with the agenda addressing variously the three issues of concern. It became apparent that the accreditation issue would probably be the easiest to resolve. The task force spent many hours reviewing the accreditation standards and procedures of both APA and NASP. They overlapped to a significant extent, although the wording was different in some cases. Significant differences were also found. For example, APA placed more emphasis on the bases of behavior, whereas NASP emphasized more knowledge of education, particularly special education, issues.

The primary objective of the task force became the development of a common set of standards and procedures that could be used by a combined team of APA and NASP representatives reviewing school psychology programs. Two primary issues, in addition to the production of a common review manual, had to be resolved. The first was the composition of the team. The task force finally determined that APA and NASP would each have a representative, trained as a site visitor by only the organization he or she represented. The third member would be an individual who had been trained in each organization's accreditation procedures.

The second issue concerned which team members would be responsible for reviewing the nondoctoral portions of a training program. There were a large number of such programs, many of which were affiliated with a doctoral program. This was obviously important to APA because it could not appear that an APA representative was reviewing and recommending an accreditation decision for a nondoctoral program. However, there was much to be gained by a doctoral program with such a one-time combined visit. If successful, the program would receive accreditation by both APA and NASP/NCATE. If unsuccessful, the program, if it wished to appeal, would have to follow the appeal procedures of each organization.

In the end, the task force did not accomplish everything it set out to accomplish. It developed a combined standards and procedures manual, and APA's Council of Representatives and NASP's governing board approved it. However, at this point NCATE reneged on its commitment to the process. The executive director of NCATE changed, and the organization moved to a new system involving accreditation of the Teacher Education Unit on a campus with specific programs reviewed through a folio process. Thus, the work of the task force on a joint accreditation review process and the interorganizational cooperation fostered by generating such a process was lost.

Several important lessons may be gleaned from this development process. First, interorganizational cooperation can be successful, even on matters in which there are widely divergent positions. Obviously, chances of success are more likely where two organizations are involved rather than three or more.

Second, as accreditation reviews have become even more expensive, organizational cooperation on such matters may become more desirable. The work of the joint task force may be useful as a model for such efforts.

Third, APA's position of not accrediting nondoctoral programs was a major obstacle in developing the joint accreditation process. Because of this position, APA has no voice in the program standards that affect thousands of school psychologists. If

continues

> **BOX 1.1 (continued)**
>
> APA's position with regard to accrediting nondoctoral school psychology programs had been different at the time of the task force's work, it is interesting to speculate on the possible outcomes. Division 16 may have gained many more members and APA would probably be a major force in establishing standards for the thousands of psychologists that work in the schools. As it turned out, APA lost a glorious opportunity to advance its standards and learn a valuable lesson that may have helped in dealing with the accreditation of other nondoctoral programs now being formed.

immediate predecessor, Meredith Crawford, did was to take him to meet Richard Millard who had assumed the presidency of COPA the year before. The influence of Millard and his leadership team was more conceptual than procedural. Fundamental to his thinking was the concept of quality in higher education and how it should be defined and operationalized through the accreditation process, the issue around which accreditation began. He related the quality of an institution or program to the coherence of its elements in achieving its educational objective or objectives (Millard, 1983). Such a model of quality can be applied to any type or level of organization, thus respecting the diversity of institutions that has been the hallmark of American higher education and allowing assessment of program quality within the context of each institution's mission as well as that of their national profession. This model further argues against the elitist model of higher education, the idea that there is a single standard for quality with a linear, hierarchical order of education institutions and programs founded on this one standard or set of standards. The reputation model of higher education is an example of the latter.

Similarly, what might be referred to as the contextual aspect of the model of quality argues against the antithesis of the elitist model, namely the notion that accreditation should simply certify compliance or threshold satisfaction with a specified minimal set of education standards or criteria, the "gate-keeping" function of accreditation. Although it is certainly true that accreditation serves the public in such a function, simply ensuring that some form of minimal standards are met by those accredited programs presumes that educational quality is a static entity, standard across types of institutions and programs. It also fails to challenge institutions and programs beyond satisfying externally imposed minimal standards or criteria. Indeed, such a conceptualization of quality relies on bodies external to education institutions and programs to set standards, thus placing the control of "self-regulation" outside rather than inside the education institution or program.

Finally, quite related to the institution or program's responsibility for self-regulation, Millard's conception of quality places significant emphasis on the process of self-study, the cornerstone of accreditation (see Box 1.2). Self-study in this instance reflects both a process and an outcome. The process is the engagement of administration, faculty, and students in a reflective analysis of the institution's or program's mission, goals, and education objectives; analysis of how resources and education processes are or are not brought to bear on those; and an assessment of the manner and extent to which educational outcomes reflect the fulfillment of the same. The outcome of self-study is a major report prepared by the institution or program for the accrediting body (regional or specialized) that is framed in response to that body's accreditation standards or criteria. Much attention in accreditation is rightfully given to the site visit, that part of the accreditation process that brings to the campus a review team of peers who are not associated with the institution or program and whose principal task is to verify firsthand the validity of what is contained in the self-study report. It is with the self-study, however, that the accreditation process begins and, ideally, continues over time. Properly conceived, the self-study is a dynamic mechanism for continuous reflection and change by an institution or program, not merely a reporting requirement that occurs as a discrete and discontinuous event in time. Kells (1995), who has written most extensively about self-study in accreditation, addressed its significance in terms of education institutional rights and responsibilities (Kells, 1983b), improving institutional performance (Kells, 1983a), and as a context for the roles of accrediting bodies in fostering self-regulation (Kells, 1983c). Of interest in the history of CoA, in this regard, is that the U.S. Office of Education in a 1975 review of psychology's accrediting practices expressed concern about the adequacy of the CoA's self-study requirements for accredited programs, specifically with regard to periodic reexamination of program goals.

One of the central functions of COPA, and a point of historical controversy that it inherited, was the accrediting body recognition process. With the establishment of COPA came a Committee on Recognition and a formal set of procedures and recognition criteria or provisions. Throughout the life of COPA, unfortunately but not surprisingly, was political pressure primarily from higher education associations representing university presidents to curtail what that community perceived to be the proliferation and intrusiveness of specialized accrediting bodies. In point of fact, the increase in numbers of professional and vocational accrediting groups seeking recognition from COPA during the 1980s was attributed largely to one of two categories of specialized program. Some were professional programs located in free-standing, single-purpose institutions, not universities. The others, while located in universities, were granted legitimacy in the first place not by the fact that they were accredited by a professional body, but rather that the universities in which they were located had initiated degree programs in those profes-

BOX 1.2
The Continuing Importance of Understanding the Self-Study Process

Clyde A. Crego, PhD, Counseling and Psychological Service, California State University, Long Beach, and University of Southern California, Los Angeles

Over the past 30-some years, I have been involved in American Psychological Association (APA) accreditation activities in numerous ways—as a consultant to many programs, as a site visitor, as an accreditation appeals panel member, and as a director of programs. In that time, I have observed several changes in the process. Most notably, the process has moved from the premise that the responsibility for quality assurance rests with an external body (i.e., APA) to an assumption that continuous improvement is the responsibility of the program itself. Although this change in orientation mirrors that which has also occurred in other societal sectors, including medical centers and corporations, the challenges in applying the concept to professional training programs have been significant. APA is to be commended for its early initiatives in this arena.

The critical quality determinant in today's accreditation process is the program's demonstrable capacity to *self*-evaluate and take appropriate corrective action on the basis of that evaluation. Although the evaluative criteria are those agreed to by the member programs (as well as some imposed by other regulatory agencies), it is each individual program's responsibility to ensure that an effective and ongoing process of self-regulation exists.

In earlier years, self-study was clearly an activity engaged in only as a prelude to the site visit for initial or re-accreditation. Whether we would admit it or not, it was an episodic event engaged in every few years, then tucked away to be dusted off prior to the next review cycle. It did not guide a great deal of our intervening program administration behaviors. I am pleased to see the changes that have occurred in this regard. APA is increasingly viewed as a valuable consultant rather than as the sole guardian of quality. Member programs themselves are engaging in an increasing variety of creative self-assessment processes and activities.

Nevertheless, the change process is not finished. In my extensive accreditation consulting experience, I still observe some programs relying on a checklist approach and on an assumption that the locus of quality control resides primarily with APA. The change process must continue, but the future of accreditation is, in my view, extremely promising.

sions. The accrediting bodies, for the most part, followed rather than preceded the establishment of the degree programs.

More a critic of CoA and its accrediting practices than institutions per se were the national organizations representing psychology graduate department chairs and professional school programs (i.e., the Council of Graduate Departments of Psychology and the National Council of Schools and Programs in Professional Psychology). These organizations, plus a few individuals representing institutions or nontraditional academic programs in professional psychology, represented important sources of third-party concerns expressed at the time of CoA recognition reviews by COPA and the DoE during the latter years of the 1980s, a period of discontent and reformation in psychology's accreditation history (Nelson, 1998; Sheridan et al., 1995). The concerns raised by graduate department chairs were much like those raised historically by university presidents, namely concerns about the process of accreditation being of a checklist nature, stifling innovation, and being intrusive through site visitor or accrediting body recommendations for improvement. The professional school concerns were of the opinion that a bias existed against their philosophy and practices of education for the profession relative to comparable programs run by traditional university academic departments of psychology.

As chapter 2 details, the roots of these concerns can be traced to the 1970s, when two forces external to psychology itself, and outside the sphere of accreditation, also influenced the course of events in psychology's accreditation criteria. One force was the need for greater numbers of psychologists than were graduating from university academic departments. The need for mental health services in large states and underserved areas of the country resembled the time following World War II that prompted psychology's initial involvement in accreditation activities. The closure of mental health facilities and increased social turbulence of the 1960s in urban and rural communities contributed to the need for more psychologists. Peterson (1997) speaks to some of this need in his writing about the education of professional psychologists and the history behind the professional schools of psychology and the professional PsyD degree movements, including a reference to James McKeen Cattell's thinking along similar lines some 30 years earlier (see Appendix K, this volume). The Vail Conference of 1973 also focused on societal needs for well-prepared professional psychologists (Korman, 1973). These needs prompted the rapid development of professional schools of psychology, many of which were free-standing (i.e., independent and unaffiliated with a university), involved large numbers of adjunct faculty, and trained significantly larger cohorts of students than were typical of university academic department programs. Consequently, the process of educating and training students in professional schools was quite different in most instances from traditional ways that continued in university academic departments. Sufficiently different were these professional school programs in form and function that as they applied for accreditation, they posed difficulties for the CoA in its interpretation of the accreditation criteria in effect at the time, given also that most of the CoA members at that time had not had experience as faculty of professional schools. Despite the fact that the CoA's revised accreditation criteria in 1973—which were made on the basis of recommendations of a special commission on accreditation and a national conference—had opened the door for diversity of professional education and training program models, the historic scientist–practitioner model remained the one with which most psychologists involved in the accreditation process had experience. Thus, it required time and experience with new models of professional education before the CoA could become comfortable with the diversity of programs it was being petitioned to accredit.

The other external force operative in the 1970s resulted from a court of law action in which a judge rendered an opinion to the effect that the profession of psychology is amorphous relative to other professions, having no clear corpus of knowledge or skills to differentiate it from other mental health and human services professions. This opinion led to a series of national conferences (see Appendix J, this volume) sponsored by the APA and the National Register of Health Service Providers in Psychology (National Register) and other bodies to define such a body of knowledge and related education requirements in relation to credentialing in psychology (Wellner, 1978). This body of knowledge about which consensus was achieved, especially among those concerned with professional education and credentialing in psychology, became known as the core curriculum in professional psychology. It was institutionalized in the CoA's revised accreditation criteria of 1979 and the designation criteria adopted in the 1980s by the National Register and the Association of State and Provincial Psychology Boards to differentiate graduates from doctoral programs in psychology from other related but different disciplinary programs. In the accreditation process, there was a tendency for these curriculum requirements to be translated into specific course requirements, even though the accreditation criteria did not mandate courses per se.

What is important about these issues in the context of this chapter is that COPA became, within the psychology community, a trusted independent forum with authority to hear the complaints or concerns of parties affected by accrediting agency practices, in this case the practices of CoA. Having served two terms on the COPA Committee on Recognition, the senior author can attest to the importance of this function during the COPA era, not only for psychology but for all communities affected by accreditation. In a very real way, the forum for third-party comment in the accrediting agency recognition process, just as it does in the accreditation of institutions or programs by the recognized accrediting bodies, attests to the principle of public accountability. The formal complaint process established by accrediting bodies and their recognition authorities is another manifestation of the same principle.

TIMES OF CHANGE FOR ACCREDITATION: THE TURBULENT 1990S

In psychology, three major forces became increasingly critical of accreditation during the 1990s: (a) those who represented the academy in traditional university departments of psychology with the research (PhD) degree models; (b) those who represented the newer and growing number of professional schools with professional (PsyD) degree models; and (c) those who represented the profession outside the academy, the practitioners of psychology (see Box 1.3). Each had different concerns about accreditation and, indeed, about the perceived control or influence on accreditation of one or both of the other constituencies. On the other hand, there were common concerns about lack of adequate representation on the CoA, about the types of decisions made by CoA, and about the process of accreditation itself from a cost–benefit perspective. Sheridan and colleagues (1995) summarized these issues of discontent that reached a peak during the late 1980s and early 1990s, resulting ultimately in reformation of the CoA and the most complete overhaul of its criteria (now referred to as *guidelines and principles*) and procedures for accreditation.

Prior to that outcome, the CoA had requested in the mid-1980s that the APA Education and Training Board commission a task force to review and make recommendations about changes in the scope, criteria, and procedures of accreditation. The task force was appointed in 1985, chaired initially by Sandra Scarr and subsequently by Jill Reich, both academic department chairs, with broad representation from academic and practice communities. Its final report (APA Education and Training Board, 1989) provided extensive recommendations on the basis of a set of principles, some long-standing and some relatively new in the history of psychology's accreditation. Perhaps the defining characteristic of the task force recommendations, however, were outcomes-based standards for accreditation founded in turn on program goals and objectives in education and training, including a self-evaluation standard for the program. The influence of COPA, especially the thinking and writing of Richard Millard and William MacLeod was clear, albeit perhaps unknown directly to many of the task force members or, indeed, the countless numbers of academic and practitioner colleagues who reviewed, critiqued, and finally accepted what the task force had recommended. The implementation through final approval of the APA Council of Representatives was tabled, pending the CoA's reformation which, at the time the report was received by Council, was at a very critical state.

Another significant, highly integrative report received by Council within a short time of the task force report was one written by the Joint Council on Professional Education in Psychology (JCPEP; Stigall et al., 1990; see Appendix H, this volume). Formed initially by members of APA divisions whose members were primarily practitioners of the profession rather than academ-

BOX 1.3
Supporting the Evolution of Practice
Arthur L. Kovacs, PhD, California School of Professional Psychology, Alliant International University, Los Angeles

When I completed my graduate education and entered independent practice in 1958, I knew little about the American Psychological Association's (APA's) approval process and probably cared even less. I had no inkling whatsoever that, over the course of my professional life, accreditation would occupy a significant number of my waking hours.

The forced change in my perspective began when I was chosen in 1969 to be the Founding Campus Dean of the California School of Professional Psychology (CSPP), Los Angeles. CSPP–Los Angeles was part of an oncoming wave of emerging professional school programs. Those of us who were responsible for CSPP's destiny made a commitment from the beginning to secure all necessary and desirable credentials for the program: approval from the California State Department of Education, regional accreditation from the Western Association of Schools and Colleges and, yes, APA accreditation. My own preparation for what was to await me began the first week instruction started on the campus; I had secured the then-extant guidelines for APA accreditation and began to practically memorize them. The process gave me quite an education.

Over the almost 8 years of my tenure, I had to make sure we got ready for 13 different site visits! Four of these were from the APA Committee on Accreditation (CoA), and as a result, CSPP–Los Angeles moved in stages from being a new program that was about to have a consultation visit, on through provisional status, and arriving eventually at its present recognition as a fully approved program.

Even though I subsequently returned to my first and most passionate love, the practice of psychology, and now teach only two graduate courses a year, I could never forget my commitment to the education of those who would succeed me and to the process of accreditation itself, wanting it to serve as best it could as the guardian of quality in the preparation of professional psychologists. I have attempted to actualize my continuing concern by my activities in a variety of venues: serving for a decade as the liaison from APA's Division of Psychologists in Independent Practice to APA's Board of Educational Affairs; serving as the Division's Education and Training Committee Chairperson; being one of the organizers of the Joint Commission on Professional Education in Psychology; serving a term on the CoA itself; and, as a member of APA's Council of Representatives, crafting a variety of pieces of legislation setting educational policy for APA and helping to restructure how APA carries out its accreditation function.

Over the years I have come to appreciate that the accreditation dynamic in APA is one constantly fraught with a clash of values. On the one hand, many entrusted with responsibility for doctoral and postdoctoral education and training oppose accreditation standards of any sort that threaten to homogenize education for practice, seeing them as a brake on academic freedom and creativity. On the other hand, those most connected with practice have been frequently dismayed by what seems to be insufficient rigor in the accreditation guidelines or in their application to programs. The leadership of the practitioner constituency in APA has frequently noted a public need for more uniformity in the education of psychologists.

The adoption of a revised structure for APA's CoA about a decade ago created a forum for thoughtful management of these competing values. The guidelines and procedures for accreditation crafted by the first members of the reformed CoA made good progress in developing an altered system that most agree serves the needs of chairs, directors, students, practicing professionals and, most of all, the public in a better fashion than has been achieved before.

Yet given the rapid changes in American psychology, the accreditation reform accomplished to date only serves to highlight additional layers of complexity and a range of difficult problems. I discuss some of them below.

- How can the CoA be given sufficient delegated authority and responsibility to meet the requirements for autonomy demanded by the U.S. Department of Education and yet be responsive to the policies of the association? Or should the accreditation function be lodged in an interorganizational consortium rather than in APA itself?
- How can the CoA accommodate new areas of focus and specialization in the field? How can the new specialties get "seats at the accreditation table," and how can they participate meaningfully in the accreditation of their emerging programs?
- How does the CoA need to respond to the fact that fewer and fewer psychologists will find careers in or be trained

continues

> BOX 1.3 (continued)
>
> to be mental health professionals given that most of its present guidelines help direct the education and training of such individuals?
> - How will the CoA respond to the chaos in the taxonomy of professional psychology? The CoA presently recognizes "specialty programs" of clinical, counseling, school, and combined programs in its listing, and every young professional graduates not as a general professional psychologist but as a clinical, counseling, school, or some other kind of psychologist. Yet, the CoA uses only a single set of common guidelines to evaluate our doctoral programs. What is the public to make of a profession that has only specialists and no generalists, particularly when state licensure is itself generic and founded on a single common examination?
>
> To take a fresh look at some of these problems, APA created the Commission for the Recognition of Specialties and Proficiencies in Professional Psychology (CRSPPP). CRSPPP is attempting to develop a new taxonomy that might better communicate with the public, but the CoA does not want to be told what its prerogatives are to be. And finally, the American Board of Professional Psychology (ABPP) recognizes individual practitioners as specialists, but ABPP has a set of specialist categories different from that of either CoA or CRSPPP. The public is not being well served by these identification confusions.
>
> I hope to stick around for at least a few more years so I might discover the answer to these extremely complex conundrums—and, if I am fortunate, even be privileged to help shape a few of their parts before my career ends.

ics, and chaired by Tommy Stigall, JCPEP served the important purpose of summarizing concerns about accreditation and professional education in psychology from the perspective of those in practice and the regulation of practice (e.g., licensing boards). The report acknowledged and integrated principles and recommendations of prior national conferences on professional education and training and the previous work of the Task Force on Scope and Criteria for Accreditation. A distinctive feature of these recommendations, however, as described in chapter 4, was the delineation of professional practice competencies expected at the doctoral level of education and training in psychology. Although the articulation of expected competencies was less specific in the accreditation guidelines developed a few years later by the new CoA, the construct of competency-based assessment was adopted, as was the outcomes-based program evaluation model set forth by the Task Force on Scope and Criteria for Accreditation.

The fundamental principle of public accountability was foremost in the thinking of those who "rewrote the accreditation script" for psychology. The influence of COPA principles of good practice and provisions of recognition, an outgrowth of the earlier NCA principles, provided a foundation for the development of APA's *Policies of Accreditation Governance* approved by the Council of Representatives in August 1991, thereby authorizing the new CoA and its authority for accreditation. Questions about accountability and authority with regard to policies and practices of accreditation arose later in the decade, leading to a request by the DoE for clarification of responsibilities within the APA for various accreditation actions, policies, and procedures. But the functions of the accrediting body and the principle that underlies the CoA's new membership domains, articulated in the *Policies of Accreditation Governance*, were derived from the COPA recognition provisions. Moreover, that fact lent considerable authority to the APA policy document within which the new CoA would function with relative autonomy. CoA is the sole authority for all accreditation decisions and has responsibility for the formulation and promulgation of accreditation policies, procedures, and criteria, as well as authority to carry out accreditation processes in accordance with those guidelines and within the framework of nationally recognized good practices of accreditation.

THE DEMISE OF COPA AND THE ADVENT OF CHEA

It was scarcely a year after the new CoA was formed that the COPA Board of Directors voted to dissolve that organization effective January 1, 1994. Leading to the demise of COPA were the historical forces of tension in accreditation. COPA had tried to be an effective forum bringing together the specialized and regional (institutional) accreditators and those representing the presidents of universities and colleges. However, in the eyes of some, COPA never achieved equity in those relationships. COPA had also tried to represent the values of the voluntary nongovernmental accreditation process in reducing government regulatory activities in higher education, but had not, in the eyes of others, succeeded.

Accreditation had been a national lightening rod for discontent with myriad issues in higher education during the 1980s. Even the honored status of higher education in America itself was under attack (e.g., Bloom, 1987). Proprietary institutions had increased in number and, in the opinion of many, without proper quality control. Federal government financing of students through loans had increased, as had student loan defaults. State higher education agencies were demanding more control over public higher education institutions in the name of public accountability. Higher education associations were advancing new models of quality assessment in higher education. And, stimulated by the writings of Ernest Boyer (1990), the former U.S. Commissioner of Education and subsequently president of the Carnegie Foundation for the Advancement of Teaching, many were redefining scholarship within the academy and its relationship to the community at large. In the face of all these challenges, in the final analysis many perceived COPA as being relatively impotent in regard to formulating and advocating for public policy on higher education in government legislation and regulations. With a few exceptions, most of its constituent members in the end became disaffected, the specialized and regional accreditors once again going off separately to reform or rejuvenate their own councils, and those representing the university and college leadership community, the most powerful constituency, assuming leadership to form the sequel to COPA.

COPA was immediately replaced by an interim organization named the Council on the Recognition of Postsecondary Accreditation (CORPA), signaling by its name what was considered to be the vital nongovernmental role in recognition of accrediting bodies. Although the regional and specialized accrediting agencies were represented in the establishment of CORPA and its bylaws (the senior author being one of two representatives from the specialized accreditation community to serve on that interim body), it was clear that CORPA would be much more under the influence of the college and university presidents and the organizations representing their interests. Until a more permanent replacement for COPA could be designed, it was agreed that CORPA would carry out its recognition function under the provisions and procedures established previously by COPA.

In 1993, motivated by what appeared to be an increased disregard for specialized accreditation by others of the former COPA constituencies, the Association of Specialized and Professional Accreditors (ASPA) was formed. At about the same time, led by the regional accrediting agencies, the National Policy Board on Institutional Accreditation was likewise established. ASPA's purpose was to carry out the functions formerly fulfilled by COPA, except for the recognition function, especially the role of reaffirming principles of good practice in accreditation and a more aggressive public affairs posture in helping the general public and other publics (e.g., government, academic institutions) understand the role and value of specialized (professional) accreditation. ASPA continues to function at this time in such capacity. Its "Code of Good Practice," based on principles formerly set forth by COPA, was formally endorsed by the CoA and is embodied in the principles, policies, procedures, and guidelines for accreditation implemented by the current CoA. Without recognition authority, ASPA functions essentially as an informal peer consultation body, a forum for discussion and debate among specialized accrediting agencies about good practices in accreditation, and an independent voice for specialized accreditation in public forums on higher education, including legislative and regulatory activities of the government. As such, it represents the professions in higher education.

In April 1996, CORPA was replaced by the Council of Higher Education Accreditation (CHEA) as the national, nongovernmental oversight authority for accreditation. It was established by majority vote of college and university presidents, with a clear signal to the public that higher education institutions themselves were now ready to assume responsibility for the self-regulation process of accreditation. CHEA's membership and controlling constituency is that of postsecondary education institutions, not accreditors. Accreditors have a voice but not a vote in CHEA's affairs. Its president, Judith Eaton, brings a distinguished background of university executive administration to bear on CHEA's leadership (McMurtrie, 1999) and has established a clear presence of higher education accreditation in government and nongovernment circles, among the latter most notably national associations representing higher education institutions. The three areas of service expected of CHEA were (a) representing the accrediting community to the federal government, (b) bringing together accreditors and academic leaders to coordinate and enhance the accreditation process, and (c) serving as a clearinghouse for best practices in quality assurance and accreditation. Specific priority issues for CHEA to address were the relationship of accreditation to student learning outcomes, increasing cooperation among regional and specialized accreditors, and the challenge of distance education for accreditation. Ultimately to these priority issues are to be added those of clarifying relationships between accreditation and quality assurance as well as between accreditation and public accountability.

CHEA's recognition function is expected to be rigorous in regard to provisions for recognition and enforcement of the same. CHEA's (1998, p. 3) policies and procedures for recognition of accrediting organizations stated three basic purposes of the recognition process:

- *To advance academic quality:* To confirm that accrediting organizations have standards that advance academic quality in higher education; that those standards emphasize student achievement and high expectations of teaching and learning, research, and service; and that those standards are developed within the framework of institutional mission.
- *To demonstrate accountability:* To confirm that accrediting organizations have standards that ensure accountability through consistent, clear, and coherent communication to the public and the higher education community about the results of educational efforts. Accountability also includes a commitment by the accrediting organization to involve the public in accreditation decision making.

- *To encourage purposeful change and needed improvement:* To confirm that accrediting organizations have standards that encourage institutions to plan, where needed, for purposeful change and improvement; to develop and sustain activities that anticipate and address needed change; to stress student achievement; and to ensure long-range institutional viability.

These goals provide the framework for the CHEA recognition standards along with standards that pertain to appropriate and fair procedures in decision making and continually reassessing one's accrediting practices. In 2002, CHEA granted continued recognition to the CoA as the accrediting body for professional education in psychology following the CoA's formal review by CHEA. In achieving that recognition, the CoA conducted a major self-study demonstrating that in practice the Policies for Accreditation Governance (APA Council of Representatives, 1991) and the CoA's Guidelines and Principles for Accreditation of Programs in Professional Psychology (APA Committee on Accreditation, 2000) are consistent with the standards and criteria for CHEA recognition of accrediting bodies.

THE HEAVY HAMMER IN ACCREDITATION: U.S. DEPARTMENT OF EDUCATION

No account of accreditation during the 1990s would be complete without mention of the role played during those years by the federal government, namely the DoE. On the heels of much national discontent with accreditation during the 1980s, prompted by questions about public trust in accreditation and the accountability of higher education institutions, the DoE moved aggressively into the area through its authority for recognizing accrediting bodies. Recall that public funding of higher education, as in student loans, had been linked some years earlier to accreditation being granted by an accrediting body recognized by the DoE. In 1992, on the occasion of congressional reauthorization of the Higher Education Act of 1965, many in the Congress were doubtful that the quality of higher education could be assured by an accreditation system that was self-regulated by the academic institutions and agencies that accredited them. Congress was particularly concerned about the public accountability of institutions, graduates from which had high student loan default rates, and held accrediting agencies responsible for this state of affairs, especially the regional accrediting bodies that had a gatekeeping function with regard to Title IV funds for student loans. The result of this concern was a tightening of legislative authority by the federal government over the accreditation process, implemented through a major revision of DoE regulations that directly affected the recognition of accrediting bodies: The implications of this change were that academic institutions (or programs in some cases) would not receive federal funding for students if they were not accredited by a regional (or in some cases specialized) accrediting body recognized by the U.S. Secretary of Education. The flipside of this change, of course, was that to be recognized by the Secretary, the regional (or specialized) accrediting bodies had to adhere to the regulatory provisions of the Secretary's standards for recognition. Moreover, the new legislation and resulting federal regulations authorized a much stronger role for the states in monitoring both higher education institutions and accreditors through what was called State Postsecondary Review Entities (SPREs). If no other effect were to be forthcoming from this change, the reporting requirements for higher education institutions and accrediting agencies were to be significantly increased.

The SPREs never materialized to any great extent (in part due to lack of funding), and were eventually eliminated from the statute when it was amended 4 years later in 1998. Other changes were made at that time in the act, and resulting regulations rendered the recognition standards somewhat more flexible. For the CoA, however, DoE recognition would become a major preoccupation during the 1990s. Its last review by DoE prior to the new regulations had been in 1992, the formative years for the new CoA. DoE granted a 5-year period of recognition with attention focused on resolving tensions among the different communities with invested interest in accreditation, reinvigorating the demonstration of reliability and validity of accreditation procedures and standards, and making more public certain aspects of the accreditation process.

In 1997, CoA's first review under the new DoE regulations resulted in continued recognition for 2 rather than 4 years. Issues of concern to DoE had to do with accreditation procedures and standards, notably clarifying or developing statements and procedures specific to each of several new recognition standards. Foremost among these standards, reflecting the national education assessment movement of the 1990s, was the student achievement standard: that is, a requirement of specific documentation of student achievements and other learning outcomes, including outcomes following graduation. Also included were standards related to student complaints (including requirements for recording keeping on the part of the education institution or program and accrediting body), public disclosure of accreditation outcomes (including notation of problems that need to be addressed by the education institution or program), how programs are monitored on cited deficiencies by the accrediting body, and time periods allowed for programs to correct deficiencies before being placed on probation or dropped from accredited status. Public accountability was at the heart of all these issues. The CoA responded to each of these in a major revision of its operating procedures and in 1999 was recognized by DoE for another 5 years.

WHAT DOES THE FUTURE HOLD FOR ACCREDITATION?

Clearly, higher education in America is not today what it was a century ago or even 50 years ago. Although it continues to be what many refer to as a "major export" service of our country in the globalization of higher education, it is also subject internally to an increasing rate of change. Economics, demographics, and computer telecommunications technology are shaping higher education into new paths that pose major challenges to firmly held values and beliefs. The public demands on higher education are greater and more diverse than ever. Emphasizing the diversity of the public's needs for education, and the corresponding diversity of institutions, curricula, and pedagogical methods for meeting those needs, Millard (1991) reminded us that "educational quality needs to be defined not in terms of reputation or resources but in terms of excellence in kind and thus in terms of effective use of resources to achieve appropriate educational objectives" (p. 268).

What lies ahead for accreditors and accreditation? Philosophically and operationally, continued attention will be given to issues of higher education quality assessment and enhancement through the self-regulatory accreditation process, challenged by continued and varied demands for public accountability in an environment with changing demographics, economics, and technology for teaching and learning (Ewell, 1994). These external forces will impact accreditation in psychology as a profession to a greater extent than has historically been the case. Changes of the past few years in governmental (DoE) and nongovernmental (CHEA) oversight of accreditation are likely to create a new framework for thinking about accreditation in which the collaboration of accreditors and academic institutions serve the public through external accountability and internal quality enhancement. The regional accrediting agencies already are moving toward new models of accreditation, all of which place increased responsibility on the higher education institution for self-regulation in quality assessment and enhancement.

For the CoA, elements of this shift in model are also in place. The only potential barrier between the CoA's present process of accreditation and the next generation of thinking about accreditation is that common human experience of "cultural lag" in regard to change and the inertial effect of continuing on a familiar path. To the extent such a barrier exists, it is likely to be less for members of the CoA than for the diverse constituencies they represent, most of whom are not engaged on a regular basis, intellectually or otherwise, with issues of accreditation or, for that matter, with strategic issues of change in the academy or profession. Consequently, it becomes the responsibility of the CoA to move the profession forward with regard to how it thinks about assessing and enhancing the quality of professional education and training in psychology. Most of all, in so doing, it must be the conscience of the profession for ensuring that the public is well served and that its policies and actions as an accrediting body meet the standards of public accountability as set forth in good practices of accreditation endorsed by government and nongovernment authorities.

REFERENCES

American Psychological Association, Committee on Accreditation. (2000). *Guidelines and principles for accreditation of programs in professional psychology*. Washington, DC: Author.

American Psychological Association, Committee on Training in Clinical Psychology. (1947). Recommended graduate training programs in clinical psychology. *American Psychologist, 2,* 539–558.

American Psychological Association, Committee on Training in Clinical Psychology. (1948). Clinical training facilities: 1948. *American Psychologist, 3,* 317–318.

American Psychological Association, Committee on Training in Clinical Psychology. (1949). Doctoral training programs in clinical psychology: 1949. *American Psychologist, 4,* 331–341.

American Psychological Association, Council of Representatives. (1991). *Policies for accreditation governance*. Washington, DC: Author.

American Psychological Association, Education and Training Board. (1970). Accrediting procedures of the American Psychological Association. *American Psychologist, 25,* 100–102.

American Psychological Association, Education and Training Board. (1989). *Final report of the Task Force on Scope and Criteria for Accreditation*. Washington, DC: Author.

Bemis, J. F. (1983). Regional accreditation. In K. E. Young, C. M. Chambers, H. R. Kells, & Associates (Eds.), *Understanding accreditation* (pp. 167–186). San Francisco: Jossey-Bass.

Bender, L. W. (1983). States and accreditation. In K. E. Young, C. M. Chambers, H. R. Kells, & Associates (Eds.), *Understanding accreditation* (pp. 270–288). San Francisco: Jossey-Bass.

Bloom, A. (1987). *The closing of the American mind*. New York: Simon & Schuster.

Bok, D. (1990). *Universities and the future of America*. Durham, NC: Duke University Press.

Boyer, E. (1990). *Scholarship reconsidered: Priorities of the professorate*. Princeton, NJ: Carnegie Foundation for the Advancement of Teaching.

Cardoza, M. H. (1975). *The association process: 1963–1973*. Washington, DC: Association of American Law Schools.

Chambers, C. M. (1983a). Federal government and accreditation. In K. E. Young, C. M. Chambers, H. R. Kells, & Associates (Eds.), *Understanding accreditation* (pp. 233–269). San Francisco: Jossey-Bass.

Chambers, C. M. (1983b). Council on Postsecondary Accreditation. In K. E. Young, C. M. Chambers, H. R. Kells, & Associates (Eds.), *Understanding accreditation* (pp. 289–314). San Francisco: Jossey-Bass.

Council for Higher Education Accreditation. (1998). *Recognition of accrediting organizations: Policies and procedures.* Washington, DC: Author.

Ewell, P. T. (1994, November/December). Accountability and the future of self-regulation. *Change,* pp. 25–29.

Flexner, A. (1925). *Medical education.* New York: Macmillan.

Glidden, R. (1983). Specialized accreditation. In K. E. Young, C. M. Chambers, H. R. Kells, & Associates (Eds.), *Understanding accreditation* (pp. 187–208). San Francisco: Jossey-Bass.

Jones, D. P. (2002). *Different perspectives on information about educational quality: Implications for the role of accreditation.* Washington, DC: Council for Higher Education Accreditation.

Kells, H. R. (1983a). Improving institutional performance through self-study. In K. E. Young, C. M. Chambers, H. R. Kells, & Associates (Eds.), *Understanding accreditation* (pp. 119–132). San Francisco: Jossey-Bass.

Kells, H. R. (1983b). Institutional rights and responsibilities. In K. E. Young, C. M. Chambers, H. R. Kells, & Associates (Eds.), *Understanding accreditation* (pp.107–118). San Francisco: Jossey-Bass.

Kells, H. R. (1983c). Roles of accrediting bodies. In K. E. Young, C. M. Chambers, H. R. Kells, & Associates (Eds.), *Understanding accreditation* (pp. 154–166). San Francisco: Jossey-Bass.

Kells, H. R. (1995). *Self-study processes: A guide to self-evaluation in higher education* (4th ed.). Phoenix, AZ: Oryx Press.

Korman, M. (Ed.). (1973). *Levels and patterns of professional training in psychology.* Washington, DC: American Psychological Association.

Lenn, M. P. (1987). Accreditation, certification, and licensure. In M. A. F. Rehnke (Ed.), *Creating career programs in a liberal arts context* (pp. 49–63). San Francisco: Jossey-Bass.

Lenn, M. P., & Campos, L. B. (Eds.). (1998). *Multinational discourse on professional accreditation, certification, and licensure: Bridges for the globalizing professions.* Washington, DC: The Center for Quality Assurance in International Education.

McConn, C. M. (1935). Academic standards versus individual differences—The dilemma of democratic education. *American School Board Journal, 91,* 44.

McMurtrie, B. (1999, November 12). Assessing the group that assesses accreditation. *Chronicle of Higher Education,* pp. A41–A42.

Millard, R. M. (1983). Evolution of accrediting standards. *Council of Postsecondary Accreditation Newsletter, 8,* 2.

Millard, R. M. (1991). *Today's myths and tomorrow's realities.* San Francisco: Jossey-Bass.

Nelson, P. D. (1998). Accreditation of education and training programs: American Psychological Association. In A. S. Bellack & M. Hersen (Series Eds.) & A. N.

Weins (Vol. Ed.), *Comprehensive clinical psychology: Vol. 2. Professional issues* (pp. 47–60). London: Pergamon Press.

Nelson, P. D., & Aletky, P. J. (1987). Accreditation: A link between training and practice. In B. A. Edelstein & E. S. Berler (Eds.), *Evaluation and accountability in clinical training* (pp. 231–252). New York: Plenum.

Peterson, D. R. (1976). Is psychology a profession? *American Psychologist, 31,* 572–581.

Peterson, D. R. (1997). *Educating professional psychologists: History and guiding conception.* Washington, DC: American Psychological Association.

Sears, R. R. (1947). Clinical training facilities: 1947. A report from the Committee on Graduate and Professional Training. *American Psychologist, 2,* 199–205.

Selden, W. K. (1960). *Accreditation: A struggle over standards in higher education.* New York: Harper & Row.

Sheridan, E. P., Matarazzo, J. D., & Nelson, P. D. (1995). Accreditation of psychology's graduate professional education and training programs: An historical perspective. *Professional Psychology: Research and Practice, 26,* 386–392.

Stark, J. S., & Austin, A. E. (1983). Students and accreditation. In K. E. Young, C. M. Chambers, H. R. Kells, & Associates (Eds.), *Understanding accreditation* (pp. 211–232). San Francisco: Jossey-Bass.

Starr, P. (1982). *The social transformation of American medicine.* New York: Basic Books.

Stigall, T. T., Bourg, E. F., Bricklin, P. M., Kovacs, A. L., Larsen, K. G., Lorion, R. P., et al. (Eds.). (1990). *Report of the Joint Council on Professional Education in Psychology.* Baton Rouge, LA: Land & Land.

Wellner, A. M. (Ed.). (1978). *Education and credentialing in psychology: A proposal for a national commission.* Washington, DC: American Psychological Association.

Young, K. E. (1983). Prologue: The changing scope of accreditation. In K. E. Young, C. M. Chambers, H. R. Kells, & Associates (Eds.), *Understanding accreditation* (pp. 1–16). San Francisco: Jossey-Bass.

2

THE HISTORY OF ACCREDITATION OF DOCTORAL PROGRAMS IN PSYCHOLOGY

ELIZABETH M. ALTMAIER

In recent years, graduate education and training in psychology has experienced several shifts in focus defined by the criteria for accreditation, those shifts partially determined by the interests and concerns of specific faculty and staff involved in training and partially by larger issues in the discipline and profession of psychology. In this chapter I consider the evolution of accreditation of doctoral programs in psychology, with a focus on the influences of both internal and external forces.

THE INITIATION OF ACCREDITATION

As is detailed in chapter 1, initial work in accreditation took place in 1946 and 1947 when the then-named Committee on Graduate and Professional Training received from the Board of Directors of the American Psychological Association (APA) a request from the Veterans Administration for a list of schools that had adequate facilities for doctoral training and thus required minimal financial assistance to train the increased number of service providers required by returning veterans. To develop such a list, the committee first determined what aspects of a school's functioning were essential to quality training. The domains considered were staff, both clinical and nonclinical; curriculum; and departmental facilities.

The domains emphasized in this first set of accreditation criteria were determined by the committee's assumptions about quality training, stated as follows: "The reason for this [emphasis on criteria] lies in the committee's assumption that competent professional psychologists supplied with adequate tools and working in a satisfactory organizational matrix, may be relied upon to produce effective training" (Sears, 1947, p. 200). Thus, the accreditation criteria focused primarily on people—those people who were doing the training—and the tools—the facilities that they possessed. Specific criteria had to do with number of staff, degree of staff training, curriculum requirements, and practicum facilities. In the Sears (1947) report, the extent to which 40 institutions met the committee's 13 criteria was enumerated.

This first attempt at clarifying criteria for accreditation was acknowledged to be a work in progress, and in March of 1947, the APA Board of Directors authorized a special committee on training in clinical psychology to develop a more carefully articulated set of criteria. This committee reported back to the board in September with a new set of criteria accompanied by a discussion of training issues (APA Committee on Training in Clinical Psychology, 1947). The report focused heavily on broad principles that committee members believed would lead to quality education:

> The general principles which underlie the graduate program appear to us of primary importance—in fact, much more important than the details of the program. If clarity in the formulation of goals exists, there should be relatively little difficulty about agreeing on the means for implementing them. (p. 543)

Rather than establishing standards that pertained to "details of the program," the committee chose to define principles or guidelines that should underlie all clinical training irrespective of institution or department (see Appendix C, this volume). Exhibit 2.1 outlines these general principles. It is important to note that these principles can be characterized by three overarching values in education and training. One such value is breadth of training (generalism) as opposed to depth (specialization). The early committee members believed that general training was of more value than "technical goals." A second value is the competence of the psychologists doing the training, in other words, the qualifications of the faculty. The quality of the faculty was felt to be paramount in setting the general atmosphere of training. A third value is the integration of practice and research throughout the training program. The committee gave equal value to the societal implications and applications of clinical research.

EXHIBIT 2.1
Graduate Professional Program General Principles

The general principles which underlie the graduate program appear to us of primary importance—in fact, much more important than the details of the program. If clarity in the formulation of goals exists, there should be relatively little difficulty about agreeing on the means for implementing them. . . .

Against this general background the principles which we consider important are the following:

1. A clinical psychologist must first and foremost be a psychologist in the sense that he can be expected to have a point of view and a core of knowledge and training which is common to all psychologists. . . .
2. The program of education for the doctorate in clinical psychology should be as rigorous and extensive as that for the traditional doctorate. . . .
3. Preparation should be broad; it should be directed to research and professional goals, not to technical goals. . . .
4. . . . the program calls for study in six major areas: a. General psychology; b. Psychodynamics of behavior; c. Diagnostic methods; d. Research methods; e. Related disciplines; f. Therapy. . . .
5. The program should concern itself mainly with basic courses and principles rather than multiple courses in technique. . . .
6. Courses should be scrutinized for their content, rather than judged by their titles. . . .
7. The specific program of instruction should be organized around a careful integration of theory and practice, of academic and field work, by persons representing both aspects. . . .
8. Through all four years of graduate work, the student should have contact, both direct and indirect, with clinical material. . . .
9. Equally important is the need for contact with normal material. Opportunities should be provided to enable the student to become acquainted with the range of normal and borderline persons who never establish clinical contact. . . .
10. The general atmosphere of the course of training should be such as to encourage the increase of maturity, the continued growth of the desirable personality characteristics. . . .
11. The program should do everything possible to bring out the responsibilities associated with the activities of the psychologist. There should be persistent effort to have the student appreciate that his findings make a real difference to a particular person and to that person's immediate group. . . . (APA Committee on Training in Clinical Psychology, 1947, pp. 543–544)

This committee (renamed the Committee on Training in Clinical Psychology) then operated as a committee on accreditation. It initially received information from programs via questionnaire but later made regular visits to programs. It assessed the degree to which programs met or failed to meet the criteria that were being developed in an ongoing way, and it issued annual reports in the *American Psychologist*, all aspects of accreditation that are similar to those currently in place.

Given the history of accreditation during the subsequent 50 years, it is essential to consider the intent of the people who influenced accreditation through the initial iterations of criteria. In 1948, APA's Policy and Planning

Board stated, "The ideal program is a general pattern, not a blueprint. There must be a recognition that quite different paths lead to the same goals. Experimental, forward looking programs must be encouraged in a rapidly changing field like clinical psychology" (p. 190). Perhaps more emphatically, the board reminded psychologists that "any 'ideal' training program such as that presented by the Committee on Training in Clinical Psychology . . . should be understood as presenting a general pattern of training toward certain goals, rather than as a blueprint for curriculum organization" (p. 190). The clear intent of psychologists was to foster diversity within parameters of commonly agreed-on guidelines of training.

It is unfortunate that the result of this emphasis on diversity within common parameters did not yield widespread agreement on methods and outcomes in graduate education. In fact, as early as 1949, the committee noted in its annual report published in the *American Psychologist* that there was considerable dissatisfaction on the part of departments who were being accredited. Department faculty believed that the results of integrating clinical training into their previous departmental emphasis on science did not work very well. Department faculty also questioned the validity of training and practice, feeling that psychological approaches to testing and treatment had not yet been validated with scientific evidence. Committee members themselves visited programs, thus interacting directly with departments who disagreed with their approach. Their 1949 report stated that their visits to departments were met with a range of responses, varying from acceptance and appreciation to an "honest conviction" that the committee was a "usurper of power and authority," thereby eroding the quality of departments' training and education.

However, the APA Committee on Training in Clinical Psychology (1949) responded with a vigorous defense of the content and process of accreditation:

> We are convinced of the importance of setting standards and evaluating performance in clinical training. In fact, we see this process as inevitable if clinical psychology is to establish itself soundly and be a credit to psychology as a whole. We have set up criteria and administered procedures in ways that seemed best. We are neither satisfied that they are perfect nor persuaded that they are dangerous or ineffective. (p. 340)

In this quote, there appears the first evidence of discrepancy between what goals were intended via accreditation versus what outcomes were actually achieved. Sheridan, Matarazzo, and Nelson (1995) commented that each of the early training conferences also noted similar discrepancies. In the discussions that took place at the conferences, both sides of the controversy were expressed: the need for accreditation to enhance quality in graduate education and to protect the public and the need for faculty at institutions of higher education to have control over their curriculum.

It is important to consider how a process created with good intentions with input from a range of departments involved in training resulted in such a degree of conflict. One answer might be suggested by a statement in the guide for site visitors published by APA in 1954:

> The underlying principle or hypothesis in our procedure of evaluation is that there are discernible differences in the nature and quality of doctoral programs in clinical psychology which are related to the competence of the graduates of the programs. While a controlled test of this hypothesis is impossible at the present time, the procedures of evaluation should be conducted as nearly as possible in accordance with an experimental design which will make such a test possible in the future, even though definitions of competence have not been agreed upon and although it is certain that such definitions will change with the development of the profession of clinical psychology. (p. 3)

This statement suggests that neither the definitions of competence nor the desired outcomes of training were clear to the committee, but the committee members were nonetheless proceeding along an evaluative path. It may be the case that in their decision making, the committee relied on what the members knew to be familiar, and that was the particular emphases of their own departments. Certainly the site visitor guide anticipates this concern in stating that "while the visitor may disagree personally with certain details of these APA standards and reports, he [sic] is under obligation to represent them faithfully in his work of evaluation" (p. 1).

The difficulties and tensions led to a request to the Education and Training Board of APA in May 1960 that the committee be disbanded. In justifying this request, the committee noted that there were patterns of societal control in place, such as the increase of licensing laws in many states, the establishment of the predecessor to the American Board of Professional Psychology, and the rapidly accelerating growth of state psychological associations. The committee also cited the burdens of reviewing too many programs and continuing conflicts with departments who preferred the committee to assume advisory functions and consultation functions as opposed to evaluative functions. However, at their May 1960 meeting, the Education and Training Board decided to continue the evaluation of doctoral programs in clinical and counseling psychology.

The early stage of accreditation revealed several tensions that have persisted to the present. First is the issue of standards versus principles. Are there going to be clear, specific prescriptive standards that apply to all programs in psychology, or are there going to be universal principles on which the education and training community agree, in the application of which there can be a degree of flexibility? An example of this issue is the role of practicum in doctoral education. Should there be a prescribed number of supervised hours required of all students irrespective of the emphasis on practice in the program? Or should a program be allowed to set its own requirement? In the current iteration of this conflict, practitioners in the field typically argue the former, whereas faculty argue the latter.

Second is the issue of the purpose of accreditation. Accreditation is commonly cited as a means of protecting the public by assuring commitment to certain principles of quality among those members who voluntarily participate. However, the public can be protected by assessing adequacy or by enhancing quality; those two different versions of protecting the public are in some conflict. If adequacy is sufficient for accreditation, will programs continue to develop toward excellence, or will they settle for less than excellence?

Third is the validity of various models of professional education and training. Tension existed in departments in which faculty tried to integrate clinical training into a department that had formerly emphasized science. Early documents from the committee frequently refer to this tension. During their visits to departments, they found that some faculty considered integrating clinical training into academic training as a great experiment worthy of considerable effort. However, other faculty refer to this change with great alarm. As chapter 1 describes, however, during this early stage of accreditation, the number of accredited programs slowly increased, the specialty of counseling psychology became included in the purview of accreditation, and the specialty of school psychology began to desire accreditation for their own doctoral training.

THE MIDDLE STAGE OF ACCREDITATION

In the 1970s and 1980s, there was a dramatic growth in the number of doctoral psychology programs. At the end of 1968, there were 199 accredited programs (doctoral and internship); by the end of 1978, there were 278 (a 40% increase); and by the end of 1988, there were 593 programs (a 113% increase in 10 years). This growth likely came about for two reasons. First, there was a corresponding rise in the number of research universities capable of developing a doctoral program in clinical or counseling psychology. These two decades were the end of the "golden age" in American higher education in which state and federal financial support increased rapidly, and many universities built up their research facilities, faculty, and doctoral degree production. There was an increase in the number of institutions granting the PhD, in psychology and other areas, and in the number of students enrolled in doctoral programs in psychology. These institutions needed new faculty, and the graduates of newly accredited programs found positions in departments offering doctoral training programs. The field also needed psychologists interested in applied and practice careers. The number of positions in colleges and universities, including in counseling centers and student health centers, grew rapidly, as did positions in hospitals and community mental health centers.

This time period also represented a stage of self-reflection on the part of psychology. A series of national conferences considering important issues in psychology began in 1949 and continued rather steadily; many of these took place during these two decades. (Appendix J, this volume, contains a complete listing of all national conferences and their reports.) Each of those conferences resulted in position statements and follow-up and implementation plans, which resulted in attempts to change various policies and practices in graduate education. The growth of these conferences was likely due to several reasons. First, the initial conference (the Boulder Conference) resulted in the clear articulation of a training model that received widespread support: the scientist–practitioner model, also known as the Boulder model of training. Additionally, the process of coming together in small groups and developing positions and plans was itself of benefit to graduate education, allowing recently opened programs to have interactions with more experienced programs over difficult issues. Last, the increase in financial support available for the conferences from institutions and from other sources had a positive effect on their occurrence.

Finally, the number of programs emphasizing practitioner training, a new model of graduate education in psychology, increased during this time period. In 1973, the Vail Conference (Korman, 1976) promoted a broadening of models of training past the then-typical scientist–practitioner model to include a professional model of training for students committed to practitioner careers. The first professional school was established in 1969 when the California School of Professional Psychology was founded with help from the California Psychological Association. Students were admitted to the first campuses (San Francisco and Los Angeles) in 1970. In 1982, only 12 years later, there were 44 such programs. Although these two decades contained a dramatic growth in the overall number of programs providing doctoral-level education and training to psychologists, the number of graduates illustrates a substantial increase of training within practitioner models.

After 20 years with essentially one set of accreditation criteria, two new sets of criteria were promulgated in a 10-year period: the 1973 criteria and the 1979 criteria. As an introduction to these changes, in 1968 what was then known as the Committee on Evaluation established a Commission on Accreditation to articulate principles to govern the necessary next steps in accreditation. In fact, the committee was given the broad mandate to study accreditation in all of its ramifications. The commission issued a report in July 1969 that summarized their recommendation that APA carry out accreditation under policies that recognize differences among institutions and their educational goals, that value diversity, and that promote a variety of pathways to achieving educational goals. The commission also stated that accreditation should (a) stimulate the educational effectiveness of the institution as a whole, (b) foster innovation and diversity among content and techniques, (c) clarify to the public the range of activities performed by psychologists, (d) protect the consumers, and (e) enable students to choose programs that best meet their own goals. An important change, further described in chapter 3, was the addition of internship programs to the scope of accreditation. The Committee on Evaluation accepted these reports and used them as a basis for a final document developed by the Committee on Evaluation (renamed the Committee on Accreditation [CoA]) in January 1971 and published by the APA in January 1973.

The 1973 criteria again outlined principles regarding quality training rather than prescriptive standards. It is important to note that the committee accepted a diversity of training models and that it counseled programs to articulate their training model and goals within which they would be held responsible for their own outcomes, a hallmark of the *Guidelines and Principles* (APA Committee on Accreditation, 2000) some 25 years later. Some of these principles concerned historically familiar ideas: breadth as opposed to depth; integration of theory, practice, and research; the competence of faculty, and so on. However, the 1973 criteria concerned themselves with a new domain of evaluation, that of students. General principles expressed the need for program faculty to concern themselves with the development of the student as a "mature, effective psychological being" as well as with the development of the student's knowledge and competencies. Additional language demanded that faculty assess students' progress continually and that students should regularly receive feedback from faculty.

Two forces arose in the mid-1970s that caused psychology to reexamine these criteria for accreditation. One force was an increasing concern with credentialing. In the mid-1970s, the National Register of Health Service Providers in Psychology and the APA cosponsored a conference on credentialing that set the stage for a shift away from principles to an emphasis on standards. This force was a voice for prescriptive standards in accreditation, for a need to articulate common required training experiences across all programs deemed to be offering training in professional psychology. The second force was the outgrowth of the Vail Conference, with increased emphasis on patterns and levels of training and a corresponding growth in the number of professional programs with models quite different from the then-familiar scientist–practitioner model.

In 1976, the Council of Representatives requested that the Education and Training Board establish another task force on accreditation. It considered several key issues in formulating the 1979 criteria, a blend of familiar areas of conflict and new areas of interest. The first issue was one of generality versus specificity. To what degree should the accreditation standards be general and to what degree should they be specific? The second issue was the increased recognition that quite different models of training exist. More to the point of accreditation, can the same criteria be used to judge a program that uses the scientist–practitioner model to train future academics and a program that uses a professional school model to train future clinicians? The third issue was an increased recognition that psychological service providers were underserving minority populations and that training practices and patterns might be contributing to this underutilization. Psychologists struggled with how to meld APA's commitment to a just and free society into principles and practices of accreditation. The fourth issue was that of a core curriculum. Does everyone who considers himself or herself a psychologist need to have taken the same courses in graduate school? Is there certain content everyone needs to know to be a psychologist?

The resulting 1979 criteria, published as the *Accreditation Handbook* (APA, 1980), combined principles and standards, attempting to define a middle ground that, in some cases, would incorporate principles and, in other cases, would incorporate standards. The *Handbook* stated this goal as follows: "the current Criteria represent a balance between 'rigid specification' and 'guiding principle' prescription" (p. I–2). Thus, for example, the 1979 criteria defined 400 as the minimum number of required practicum hours, a standard, but also principles about what practicum training is meant to achieve. Another example is in the section on faculty. Principles articulated necessary diversity for faculty, as well as their qualities (e.g., experienced, productive individuals; large enough in the aggregate to ensure availability to students). Standards said the faculty had to be licensed in their state, and the program should be directed by a senior faculty member with "evidence of professional leadership" (e.g., diplomate, fellowship status in APA).

There were both positive and negative consequences of the 1979 criteria. On the positive side, the 1980s and 1990s demonstrated continuing growth in the number of accredited programs and in their diversity. On the negative side, these criteria generated a history of unresolved tensions, both in and around the criteria for accreditation themselves and concerning the process of accreditation in general.

Somehow the intent of the 1979 criteria to carefully combine standards and principles, emphasizing the need for programmatic diversity and innovation, did not get carried out. Two reasons may explain the discrepancy between what was intended and what was achieved. First, there is an unresolved, and perhaps unresolvable, tension between assessing for *adequacy* versus assessing and promoting *excellence*. Standards that are prescriptive set a lower boundary above which programs are expected to function, but how much of the function above that boundary is determined at the program level? Principles or guidelines are meant to be aspirational in nature and thus by definition inspire programs to levels of excellence.

Second is the burden that the activities pertaining to accreditation place on CoA members. The structures in place for program review within the CoA and within APA did not change, despite the increase in programs needing review, and the burden simply meant that committee members may not have been able to think carefully about their decisions. A related concern is the increase in the use of site visitors to evaluate program quality. In the 1970s, the CoA turned to experienced senior faculty to conduct the site visits and provide reports of program functioning to the committee. As the number of programs grew, more site visitors were needed, and their seniority in the field was not assured. Thus, the committee developed a checklist that was inserted in the *Handbook* with abbreviated descriptions of accreditation criteria to guide site visitor review. Unfortunately, the checklist became the criteria, and the term *checklist mentality* described a limited evaluation that concerned itself with specifics rather than the broad evaluation necessary to ensure program functioning within the criteria.

The committee made one additional change to the 1979 criteria. As is detailed in Box 2.1, the applicability of the accreditation criteria to faith-based institutions was tested because in such institutions faculty hiring, student recruitment, and curriculum planning are guided by institutional faith or creedal statements. Footnote 3, approved by the Council of Representatives in 1980, allowed the institution to apply for an exception to APA criteria if the institution could document procedures by which it assured that accepted practices of academic freedom, faculty and student rights, and training and research were not eroded by discrimination in selection of faculty and students on the basis of allegiance to a creedal oath.

CURRENT STATUS OF ACCREDITATION

In 1989, the APA, in the form of the Interim Board of Educational Affairs, took a serious look at accreditation governance and convened, in 1990, a meeting of a small group to develop recommendations about the future governance of accreditation. Box 2.2 gives a personal voice to these events. Participants in this group were chosen to represent the full spectrum of perspectives and responsibilities relevant to accreditation: graduate education and academic institutions, professional programs (academic and internship), public consumers of professional education, and professional practice service institutions and settings. The group developed a proposed governance structure, with the recommendation that national organizations of psychologists be represented on a new accrediting body. The CoA received this report in 1990. Two other reports were forwarded to the committee, each recommending more prominent roles for practitioners in the accreditation process: one from the Joint Council on Professional Education in Psychology that is described in more detail in chapter 4, and one from the Council of Representatives by initiative of Division 42 and the State of Virginia.

Governance groups throughout the APA and professional psychology were given the opportunity to comment on these proposals. The CoA was then asked to develop its own recommendations for the structure and func-

BOX 2.1
Religion and Educational Standards at the Crossroads
Dorothy E. Holmes, PhD, Department of Clinical Psychology, George Washington University, Washington, DC, and Baltimore–Washington Institute for Psychoanalysis

In the 3 years that I served on the Committee on Accreditation (CoA), culminating in my chairpersonship in 1980, the pivotal experience for me was my participation and leadership in the task of considering Fuller Theological Seminary's application for accreditation of its clinical psychology program. Determining the accreditation worthiness of Fuller's program tested the soundness and resiliency of the principles and procedures of accreditation, and of the members of the CoA, more stringently than any other task or challenge during my years of service. It was a watershed in the history of accreditation because Fuller's faith-based decisions on faculty and staff hiring and student admissions meant the probable exclusion of otherwise qualified people on the basis of creed. For most on the CoA, such practices were detested as intolerably discriminatory. The acuteness of the problem was accentuated because it was a time in the history of the American Psychological Association (APA) when its governing bodies were mandating widespread nondiscrimination policies with respect to race, gender, and culture and the necessity for didactic and clinical training across this spectrum. As an African American woman and the first African American CoA Chair, I was especially attuned to the issues and the challenges the Fuller situation presented.

At times in the process, the likelihood of accrediting Fuller's program seemed improbable, but we toiled on, looking for a workable compromise solution. Only in retrospect do I see the elegance of the solution to which we came. At the time it seemed smartly pragmatic. The final decision to accredit the program was founded on requiring Fuller to fully disclose its policies and to pledge itself to providing systematic exposure of its students to training experiences in diversity beyond the confines of its program's offerings.

Why do I consider the solution elegant? It brought to full consciousness the possible limitations in freedom one would experience in deciding to become a faculty member or student at Fuller. Even if an aspirant to Fuller personally considered Fuller's practices favorably, APA identified them as limitations. Thus, if only for a moment in time, it becomes necessary for prospective

continues

> **BOX 2.1 (continued)**
>
> faculty members and students in religiously based institutions to consider these factors as limitations per se and to consider their possible negative ramifications (e.g., possible adverse effects on faculty and student rights and on academic freedom). Then, one can weigh them along with one's possible other views of these factors and the range of usual criteria one considers in evaluating the quality of a graduate program.
>
> In the Fuller decision, APA did its best to assure that the selection of a faith-based psychology training program would be founded on choice—that is, setting one's course with full awareness and knowledge of options and consequences. As I remember the work of the committee on this issue, the thought processes involved were intense, but the deliberations were without rancor. A very high purpose seemed to bind us together in constructive reflection and work. With the Fuller decision, APA set the bar high and did so with equanimity and grace under duress. It did itself proud.

tion of a new accrediting body. In its response to that charge, the CoA recommended that a new committee be instituted that would have representatives of five domains: (a) academic administration at departmental or higher levels, (b) professional practice, (c) education and training, (d) consumers or the public, and (e) students. In 1991, the Council of Representatives approved this new committee governing accreditation. The new committee, also named the Committee on Accreditation, consisted of 21 people representing the above domains and constituencies. Further, the Council of Representatives charged the new committee with reviewing current policies and practices to determine any necessary changes in scope (the types of programs to be accredited), criteria (the standards on which accreditation decisions would be made), and procedures to be followed by site visitors and decision makers.

The new committee was successful at its task and developed revised statements of scope, criteria, and procedures, the *Guidelines and Principles* (APA, 2000). In the new model, formally accepted by the Council of Representatives in 1995, were definite changes in several aspects of accreditation. First, the committee broadened the scope of accreditation to include doctoral training programs that lead to preparation for the delivery of psychological services in clinical, counseling, or school psychology; combinations of the above; and "emerging substantive areas of psychology." Thus, for the first time, accreditation was intended to be available to programs preparing providers for newer specialty areas of practice. Accreditation was continued

BOX 2.2
Personal Reminiscences

M. Marlyne Kilbey, PhD, Department of Psychology, Wayne State University, Detroit, Michigan

I served on the Committee on Accreditation (CoA) from 1988 through 1991 and chaired it in 1990. There are three things that I remember vividly about CoA service, and I'd be surprised if everyone who ever served on the committee did not echo them. One was the incredible amount of work involved. When I unpacked the first box of materials, I feared that I had ruined my life by agreeing to join the CoA. Although the going was slow at first, I did learn to review an accreditation packet both thoroughly and quickly. My second memory is of the collegiality of the CoA. I served as a generalist, meaning that I was one of the few, if not the only, basic scientist on the CoA. Yet, regardless of training or work experience, CoA members shared a fairly uniform idea of what comprised a solid program and what indicated problems. The third memory I have is of the program reviewers and the American Psychological Association (APA) staff. The CoA's difficult job was made possible because of the incredibly solid work done by the psychologists who reviewed the programs. Even then, the CoA's work would not have happened had it not been for the painstaking and methodical work of Paul Nelson, Elizabeth Hilt, and Jane Winston. Less able people would have had chaos where these had fashioned order.

During my tenure on the CoA, work was under way to adapt the accreditation guidelines to take into account the developments in the field between 1970 and the mid-1980s. Jill Reich had chaired a task force that outlined how these changes might proceed, but it was apparent that if changes were to take place, various groups would have to be assured that their points of view would be valued by future CoAs. One of these groups was the Council of Graduate Departments of Psychology (COGDOP). I was a member, so I invited Paul Nelson to attend our meeting that year (1989) in San Antonio to talk informally with people about the CoA structure. Manny Donchin and other COGDOP leaders, Joe Matarazzo, Paul Nelson, and I met over beers in a hotel on the River Walk, and Paul sketched out a plan on a cocktail napkin that identified four major groups that were best qualified to determine the ideal size and structure of a future CoA. APA then planned a special

continues

> BOX 2.2 (continued)
>
> meeting of representatives of those groups to be held in Washington, DC, in 1990, which I chaired.
>
> The core concept was that there should be four communities represented on the new CoA as domains of perspective and responsibility: namely, (a) representatives of academic departments or colleges (administration), (b) academic and internship programs in professional psychology (training directors), (c) practitioners (independent and institutional practice), and (d) the general public. This composition adhered to principles of good practice in accreditation set forth by the Council on Postsecondary Accreditation. But the sticky issues had to do with how many seats on the CoA to allocate to each domain from the various constituencies. Debate was long and often hot at the meeting, but in the end the group agreed that COGDOP and practitioner groups were to have 4 seats each; 8 seats were to be allocated across the training director communities, with no more than 2 representatives per organization; and 3 seats were to be allocated to public representatives, including a student. When the plan went before the APA Council, they changed the number of seats allocated to the training director communities to 10. Although it took lots of work from many people to articulate this plan and build consensus to support it, I must say that it has worked well, and accreditation of psychology training and internship programs has continued to be held in high regard by people within and outside the profession.

for predoctoral internship programs. And last, accreditation was made available for postdoctoral training programs in specialized fields of professional psychology. Thus, the scope of accreditation was broadened, and the number of programs who could participate in this system of peer review would be dramatically expanded. As it has turned out, the CoA has yet to enact governing language that would define the emerging areas, and so this intent of the new committee has not yet become reality. And, as Box 2.3 details, political issues have continued to thrust themselves into the working environment.

A second major change was in the philosophy of reviewing program adherence to criteria and standards. In the previous systems, as outlined above, there were specific criteria regarding doctoral training (prescriptive) as well as guiding principles. In the new system, examining a program's adherence to its own stated philosophy, models, and missions; considering how well a program was developed and organized (coherence); and determining how effec-

BOX 2.3
Almost a Convert

Virginia E. O'Leary, PhD, Department of Psychology, Auburn University, Auburn, Alabama

I took my seat on the Committee on Accreditation (CoA) very skeptical about both the politics and the process. I had not been allowed to take a position on the 21-person committee after I was appointed as a Council of Graduate Departments of Psychology (COGDOP) representative (one of four and the only one who was on the COGDOP Executive Committee). Indeed, the fact that I was not seated on the committee upon my appointment to it occasioned my resignation from the American Psychological Association (APA). After the person who blocked my appointment was no longer in a position to do so, I was seated. I was not expecting much. A 21-member committee is unwieldy, at best. A 21-member committee representing a variety of disparate interests among groups with a long history of fervent disagreement is fraught with peril. I was sufficiently skeptical that I participated eagerly and actively in the Accreditation Summit organized by the American Psychological Society in anticipation of the need to locate the accrediting body for psychology outside of the political reach of the APA.

My first meeting with the committee was a pleasant surprise. Relations among representatives of different psychological organizations with stakes in accreditation were cordial. Everyone appeared clearly committed to affecting a workable compromise, and most were working hard at keeping their personal and political agendas in check. This was due in no small part to the first chair of the committee, who was dedicated to keeping the group talking until consensus was reached. For the most part her strategy worked. Only once in the first few years of the committee's existence was the group forced to a vote on a controversial issue—postdoctoral training. That vote was a triumph for the guild interests within APA, and I still consider its outcome unfortunate, especially as I do not believe that everyone on the committee clearly understood its implications.

I chaired a subcommittee to explore master's-level accreditation. We recommended that the committee consider the issue as part of its mission. The issue was tabled and has not been pursued. I find that shortsighted, as the changes in the delivery of

continues

BOX 2.3 (continued)

mental health services in the past decade have increased reliance on master's-level clinical practitioners around the country, practitioners who are not governed by an accrediting body recognized by the U.S. Department of Education (although the Interorganizational Board for Accreditation of Masters in Psychology Programs, now named the Masters in Psychology Accreditation Council, may obtain such recognition in the future). In this instance, I believe the committee acted myopically to serve the interests of the guild and to ignore the interests of the general public. I remain disappointed that we failed to assume responsibility for overseeing the training of master's students in psychology, many of whom are "products" of the graduate departments of psychology that house the doctoral programs accredited by the CoA.

Still, we did forge a document that was generally acceptable to the many stakeholders involved, and the system we designed works. Accreditation is no longer granted on the basis of a long checklist with no real assessment of the overall quality of the program in question. The process involved in writing the new accreditation guidelines was noteworthy for the commitment evidenced to quality and fairness. The endeavor was arduous at times, but a great deal of thought went into the document, and both the profession and the public are generally well served by the outcome.

But the story is not over yet. I believe that some members of APA's Board of Directors continue to try to intrude into the affairs of the committee, which is administratively housed within, but not of it. Such intrusion places the staff of the committee in an untenable position and threatens the integrity of the committee and of the accreditation process. Particularly troubling is the fact that in the years since the committee's inception, the original members of the committee who were keenly aware of the delicate balance they were entrusted to maintain have been replaced with members who are disinclined to maintain that balance. Illustrative of this point was a recent vote by the committee to accept a Board of Director's liaison on the grounds that the committee "has not yet achieved independence from APA." This is coupled with the fact that the committee's repeated attempts to obtain independent counsel have met with failure, and the recent emergence

continues

> of interest in codifying the criteria necessary to achieve or maintain accreditation is a long way off. Indeed, until the CoA ceases to rely on APA for any reason, I believe the question of whose interests it represents (and serves) will persist. Despite my generally favorable experience as a committee member, until that issue is resolved and I am confident that the integrity of the original committee's philosophy of rendering a summative judgement about the quality of each program reviewed for accreditation has been preserved, I will remain a skeptic.

tively the program was able to demonstrate scientific, professional, and procedural outcomes became paramount. Although this change was anticipated in the wording of previous iterations of accreditation criteria, the current *Guidelines and Principles* (APA, 2000) make the linkage of the mission/model and outcome data an explicit aspect of evaluation.

Under the "new" criteria, programs were to be examined within eight general domain areas: (a) the eligibility and institutional setting; (b) philosophy, objectives, and curriculum plan; (c) resources; (d) attention to cultural and individual differences and diversity; (e) student–faculty relationships; (f) self-assessment and quality enhancement methods; (g) methods of public disclosure; and (h) the relationship with the accrediting body. Essentially, the review shifted from the former checklist to a new consideration of the breadth and coherence of the program's philosophy, resources, and outcomes. The *Guidelines and Principles* stated the goal of this new focus as follows:

> The accreditation review process will place great emphasis on the outcomes or products of a program's training efforts. Resource and process evaluations of programs will continue, but such evaluations are not designed to discourage experimentation, innovation, or modernization with regard to teaching methods or curricula. (APA, 2000, p. 4)

This philosophy, and the new procedures, placed great emphasis on outcomes and how those outcomes are reflected in the relationships of goals and objectives. The program's goals and objectives represent the standards against which the outcomes are measured, and thus each program's evaluation is specific to its own plans and achievements.

Some aspects of accreditation were not changed. First, there was a continuing emphasis on principles that should underlie effective training in any clinical, counseling, school, or professional psychology program. These principles are contained in the preamble and essentially are the following:

- Preparation for practice at the entry level (doctoral) should be broad and professional in its nature rather than narrow and technical.

- Advanced training (at the postdoctoral level and beyond) should reflect the changing and growing knowledge of the discipline of psychology and be responsive to the needs of consumers.
- Both science and practice are necessary for excellence in training in professional psychology. Although programs may place differential emphasis on these two areas, all graduates of psychology programs must understand the mutuality of science and practice for the future of psychology.
- Programs must have a clearly defined series of goals for their training and have carefully articulated plans for achieving these goals.

This is a remarkably exciting time in the history of accreditation. It is 50 years, more or less, since its beginning, and now psychology is starting off on a new and different path. The current CoA, as is explained in chapter 5, is grappling with issues concerning the implementation of the new criteria and with related concerns. As an example, site visitors now need to be trained to examine program functioning in a different way than they had before. Also, program directors and program faculty, as well as internship staff, must be able to produce outcome data that demonstrates programs are meeting their training goals. Gathering these data from current students and from alumni is a new task for many training programs, and APA has attempted—through training workshops—to assist program faculty and staff in conceptualizing what data are needed and how best to gather them.

THE FUTURE: CRISES AND CHALLENGES

The effectiveness of psychology's accreditation efforts rests somewhat uneasily on the effectiveness with which psychology as a field copes with several distinct challenges for the future.

The first challenge is a crisis in higher education that stems from many sources. A troubling level of disaffection exists in the work of colleges and universities. Academics lack support among the general public, even among those who claim to be knowledgeable about the work of colleges and universities. Criticisms focus on the quality of undergraduate education, the degree to which faculty are teaching as opposed to conducting research, and how overseers of higher education (boards of regents, state legislatures, the general public) can have appropriate and adequate input.

There are also increasing financial constraints in higher education. Institutions probably peaked in their funding levels in the 1970s, and these resources have been diminishing ever since. It is not unusual now for a state university to derive less than a third of its budget from general fund (tax payers') money. The remaining dollars must be obtained through tuition, extramural funding of research, private donations, and other revenue streams.

There are also increasing demands from students. However, these students are not 18-year-old freshmen who have just graduated from high school. The new students on college campuses have family and work demands that compete with their studies, they have very different personal circumstances than younger students, and they intersperse periods of education with periods of work. This is a kind of student that not all institutions are well equipped to handle.

A fourth aspect of the crisis is morale among faculty. Faculty cannot help being affected by trends in un- and underemployment in university settings. Whereas some faculty in fields with access to outside funding or in institutions with better resources remain excited and invigorated, morale has dropped in some disciplines and settings with a correspondent increase in sad, angry, and frustrated faculty members whose careers are not turning out in ways they had imagined.

Another major challenge is the challenge of technology. It is impossible to pick up a journal concerned with higher education and not read about technology. Technology is going to affect graduate education in psychology in two important ways. One is that technology can and probably will transform the interaction between faculty and students, particularly in allowing students increased flexibility in the ways that they "learn." Learning will no longer be confined to classrooms, lectures, and books. All of the traditional ways of helping students learn are going to undergo a dramatic change. An example is the use of "electronic office hours." Second, technology is going to transform the definition of teaching. Institutions already use the term *distance learning* to embody this concept, and virtually every institution of higher education is struggling with how it can, will, or should deliver instruction over a distance.

Psychology has begun to consider how distance learning can interact with education. The APA Task Force on Distance Education and Training in Professional Psychology (2002) recently issued their report on Principles of Good Practice. In it, the task force outlined nine domains relevant to distance education (e.g., access, faculty and student technical support, library and learning resources) and identified issues related to quality assessment within each domain. Of particular relevance to this chapter are emphases in this report on how programs must organize training to be "sequential, cumulative, and graded in complexity" (p. 24), a characteristic of all doctoral programs.

A third challenge is that of diversity. The CoA over its history has changed a good deal in its emphasis in this area. In more recent years, criteria related to the diversity of students and faculty and to the degree to which students receive instruction in working with diverse client populations have become more explicit and more enforced. That is true for several reasons. First, programs must and need to attend to recruiting and retaining students who represent the diversity that graduates will see in their clients. Second, programs must ensure that all students receive systematic and coherent learning experiences in dealing with a diverse client population. The fact that many large cities in the United States have a majority population of ethnic minorities underlines the importance of psychology embracing the training of its practitioners and researchers in diversities of racial and ethnic origin, gender, sexual orientation, religion, and culture. New guidelines for working with clients of varying ethnic and racial backgrounds challenge academic programs to prepare students with new multicultural competencies (Pope-Davis & Coleman, 1997).

The fourth challenge is the complex interplay of science, practice, and scientifically based practice. The new accreditation criteria clearly allow a program to define its own goals and training model within reasonable limits. However, these goals and models must be set against the larger discipline of psychology and the necessary and appropriate roles of science and practice. An example of this challenge is the degree to which doctoral programs and internships will be required to teach their students psychotherapeutic methods that have been designated as empirically supported. Recall that an early tension in accreditation was departments' reluctance to teach their students methods of assessment and intervention that, in the opinion of some, had not yet been empirically validated. Today's tension is whether interventions that have received empirical validation must be taught to all students and, if so, which ones.

The last challenge is that of psychology's own accreditation history. Doctoral programs have not demonstrated that the widespread adoption of accreditation as a means to achieve excellence has resulted in uniform excellence. Rather, accreditation has been misused by various programs to obtain more resources from their departmental and university administrations, to obtain a peer judgment of adequacy as opposed to excellence, and to define political issues in the larger field of psychology that are actually unrelated to accreditation. The *Guidelines and Principles* (APA Committee on Accreditation, 2000) have placed the responsibility with program faculty for defining what constitutes training in the program's model and for demonstrating that such training exists and leads to the expected outcomes. The 1947 criteria presented the idea that competent faculty, with adequate tools, and a satisfactory organizational matrix will achieve excellence in training; in some ways, psychology has returned to that conceptualization. The responsibility of achieving quality is back in the hands of faculty through processes of self-study and program enhancement.

SUMMARY

The first 50 years of accreditation suggest that accreditation distills disciplinary and educational challenges and issues to the elemental level of one program and one department. However, the process does not and will not let larger issues be shut out. The challenge is to have accreditation result in excellence, as the most recent statement articulates it, but that excellence must be achieved one by one, one program and one student at a time.

I was very fortunate to have chaired the CoA during this historic juncture. Just as the history of accreditation determines, and I think will determine, its future, so the various people involved in activities related to accreditation have each put a personal stamp on the outcome. Appendix I at the end of this volume lists members of the CoA from its inception to the writing of this text, and to them psychology owes its gratitude.

REFERENCES

American Psychological Association. (1954). *Guide for visits in evaluation of graduate programs of training in clinical psychology and in counseling psychology.* Washington, DC: Author.

American Psychological Association. (1973). *Accreditation procedures and criteria.* Washington, DC: Author.

American Psychological Association. (1980). *Accreditation handbook.* Washington, DC: Author.

American Psychological Association, Committee on Accreditation. (2000). *Guidelines and principles for accreditation of programs in professional psychology.* Washington, DC: Author.

American Psychological Association, Committee on Training in Clinical Psychology. (1947). Recommended graduate training program in clinical psychology. *American Psychologist, 2,* 539–558.

American Psychological Association, Committee on Training in Clinical Psychology. (1949). Doctoral training programs in clinical psychology: 1949. *American Psychologist, 4,* 331–341.

American Psychological Association, Policy and Planning Board. (1948). Annual report of the Policy and Planning Board of the American Psychological Association. *American Psychologist, 3,* 187–192.

American Psychological Association, Task Force on Distance Education and Training in Professional Psychology. (2002). Principles of good practice in distance education and their application to professional education and training in psychology. Retrieved September, 13, 2002 from http://www.apa.org/ed/graduate/distance_ed.pdf

Korman, M. (Ed.). (1976). *Levels and patterns of professional training in psychology.* Washington, DC: American Psychological Association.

Pope-Davis, D. B., & Coleman, H. L. K. (Eds.). (1997). *Multicultural counseling competencies: Assessment, education and training, and supervision.* Thousand Oaks, CA: Sage.

Sears, R. R. (1947). Clinical training facilities: 1947; A report from the Committee on Graduate and Professional Training. *American Psychologist, 2,* 199–205.

Sheridan, E. P., Matarazzo, J. D., & Nelson, P. D. (1995). Accreditation of psychology's graduate professional education and training programs: An historical perspective. *Professional Psychology: Research and Practice, 26,* 386–392.

3

THE HISTORY OF ACCREDITATION OF INTERNSHIP PROGRAMS AND POSTDOCTORAL RESIDENCIES

CYNTHIA D. BELAR AND NADINE KASLOW

The American Psychological Association's (APA) Committee on Accreditation (CoA) has been accrediting doctoral internship programs since 1956 and postdoctoral residency programs since 1997. This chapter reviews the evolution of accreditation in both these areas, with attention to contextual issues and shifts in focus.

ACCREDITATION OF INTERNSHIP PROGRAMS

Although proposals for practical work as part of academic training in psychology date back to Lightner Witmer, the first independent internship program was offered by H. H. Goddard at the Training School at Vineland, New Jersey, in 1908. Yet, in these early years, psychology had no identification as a profession; indeed, its evolution as a science distinct from philosophy and physiology was relatively new. Although applications of psychology did occur outside the laboratory, especially after World War I, it was not until the shortage of psychologists to help World War II veterans was recognized that the government had need to identify appropriately trained psychologists. It was in this context of public service and accountability that the formalization of requirements and an accreditation process for professional education and training began.

As is detailed in Appendixes B and C in this volume, the internship was articulated as a requirement for education and training of clinical psychologists in 1947 in a report of a committee chaired by David Shakow (APA Committee on Training in Clinical Psychology, 1947). This report, later referred to as the Shakow Report, recommended that education and training in the scientist–practitioner model of clinical psychology include both a university experience and an internship sequence, thus the internship was included in the original standards for education and training in professional psychology. The internship was to occur in the third year of graduate study, after which the student would return to the university more able to conduct a clinically relevant dissertation in the fourth year. During this time, faculty in university settings had primarily academic interests; the applied experiences that were available tended to focus on the illustration of academic material (e.g., administration of psychological tests) during limited clerkships.

The internship was to be designed to provide "extended practical experience of gradually increasing complexity under close and competent supervision" (APA Committee on Training in Clinical Psychology, 1947, p. 551). In addition to clinical experience in the areas of diagnosis and treatment, the internship was also to promote experiences with other disciplines in real-world service settings. The standards called for up to one third of internship time to be devoted to research, specifically the accumulation of data that could be used later for a dissertation. Other necessities were involvement in the administrative aspects of the setting and the provision of experiences with normal populations. The setting was to be one with a commitment to training in other disciplines as well. The Shakow Report provided the foundation for the subsequent Boulder Conference in 1949 (Raimy, 1950).

In 1950, the APA Council of Representatives adopted standards for field training in clinical psychology set forth by the APA Committee on Training in Clinical Psychology (1950). These standards differentiated among laboratory, clerkship, and internship training. Expectations for internship training included (a) the subjects would be patients or clients; (b) the primary function of the intern would be the integration of various techniques; (c) the supervision would be conducted by agency personnel from an array of professions; (d) the duration of the internship could be variable, but not less than the equivalent of 11 months; (e) the time commitment could be full- or half-time; (f) the intern would engage in the intensive use of many methods with follow-up with relatively few patients; and (g) the remuneration would be a scholarship or stipend. In contrast to the trainee on clerkship, the intern was expected to take responsibility, under supervision, for clinical decisions and to operate at the level of a junior staff member, including supervision of other trainees. A significant difference between the internship and clerkship was that the intern was to receive a stipend, whereas the student on clerkship should not be remunerated and in fact "should not take responsibility for decisions regarding patients, and his [sic] work should not be utilized by the agency unless it has been done under such sufficiently close and competent supervision as to warrant its validity" (p. 596).

Concurrent with developments in clinical psychology, counseling psychology was also concerned with the development of standards. In 1951, a conference was convened to define and review the functions of the counseling psychologist. At that meeting, the Division of Counseling and Guidance followed the lead of clinical psychology and recommended a doctoral internship training sequence for its students. Standards for the practicum training of counseling psychologists were presented in 1952, with the internship described as the terminal phase of practicum, occurring after the laboratory and fieldwork stages of training. Although the internship was to be completed in an agency, the graduate program was viewed as sharing the burden of planning and evaluating the experience. The internship was to be for 1 academic year (not the 11 months required for clinical psychology) but could be halftime for 2 years. Mastery of basic skills was assumed prior to entry, and the outcome goal was "functioning as a regular junior member of the agency staff" (APA Committee on Counselor Training, Division of Counseling and Guidance, 1952, p. 186).

With the receipt of federal funds for training and more need for public accountability, issues of quality assurance in internship programs became more salient. Thus in 1956, the APA, through its Office of Accreditation, began accrediting clinical and counseling internships. Only independent agencies, that is, agencies accepting interns from more than one university, were accredited. The initial listing of accredited programs did not include "captive agencies," that is, agencies affiliated with an approved university, or programs based in Veterans Administration (VA) facilities. Of the 28 accredited programs listed in Exhibit 3.1, many continue to thrive today.

There have been four major documents specifying internship accreditation guidelines since the initial articulation of standards in the Shakow Report. These are reviewed below in historical sequence.

CRITERIA FOR EVALUATING TRAINING PROGRAMS IN CLINICAL OR IN COUNSELING PSYCHOLOGY (APA, 1958)

As is detailed in Appendix D, the "Criteria for Evaluating Training Programs in Clinical or in Counseling Psychology" (APA, 1958) essentially summarized the criteria from the more detailed Shakow Report. A separate section devoted to internship training addressed staff, prerequisites for the students accepted, content and methods of practicum training, and facilities

EXHIBIT 3.1
APA Accredited Internships (APA, 1956)

Boston Children's Medical Center
California Metropolitan State Hospital
University of Colorado Medical School
Connecticut State Hospital
Duke University Medical School Hospital
University of Illinois Neuropsychiatric Institute
Larue Carter Hospital
State University of Iowa Psychopathic Hospital
Judge Baker Guidance Center
Kings County Hospital
Langley Porter Clinic
Louisiana Hospital
University of Maryland Psychiatric Institute
Michael Reese Hospital
Nebraska State Hospital
New York University Institute of Physical Medicine and Rehabilitation
Northwestern University Medical School
St. Elizabeth's Hospital
St. Louis State Hospital
University of Tennessee Gailor Hospital
Kansas State Hospital
University of Texas Southwestern Medical School
University of Utah Medical School
Washington University School of Medicine
Western Reserve University Hospital
Wichita Guidance Center
Worcester Massachusetts State Hospital

---

for study and research. The intern's work had to be collaboratively planned with a qualified psychologist supervisor who was on site at least 50% of the time. Trainers from other fields and representatives from the intern's home university supplemented supervision. In terms of prerequisites for students, it was noted that the agency would accept only those individuals who were developmentally ready to benefit from the internship training offered, who had prior practicum experience, and who were committed to working at least half-time. The criteria that focused on content and methods indicated that the intern must have contact with a diversity of patients and clinical problems; be cognizant of the agency's mission; attend case conferences and seminars; and receive supervised training in two of the following: diagnosis, therapy, and research. Finally, the criteria stated that the intern must have a desk and private space, adequate resources and equipment, access to a library, and access to ongoing research endeavors.

Until the mid-1960s, accreditation site visit teams were composed of members of the then-named Committee on Evaluation. A problem surfaced when the number of requests for accreditation exceeded the committee's capacity for completing the required site visits. The inability to meet the demands from the field led to a moratorium on site visits to internship agencies and the recommendation that the accreditation of internships be discontinued. However, the response from the field was strong, as internships wished to retain public recognition of having met the standards of the discipline. The response prompted the APA Council of Representatives to reaffirm its commitment to the accreditation of internship programs, but proceeding to do so necessitated a redesign of the accreditation process. The committee identified panels of qualified site visitors in the field and in 1968 began work on revising the standards and criteria. Box 3.1 contains a description of the site visit experiences of a long-time internship site visitor.

ACCREDITATION PROCEDURES AND CRITERIA (APA, 1973)

As is described in chapter 2, this revision of accreditation criteria acknowledged that, although the prototypic training model had been that of the scientist–practitioner, "a need for diversity and innovation in training program development has been increasingly expressed" (APA, 1973, p. 13). This acknowledgment opened the door to alternate training models, which were later endorsed. The criteria for independent internships were in a section titled "Criteria for Accreditation of Internship Programs in Clinical and Counseling Psychology." "Captive" or "satellite" programs were to be considered in the context of the doctoral programs they served but would be evaluated using the same criteria as applied to independent internship centers.

The 1973 criteria reinforced the internship as an essential component of doctoral training programs in professional psychology. The internship experience was to be 1 year full-time or 2 years part-time and to be funded by a stipend. As recommended by the Shakow Report, it was to occur after completion of the second year of graduate school and earlier practicum work. The setting was expected to offer the intern significant responsibility for fulfilling his or her professional functions while receiving appropriate quantity and quality of supervisory support. In this document, separate discussions were offered regarding internships in clinical and counseling psychology and internships in school psychology.

The following were the criteria for the accreditation of independent clinical and counseling psychology internship training programs. Site visitors used these criteria, which were not viewed as exhaustive, in formulating their assessment of whether or not an internship experience was of sufficiently high quality to merit accreditation. First, the 1973 criteria discussed expectations regarding internship staff. Training programs were expected to provide a variety of faculty role models for trainees, be relatively stable, and be sufficient in number to accommodate the training and professional development needs of the interns. The criteria required a clearly designated and experienced training director, preferably with a diploma from the American

BOX 3.1
The Internship Component of Psychology Training
Sidney A. Orgel, PhD, State University of New York Upstate Medical University, Syracuse

In the early 1970s, I was honored to serve as a potential site visitor to internship locales seeking either initial accreditation or renewal evaluation for their already accredited programs. I soon found myself visiting between four and six internship sites each year. I preferred to visit internship program sites housed in medical schools because I had most experience with this kind of environment, having directed an internship endeavor approved by the American Psychological Association at what was then known as the Upstate Medical Center in Syracuse, New York. I soon found, however, that I was accepting invitations to visit Veterans Administration sites, state hospital programs, outpatient mental health clinics, and student counseling centers. Occasionally I was part of a larger team chosen by the host academic institution to visit their program. On such academic evaluation trips, I would be most frequently charged with evaluating the academic programs' practicum, in-house clinics, and the variety of internship sites where their students typically trained.

Was there a downside to these visits, which necessitated being away from my own campus about once every 2 or 3 months? The administration of our medical school was very pleased to have one of their faculty so involved. They thought it brought the name of our medical center to a varied group of installations involved in psychology training. Our intern cohorts were much less sanguine about their chief disappearing for 2 to 3 days with almost predictable regularity. As I look back on these relatively frequent site visits, I think I must have been doubly flattered, first that I was selected frequently enough to visit, and second, that my interns missed my supervision for even those very brief periods. I remember attempting to placate them with, "But you know I bring back here the most creative and original aspects of training that I observe at other centers!" I'm not sure they were persuaded by this hastily provided rationalization.

All of this site visiting did have some very nice effects. I slowly developed a reputation for being very knowledgeable about accreditation matters and particularly internship criteria concerning excellence. This led to my name being offered to sites wishing prior consultation before seeking accreditation of their programs. For this kind of consultation I would dry-run the program, providing them with an experience close to an actual site visit evaluation. I would avoid the temptation to be overly kind in my feedback, and instead offered my hosts a clear-cut reading of their strengths and weaknesses. I would not mince words about their readiness to apply for accreditation. This stance held up rather well over time because the view of peers in the field was that I was tough but that I would always be respectful and would not lead a budding program astray.

This all culminated in an invitation to join the Committee on Accreditation in 1979 for a term of 3 years. That period of service was an extraordinary experience with extraordinary people, making it difficult for me to focus on the highlights. I was extremely fortunate in my accreditation work to have served under two such talented, humane, and creative directors as Dr. Meredith Crawford and Dr. Paul Nelson. They shared a common philosophy: Do our work with élan and quiet competence and avoid involvement in the political arena. Work hard we did, as attested to by those 10-pound agenda books that would arrive 2 weeks prior to an accreditation meeting.

Some of the friendships formed there have continued for more than 2 decades. I see these long-term friendships as being established on a common bond of volunteerism to our profession's well-being. There is something extraordinary about such a large cohort of psychologists donating so many hours each year to the study of accreditation applications, self-study submissions, and site visitor reports as well as to the all-too-frequent meetings devoted to formulating the actual work of accreditation judgments. In addition, there are the dedicated numbers of colleagues who do the actual site visiting, a task that involves not only time away from home and the extensive strain of interviews and evaluation but also writing a comprehensive report that captures the essence of a visit.

When I have queried any of these individuals about the reasons for their willingness to donate so much labor to their profession, they tend to demur. One can only infer that what is demonstrated here is an enormous affection for their profession and some reasoning that one is obligated to return some kind of payment to a profession that has proved so personally rewarding.

Sadly, my crystal ball is as hazy as that of any prognosticator about the future of psychology accreditation. Lately one hears much talk about limiting the production of clinical doctorates because of the shortages of current position openings. I suggest there may

continues

> **BOX 3.1 (continued)**
>
> be an alternative to gate keeping for clinical programs. Perhaps accreditation will at some future time mandate that programs must demonstrate how creative and forward looking they are by providing evidence for the new and varied careers in which their graduates are playing a leading role. To an inveterate optimist, there is very little limit to future roles for our graduates.
>
> Over my years of involvement, I have seen accreditation become a much-honored aspect of American psychology's commitment to the highest standards of elegance in graduate education. To watch accreditation become even broader in its member composition, and for it to become increasingly attuned to having institutions propose what their model for training is and subsequently demonstrate their effective execution of that model, is for me a continuing source for my pride in American psychology.

Board of Professional Psychology (ABPP) or Fellow status in APA, who was responsible for the integrity and quality of the training program. Further, the criteria viewed intern interactions and collaborations with other professionals, including those from other disciplines, as desirable.

Second, with regard to the trainees, accredited programs were to have a sufficient number of interns to provide maximal levels of intertrainee stimulation. Interns were to have come from a relevant doctoral program, have completed prior practicum experience, be actively involved in evaluating their own experience, and be cognizant of the site's mission. In addition, interns were to be regarded as an integral part of the agency's professional staff.

The third set of criteria related to training activities, which "must not be overspecialized" (APA, 1973, p. 26). Programs were to provide supervision in a range of activities in the following areas: assessment, intervention, and research into the applications of psychology. Experiences with various modes of therapy and consultation, as well as program administration, were given as examples. Internships were expected to have detailed written program descriptions and close liaison relationships with graduate programs. The guidelines indicated that supervision should be sufficient in quality and quantity, and the intern should receive ongoing evaluation and feedback. There was a requirement that evidence be provided regarding program self-assessment. In addition, adequate program resources (e.g., office space, clerical support) were required.

The final set of criteria related to general administrative issues. This section covered the need for adequate administrative and financial support for the training program, institutional acknowledgment for the value of training activities by the staff, and contact with graduate programs regarding student advisement and matching of students to sites. There was also a brief comment noting the acceptability of multiple agency consortia as long as there was a staff member responsible for integration across agencies of the internship experience for the trainees.

The guidelines for school psychology internships found in the 1973 accreditation criteria were derived from a conference on internship training at Peabody College in 1963 (Gray, 1963). Of special note is the requirement that the major part of the internship be in a school setting. As with counseling psychology internships, school psychology internships were usually an academic year in length. Rather than require a variety of supervisors, guidelines were for a supervisor who had a doctorate or its equivalent in psychology and who spent one sixth of his or her work time supervising each intern.

The committee completed the 1973 revision of accreditation procedures and criteria in the same year as the Vail Conference, in which for the first time a model other than the scientist–practitioner model was endorsed for education and training in professional psychology. In addition to the practitioner model, the PsyD degree was also endorsed (Korman, 1974). In view of these major developments, the APA Council of Representatives requested yet another review of the accreditation criteria.

CRITERIA FOR ACCREDITATION: DOCTORAL TRAINING PROGRAMS AND INTERNSHIPS IN PROFESSIONAL PSYCHOLOGY (APA, 1979)

This revision of accreditation criteria, *Criteria for Accreditation: Doctoral Training Programs and Internships in Professional Psychology* (APA, 1979), explicitly recognized both the scientist–practitioner (PhD) and practitioner (PsyD) models of professional education and training; free-standing professional schools were also recognized. Each program was to specify its model, goals of training, abilities and skills of graduates, and methods for assessing program outcomes. Programs were to be evaluated in terms of the model endorsed and success in reaching goals. There were also very strong emphases on issues of diversity in faculty, students, and clientele, as well as social justice issues.

Although practicum and internship training fell under the same heading, the document provided separate criteria for the accreditation of independent internship centers. The internship was to be preceded by a minimum of 400 practicum hours, of which at least 150 hours were in direct service and at least 75 hours were in formally scheduled supervision. However, there was no longer the statement that the internship was to occur in the third year of graduate study. The criteria highlighted the importance of close relationships between doctoral and internship training programs and stated that the internship should precede the granting of the doctoral degree, underscoring its crucial importance in the preparation of independent professionals.

Because these guidelines are similar to those presented in 1973, we note only key additions or differences here. Whereas the expectation remained that internships in clinical psychology be the equivalent of 1 year full-time, the document explicitly stated that internships in school and counseling psychology could be the full-time equivalent of either an academic or a calendar year. There was also increased emphasis on the rights of interns and on intern evaluation of all aspects of their training experience. In addition, there was more focus on the need for systematic review of the preparation of intern applicants. Considerable attention was given to issues of respecialization.

The crafters of the 1979 document also paid more attention to issues of training and supervision, perhaps reflecting concerns expressed in the field. The document clearly stated that service goals were not to erode training goals and that direct service was to be carefully supervised and part of an integrated training plan. Increased attention to the supervisory process was also a part of the 1979 document, and for the first time there was a specific requirement for amount of supervision—at least 2 hours per week of formally scheduled individual supervision for each intern. Although the 1973 guidelines briefly mentioned consortia, the 1979 guidelines included a separate and detailed section on consortia. The document defined consortia internship programs and delineated the requisite administrative and training components of these programs for accreditation.

Site visitors following the 1979 criteria had an itemized list of criteria, including a description of areas in which interns should demonstrate knowledge. As chapters 1 and 2 suggest, many site visitors found this checklist to be useful and to serve as a concrete list of expectations for accreditation, but others became concerned about a checklist mentality in which presence or absence of an item was more important than issues of quality. Accreditation was challenged, albeit for different reasons, by both academics and practitioners. There were debates over the core curriculum and also increased concern about who controlled accreditation. Within the context of this questioning of standards, the Association of Psychology Internship Centers[1] and the Department of Clinical and Health Psychology of the University of Florida cosponsored the 1987 National Conference on Internship Training in Professional Psychology in Gainesville—the first and only national conference focused solely on internship training (Belar et al., 1989). Forty-

---

[1] The Association of Psychology Internship Centers (APIC) was founded in 1968 to respond to a broad array of internship issues that were beyond the scope of accreditation, most notably the procedures surrounding internship application and notification of acceptance. APIC changed its name to the Association of Psychology Postdoctoral and Internship Centers (APPIC) in 1991 to more clearly represent its membership and its growing interest in postdoctoral training. APPIC now includes 567 internship programs for a total of 2,528 full-time slots (98% of which are funded) and 77 part-time slots (57% of which are funded; APPIC, 2000). Of the 567, 431 represent APA accredited programs (76%).

eight delegates with demonstrated leadership and expertise in graduate education, internship training, or professional psychology adopted a policy statement that addressed (a) purpose of internship training, (b) timing of the internship, (c) careers in psychology for which an internship is required or appropriate, (d) entrance and exit criteria, (e) necessary processes and structure of the internship, (f) core content, and (g) financial and administrative issues.

Regarding the purpose of internship training, the policy statement notes that the "person who completes the internship training is an individual who has demonstrated the capacity to function autonomously and responsibly as a practicing psychologist" (Belar et al., 1989, p. 63). Delegates believed that 2 years of supervised experience were needed to produce an autonomous professional. Some advocated that this 2-year experience be postdoctoral; others asserted that more training was needed at the doctoral level. At that time the requirement for pre-internship practica was 400 hours; delegates did suggest increasing this to 900 hours but did not want to extend the doctoral program any longer, thus they agreed on a statement of 1 year predoctoral and 1 year postdoctoral. However, a significant shift from previous accreditation criteria was the recommendation that the dissertation should be completed prior to the internship rather than during or after the internship.

The Gainesville Conference also supported an aspirational goal that all training should occur within APA-accredited internship programs. The conference delegates detailed the importance of collaboration between the internship and graduate trainers, and delegates underscored the value that internship training must be an extension of and consistent with prior graduate education and training. They recommended at least three staff members, headed by a senior and appropriately credentialed psychologist, noting that staff should be capable of offering a diverse array of role models for the interns. The importance of conveying respect for interns and attending to interns' stress and professional needs through the organized training sequence was also highlighted.

In addressing the topic of core content and requirements, a more clearly delineated set of experiences emerged than was previously articulated. This common core emphasized the need for a breadth of evaluation and intervention experiences with diverse patient groups as opposed to specialty training. An emphasis was placed on the need for the integration of science and practice, and a value on research, application of empirical skills, and critical thinking. However, although delegates highlighted the importance of assessing outcome criteria indicative of successful fulfillment of the core requirements of the internship, they did not define outcome measures.

In terms of financial and administrative issues, the delegates noted that interns should be funded at a level commensurate with experience; they forcefully argued that unfunded positions had the potential to result in exploitation, unfair discrimination, and potential interference in the learning process.

In general, the recommendations of the Gainesville Conference were positively accepted in the field. Many graduate programs were already requiring the completion of a dissertation proposal prior to internship; many fostered completion of the dissertation itself prior to leaving campus. The model of the internship in the third year, with a return to the university for the dissertation in the fourth year, had definitely lost widespread support. With respect to other recommendations, the number of pre-internship practicum hours has been exceeded twofold, a change that has also been accompanied by the predicted concern about length of graduate education and training. These developments were probable factors in re-igniting the debate over the placement of the internship in professional education and training. The statement of the Gainesville Conference that the internship remain predoctoral had not been as well received by many faculty. In fact within the next decade, the Council of University Directors of Clinical Psychology formally voted for the internship to be postdoctoral. Not all groups were in agreement, and this issue remains one on which many groups are split internally. In fact, as noted below, it was the only issue requiring a formal vote of the CoA during its most recent revision of the criteria.

In 1991, after a rather turbulent period of conflict over "ownership" of accreditation, a newly structured APA CoA was formed as a multiorganizational body representing multiple constituencies that would both assess program quality and formulate accreditation policies and procedures. As an organization, the Association of Psychology Postdoctoral and Internship Centers (APPIC) was awarded 2 of the 21 seats. Doctoral programs (within which the internship was considered a component) were awarded 8 seats through 4 organizations: the Council of Counseling Psychology Training Directors, the Council of School Psychology Program Directors, the Council of University Directors of Clinical Psychology, and the National Council of Schools and Programs in Professional Psychology. After conducting a major self-study of its own, the APA CoA approved a new set of guidelines and procedures in 1996 that attempted to mediate tensions between the needs for academic freedom and public accountability for professional education and training. Box 3.2 details some of the initial issues involved in applying the new model of accreditation to internship settings.

GUIDELINES AND PRINCIPLES FOR ACCREDITATION OF PROGRAMS IN PROFESSIONAL PSYCHOLOGY (APA, 1996A, 1996B)

The current *Guidelines and Principles for Accreditation of Programs in Professional Psychology* (APA, 1996a, 1996b) are founded on the following principles. First, internship education and training should be broad and professional in its orientation; grounded in the current and emerging body of

BOX 3.2
Perspectives of Accreditation

Kathleen R. Boggs, PhD, Counseling Center, and Department of Educational and Counseling Psychology, University of Missouri—Columbia

Training in the new *Guidelines and Principles for Accreditation of Programs in Professional Psychology* ([G&P], APA, 1996a, 1996b) had an inauspicious beginning, partly because the G&P were so new that members of the Committee on Accreditation (CoA) were inexperienced in their practical application and partly because there was a mismatch between the backgrounds of trainers and the groups they were training (e.g., faculty from academic departments providing training for internship sites). As a new board member of the Association of Psychology Postdoctoral and Internship Centers (APPIC), I organized the APPIC workshop on August 10, 1995, in New York City prior to the American Psychological Association (APA) Convention. The workshop was to help prepare APPIC members to write self-studies under the new G&P, and I believe it was the first such group training.

The CoA Chair, Deborah Beidel, and a CoA Member, Bernhard Blom, conducted the day-long workshop, entitled "Implementing New APA Accreditation Guidelines." A record number of 84 psychologists attended, attesting to their need for education on the new accreditation criteria. They were eager to learn. Participants requested examples of training models, goals, objectives, and outcomes, although the leaders stressed the importance of programs developing their own models. As the day progressed, the emotional atmosphere became increasingly tense as participants expressed their anxiety about the new G&P by voicing their frustration over a lack of examples to help them understand what the new guidelines required.

The Psychology Internship at the University of Utah Counseling Center was one of the first counseling centers to be accredited in 1979, while I was a member of the Training Committee. Subsequently, as director of training, I led the center through the accreditation process in 1986, 1991, and 1996. In fall 1995, I prepared to instruct the staff on the G&P so we could work collaboratively to define our training model and write our self-study. We completed the self-study in spring 1996 and hosted a site visit that fall.

continues

> BOX 3.2 (continued)
>
> In August 1995, I became a member of the Interorganizational Council for Accreditation of Postdoctoral Programs in Professional Psychology (IOC). I chaired a committee that developed the manual of procedures for accrediting postdoctoral training programs. This document stimulated discussion at the IOC meeting about similarities and differences between IOC and CoA procedures. The IOC accepted the manual at the June 1996 meeting, and it was merged with the existing CoA operations for accreditation of doctoral and internship programs. This ended work on development of accreditation of general postdoctoral training programs, and the IOC turned attention to proposed models of accreditation of specialty postdoctoral programs. A Specialties Council was formed to develop a general quality assurance process to guide the development of specialty-specific accreditation standards and self-study documents.
>
> Since fall 1995, the Association of Counseling Center Training Agencies (ACCTA) has provided yearly training on the G&P with a specific focus on counseling center internships, and ACCTA and APPIC have included examples of training models and self-studies on their Web sites. APA also regularly offers training on the G&P. Thus, resources for developing training models and writing self-studies are readily available.

knowledge, skills, and competencies that define the substantive practice areas; and well integrated with the broad theoretical and scientific foundation of the discipline and the field. Second, internship education and training should be established on the existing and evolving body of general knowledge and methods in the science and practice of psychology. Third, internship training programs will be evaluated in light of their own education and training philosophy, model, goals, objectives, and methods. Fourth, an emphasis is placed on the outcomes or products of an internship program's training efforts. Fifth, and consistent with the aforementioned principles, the accreditation guidelines for internships identify and describe in detail the domains essential to the success of any training program in professional psychology. With these principles, checklists are less useful to the CoA and its site visitors (e.g., there is no specification of pre-internship practicum hour requirements). Rather, a more detailed assessment of outcomes as related to program goals is required. The expectations for program quality and description are more parallel, albeit not identical, between graduate programs and internships. The most controversial issue in this revision and the only one that required a vote among committee members, as noted above, related to the timing of the internship and the award of the doctoral degree. Once again there were advocates for a postdoctoral internship, but the final decision was to maintain the internship as a part of the doctoral program.

The eight domains assessed in the current guidelines and principles for accreditation of internship programs include (a) eligibility; (b) program philosophy, objectives, and training plan; (c) program resources; (d) cultural and individual differences and diversity; (e) intern–staff relations; (f) program self-assessment and quality enhancement; (g) public disclosure; and (h) program relationship with accrediting body. As before, programs are to be evaluated in the context of their publicly stated education and training goals, but with this revision there is increased emphasis on the self-study process and the analysis of outcomes, an emphasis consistent with national trends toward more public accountability in education and training. Collateral efforts to promote "truth in advertising" regarding program processes and outcomes have been initiated by the Council of University Directors of Clinical Psychology and recommended by the APPIC/APA Supply and Demand Conference.

GROWTH IN ACCREDITED PROGRAMS

In a report on the first 50 years of psychology accreditation, data were presented on the number of accredited internship programs by decade and percentage of change from the previous decade (APA Committee on Accreditation, 1999). As shown in Table 3.1, there was an overall increase of 71% in the number of accredited programs over the four decades.

The most recent data are from the 2001 Annual Report (APA Committee on Accreditation, 2002). Of the 466 accredited internship programs, settings include community mental health centers and child and family clinics (12%), university counseling centers and clinics (20%), VA Medical Centers and military medical centers (17%), general and state hospitals (9%), private hospitals (4%), and medical schools (6%). Additionally, there are accredited internship programs in consortia with multiple agencies (7%); other settings such as health maintenance organizations, schools, correctional facilities (13%); and mental health institutes and state hospitals (12%). In some cases, internships with common settings have formed professional associations to identify and resolve shared training issues. Box 3.3 details some of the history of one such organization.

Data from the 2001 annual report also reveal that in accredited internship programs the mean intern–staff ratio is approximately 1:2. Most interns are full-time (approximately 40 hours per week) and funded (mean stipend = $18,406). Nearly 72% of interns are female; 20% are ethnic minorities. More than 96% are from APA-accredited doctoral programs, and they have an

BOX 3.3
ACCTA and University Counseling Center Internships
Helen J. Roehlke, EdD, Counseling Center, University of Missouri—Columbia

When the Association of Counseling Center Training Agencies (ACCTA) first met as an organization in November 1977, only five counseling center internships were American Psychological Association (APA) accredited, and our program at the University of Missouri was the second of those. Although I had been involved in our 1972 site visit, I was really quite unaware of what this process actually entailed until I became the internship director myself in 1977. This first ACCTA conference, which only 13 people attended, provided a great opportunity for me to discuss internship training issues and to meet other training directors who had involvement with the Committee on Accreditation (CoA). Indeed, the pros and cons of program accreditation was one of our main topics of discussion.

Those of us already affiliated with accredited internship programs believed that accreditation provided a valuable means of quality assurance, which is a definite asset when recruiting interns. Therefore, at the 1978 meeting, we began to present accreditation workshops as an integral part of our annual conferences. We talked about our own experiences with both initial and re-accreditation site visits, answered questions, and shared our self-studies and other relevant materials. A few of us were also site visitors, and we discussed what we looked for in a program from this perspective as well. This process contributed to doubling, and sometimes tripling, the number of counseling center internships receiving APA accreditation annually. For example, by 1980, there were 12 accredited counseling center internships; by 1998, there were 68. Today, counseling center internships rank second in total numbers of accredited programs available to prospective intern applicants.

During ACCTA's 1986, 1987, and 1988 conferences, we were heavily involved in accreditation issues as focal topics of work and discussion. In 1986 the first draft of accreditation criteria revisions was circulated, and the board of directors worked very hard on developing consensual responses to these potential changes. ACCTA even sent liaisons to the CoA meeting in Washington, DC, that year and received very positive feedback on our efforts. In 1987, we invited staff from the Office of Accreditation to join us for the next 4 years. Throughout those years, APA staff offered us invaluable consultation, suggestions for setting up site visitor teams, and assistance in navigating the accreditation process. By the time we held the 1988 conference, the Task Force on the Scope and Criteria of Accreditation had been appointed, and we invited a member of this task force to discuss the issues with us. Out of that discussion, ACCTA developed a position paper that was subsequently endorsed by councils representing Counseling Center Directors and the Council of Counseling Psychology Training Programs.

Some of the accreditation issues that ACCTA discussed over the years were the same as, or similar to, those of other internship settings, such as needing uniform standards and guidelines for practice and training, supporting the training mission of the agency, and so forth. But there are two special issues for university counseling centers still operant. One is the need for training experiences and areas of expertise different from those required for other internship settings (i.e., competency in campus consultation and outreach programming; supervision of other trainees; structured and unstructured group skills; and a strong grounding in, and awareness of, normal developmental issues). The other operant issue is the relative lack of opportunities to gain significant research experience because of the heavy service demands of most agencies, which requires somewhat different accreditation criteria in this area.

By 1991, ACCTA member programs began to consider offering postdoctoral residencies. Simultaneously, various professional organizations and credentialing bodies started to talk about potential accreditation guidelines and standards for postdoctoral training programs. The latter ultimately resulted in the formation of the Interorganizational Council (IOC), on which I served as Division 17's representative and as ACCTA's liaison.

In the ACCTA 1994 meeting, we discussed the IOC's developing postdoctoral accreditation criteria. We also talked about our collective position on where the internship should be located—at the pre- or postdoctoral level—and had a lively discussion about diversity issues raised by Footnote 4 in the new accreditation guidelines, which dealt with the exemption of programs in institutions with a religious orientation that conflicted with selection and training issues related to gay, lesbian, and bisexual individuals. The other significant event that occurred at this meeting was our first site visitors training workshop. This workshop enabled many more internship training directors to receive training necessary to become site visitors, and ACCTA has continued to offer this workshop annually.

continues

> **BOX 3.3 (continued)**
>
> Thus, ACCTA has a 23-year history of working closely with the CoA and attending carefully to accreditation issues in intern training. Although I am no longer an ACCTA member, I am confident that this tradition will be carried on and the excellent working relationship between the two will persist.

average of 2,072 practicum hours prior to internship, clearly a significant difference from the 400-hour requirement of the 1979 accreditation criteria and the 900 hours recommended at the Gainesville Conference. The staff or faculty of APA-accredited internship programs is equally balanced between men and women, but minority representation is low (13.7%). For the most part, there is consistency between where individuals do their doctoral internship and their initial employment setting. For example, in 1999, there was a 75% match between internship and initial employment settings, a slight drop from 1998, when the match rate was 82%.

POSTDOCTORAL RESIDENCY ACCREDITATION

This section provides a brief history of postdoctoral education and training in professional psychology, followed by a focus on the development of accreditation processes for postdoctoral residency programs. Although postdoctoral training has a long history in professional psychology, there was no formal accreditation of postdoctoral programs until 1997, when the APA CoA approved two postdoctoral residencies, one at the Harbor–UCLA Medical Center and one at the Menninger Clinic. (Boxes 3.4 and 3.5 present the experiences of the two training directors.) As of January 2003, there were 15 postdoctoral programs accredited and several others in the pipeline. Consistent with their roots in doctoral accreditation, the VA is playing a significant role in that increase. Several VA medical center programs are currently seeking accreditation because VA Central Office has mandated attainment of accreditation to maintain funding of postdoctoral positions.

Although accreditation is relatively new at the postdoctoral level, attention to the need for postdoctoral training in clinical psychology dates back to the Boulder Conference (Raimy, 1950), the first national conference to define a training model for professional psychology. As stated above, the model of education and training articulated at that time called for a 1-year internship in the third year of graduate study. The internship was to be the primary vehicle for intensive clinical training, after which students would

TABLE 3.1
Increase in Number of Accredited Internships by Decade, 1958–1998

Year	Number of accredited internships	% Increase
1958	62	
1968	102	65
1978	138	35
1988	347	151
1998	455	31

Note. From "APA Committee on Accreditation 1998 Annual Report" (p. 15) by the American Psychological Association, Committee on Accreditation, 1999, Washington, DC: Author. Copyright 1999 by the American Psychological Association.

return to the university to complete a clinically informed dissertation. To become proficient in psychotherapy, however, Boulder conference attendees stated that postdoctoral training would be required. At the Stanford (1955) and Miami (1958) conferences, the model of a 4-year academic program followed by a 2-year postdoctoral internship was proposed for clinical psychology. That model failed to gain majority support (although it still has proponents some 50 years later), and the one-year doctoral internship was reaffirmed. However, postdoctoral training was seen as highly valued.

At the 1965 Chicago Conference, "there was no debating the advisability of postdoctoral education. Indeed, the latter was in effect regarded as an ethical responsibility for those who aspire to the status of 'expert' in selected areas of professional function" (Hoch, Ross, & Winder, 1966, p. 44). Delegates supported postdoctoral education and training as a way to obtain advanced and specialized skills and as a means for respecialization into the profession of psychology from other areas of the discipline. It is also noteworthy that delegates viewed doctoral education and training as sufficient for practice at the journeyperson level and in fact warned that postdoctoral training should not be a correction factor for deficiencies at the doctoral level. Themes of advanced training and excellence marked their descriptions of postdoctoral training, which was seen as essential for those who wished to teach, supervise, or enter independent practice.

The first conference to focus exclusively on postdoctoral education and training in psychology was held at the Menninger Clinic in 1972 (Weiner, 1973). The purpose of this meeting was not for policy development but to share information and concerns. An especially prominent concern expressed was that some programs were functioning more as trade schools, thus fostering a false dichotomy between research and clinical work. Delegates believed that clinical research was integral to postdoctoral training. However, they developed no specific guidelines for postdoctoral training.

In the 1980s, guidelines for postdoctoral training in various specialty areas of practice were developed through national conferences and meetings, for example, health psychology (Stone, 1983; Sheridan et al., 1988), clinical child psychology (Tuma, 1985), and clinical neuropsychology (INS–Divi-

BOX 3.4
Becoming the First Accredited Postdoctoral Program
James H. Kleiger, PsyD, Private Practice, Bethesda, Maryland

Postdoctoral psychology training at the Menninger Clinic, currently located in Topeka, Kansas, embodies a rich tradition spanning more than 50 years. Through a thorough apprenticeship process, postdoctoral fellows learn a unique way of conceptualizing the diagnostic process that connects them to such luminaries in our field as David Rapaport, Roy Schafer, Martin Mayman, and Stephen Appelbaum. With this keen appreciation for the history of psychology training, it was a great honor to be asked by the American Psychological Association (APA) in 1995 to be among the first programs to participate in a pilot process for accrediting postdoctoral programs.

My predecessor spearheaded this effort by participating in the national training conference that set the stage for postdoctoral accreditation to become a reality. When I assumed the position of training director in 1996, I assigned the accreditation process top priority. Nancy Garfield, an experienced training director, was of immeasurable assistance in helping me prepare for our site visit. Her feedback on early drafts was extremely helpful and paved the way for the completion of the daunting self-study questions required as part of accreditation applications.

For those unfamiliar with the self-study process, painfully answering 80 or more questions about every facet of one's training program is predictably exhausting but surprisingly helpful. We learned that our program, founded on oral traditions passed down to our teachers by their teachers, lacked many operational criteria. What was our essential mission? How did we conceive our learning objectives? What were our graduation requirements? How did we deal with problems that occurred during training? Were we adequately attuned to issues of diversity? Completion of both a comprehensive policy and procedures manual and the self-study questions, which became two vital documents, provided a thorough definition of the mission and mechanics of the program. Both continue to serve as important reference sources for incoming postdoctoral fellows during their orientation to the program.

Our site visit was arranged within a year of our completion of the self-study. For roughly 2 days, the site visitors met with senior administrators of the clinic, my training faculty, alumni of the program, and current postdoctoral fellows. They surveyed our

> records and questioned me in a collegial manner about all aspects of the program. Most helpful was their final feedback to members of the psychology discipline about the relative strengths and weaknesses of our program.
>
> We felt honored to become part of the history of APA accreditation and to follow in the footsteps of other Topeka-based psychology training programs which, in their times, were among the first to receive APA accreditation.

sion 40 Task Force, 1987), but no generic standards existed for postdoctoral training in professional psychology. At the first National Conference on Internship Training in Psychology (Gainesville Conference), delegates had raised significant concerns about the lack of quality assurance in postdoctoral training. Although their major focus was on the development of policy regarding internship training, they decried the hit or miss nature of the 1-year supervised experience required by many state licensing boards and denounced the potential for exploitation of recent graduates (Belar et al., 1989). Participants called for a subsequent national conference to articulate standards for postdoctoral training that could be the basis for accreditation processes. An additional convergent force in the field was the report of the Joint Council on Professional Education in Psychology (Stigall et al., 1990; see Appendix H, this volume). As is detailed in chapter 4, this report also spoke to the need for general standards in postdoctoral training; it provided some recommendations and called for APA to encourage the development of accredited programs.

As a follow-up to the Gainesville Conference, APPIC sponsored the first National Conference on Postdoctoral Training in Professional Psychology (Belar et al., 1993), often referred to as the Ann Arbor Conference. Held in 1992, this conference was cosponsored by APA, the ABPP, the Association of State and Provincial Psychology Boards (ASPPB), and the National Register of Health Service Providers in Psychology. Conference participants spent 4 days examining issues related to the purpose of postdoctoral training as well as program models, structures, content, processes, and entrance and exit criteria. They then adopted by acclamation a policy statement detailing standards for postdoctoral residency programs, followed by recommendations for a series of initiatives to foster excellence and innovation in training—including a call for accreditation of postdoctoral programs. With respect to accreditation, the 1989 APA Task Force on Scope and Criteria for Accreditation had recommended that postdoctoral training programs be provided access to accreditation processes, but little progress had been made to date. In fact, the CoA itself had been undergoing reorganization and, as noted above, a new model for its composition had just been approved by APA and

BOX 3.5
A Postdoctoral Program Joins the Fold
*Annette M. Brodsky, PhD, Department of Psychiatry, Harbor–
UCLA Medical Center, Torrance, California*

In 1980, I arrived in California as training director for a new program in a UCLA-affiliated county hospital. I soon realized that the first class of two predoctoral interns were bravely trying to cope without sufficient supervision in tough psychiatry inpatient and outpatient settings with patients who were severely mentally ill and had rarely or, conversely, constantly been part of the public mental health system. With much enthusiasm and a lot of help, over the next 15 years I managed to develop the program by restricting intern positions to more advanced postdoctoral fellows, offering year-long experiences in specialized tracks, and increasing the class size to between 5 and 10 fellows per year, depending on the solvency status of Los Angeles County and its public agencies. The training staff grew from 3 paid psychologists on board in 1980, plus half a dozen volunteer supervisors from the community (3 of whom are still with us), to 15 full-time paid faculty and a dozen or so volunteer supervisors from outside the community.

Throughout this period, accreditation by the American Psychological Association (APA) was the ultimate goal. Because postdoctoral programs were not being accredited, we drew from APA internship standards as much as possible. When accreditation for postdoctoral programs looked imminent, I kept in touch with APA's progress, sharing our eagerness to be among the first considered. It would mean so much for Harbor–UCLA to have *all* its training programs accredited by their professions. With the invitation to submit the initial self-study, I pleaded my case with my department chair for long overdue cleaning and painting, hiring a part-time clerk, and buying a few computers. When the site visitors noted that our physical facilities ranged from shabby to attractive, we were delighted. We try to recruit candidates to come to work in authentic World War II army barracks, complete with termites and asbestos. On the other hand, they get free lunches in the doctor's dining room!

The biggest surprise in the accreditation process was the obvious Committee on Accreditation (CoA) debate over multitrack programs at the postdoctoral level. Having been a predoctoral internship site visitor since the mid-1970s, I had seen many successful internship programs featuring specialized tracks integrated with a core experience shared by all. It made sense that at the postdoctoral level students who had completed APA-accredited internships should function as the only psychology trainees in an interdisciplinary unit as opposed to one of a group of three trainees. This was especially logical, as these students typically came from APA-accredited predoctoral internships in which they were the only intern on a unit. So, we found ourselves having to explain and convince and document how the fellows socialized, professionally and personally. Some of our former classes happy-houred excessively, whereas others met only at lunch and a few training meetings a week, preferring to spend the bulk of their time with interdisciplinary colleagues on their clinical units rather than with psychology fellows working with other clinical populations. For most psychologists, this is what real-world professional settings are like.

Of course, a public setting is synonymous with minimal budgets. To run a postdoctoral psychology program in a psychiatry department of a county hospital has always been at the pleasure of nonpsychologists in the system. To ask such a setting to pay accreditation fees separately for each track or placement of fellows would be folly. For us, being honored by our profession as an accredited program is a distinction that places us in the company of those other mental health professions who can claim accreditation. The amount of money the honor requires from the institution is a tradeoff that can quickly become too high.

Happily, we prevailed both at home and at APA. Our psychiatry department chair cared enough to find the funds and other resources in our hour of need. Our site visitors recognized the viability and necessity of a medical center model of individuals in tracks in an overarching program. Our students and faculty realized that APA accreditation, although not necessary, was worth the extra effort and time above and beyond their busy professional duties. Finally, CoA apparently worked out its problem with the classic medical center model of postdoctoral training.

Thus, the Harbor–UCLA postdoctoral program is a positive result of the culmination of the 20 some years of APA discussion, conferences, political posturing, negotiations, and plain hard work on two areas: (a) how accreditation can apply to postdoctoral programs in psychology and (b) how public service medical center programs can be excellent candidates for postdoctoral accreditation.

a variety of external organizations representing graduate and professional education and training.

In addition to the national conferences, some of the most vocal advocates for accreditation at the postdoctoral level were the specialties in professional psychology. In fact, the Midwestern Neuropsychology Consortium of Postdoctoral Fellowship Programs had already developed program self-study procedures and site visit team evaluation forms in accordance with its specialty guidelines. To promote a collaborative and cohesive accreditation process for the field, the ABPP hosted a meeting at the University of Minnesota in 1991. The outcome of this meeting was the creation of the Interorganizational Council for the Accreditation of Postdoctoral Training Programs (IOC). Over the next several years, representatives from the ABPP Board of Trustees, the ABPP specialty councils, the National Register of Health Service Providers in Psychology, ASPPB, APPIC, and APA met on a regular basis to discuss the most appropriate mechanisms for the field. Some believed that accreditation should be developed under the auspices of the various specialty councils if the APA CoA could not provide this service to the field in a timely manner. But, by 1995, the IOC had completed its work; in coordination with the APA CoA, generic guidelines and procedures had been developed that drew on the recommendations of the Ann Arbor Conference and the CoA's own newly developed guidelines for accreditation at the doctoral level. The IOC then retired but recommended the formation of the Council of Specialties to serve as the ongoing forum in psychology for issues of education, training, and credentialing among the specialties in profession.

In 1996, after a period of public review, the CoA and the APA Council of Representatives formally adopted guidelines for the accreditation of postdoctoral education and training programs in professional psychology. The accreditation process is consistent with that of the doctoral and internship levels in that it involves a professional judgment as to the degree to which a program has achieved the goals and objectives of its stated training model. A core principle is that

> Postdoctoral residency education and training in professional psychology reflect the natural evolution and expansion of the knowledge base of the science and practice of psychology, and should be of sufficient breadth to ensure advanced competence as a professional psychologist and of sufficient depth and focus to ensure technical expertise and proficiency in the substantive traditional or specialty practice areas of professional psychology for which the residents are being prepared. (APA, 2000, p. 3)

To become accredited, a program must publicly state a goal of preparation for advanced practice in a substantive traditional or specialty practice area. In addition to specifying the advanced competencies that residents are to achieve in assessment, intervention, consultation, program evaluation, supervision, teaching, administration, and professional conduct, a program must also articulate advanced competencies in strategies of scholarly inquiry. The criteria of program length specifies a minimum of 1 year, although it is acknowledged that up to 3 years may be required for some specialty areas of practice.

Postdoctoral accreditation in professional psychology was implemented in 1997 with the approval of the two general programs cited earlier. To help with the review of specialized postdoctoral programs, the APA CoA decided to augment the general guidelines with specialty-specific guidelines received from organizations that have membership on the Council of Specialties. The first two postdoctoral training programs to be accredited in a recognized specialty were Michigan State University Consortium for Advanced Psychology Training and Wilford Hall Medical Center at Lackland Air Force Base; the specialty was Clinical Health Psychology.

CURRENT ISSUES AND FUTURE DIRECTIONS

Some of the current accreditation criteria and their interpretation have been questioned in recent years given changes in the internship and employment marketplaces as well as changes in the profession. For example, although the practice of unfunded internships had long been viewed as potentially exploitive and not beneficial to the profession, the imbalance caused by the relatively faster growth of the applicant pool in relationship to internship availability has led some sites to offer unfunded positions (Boggs & Douce, 2000; Keilin, Thorn, Rodolfa, Constantine, & Kaslow, 2000; Oehlert & Lopez, 1998). However, this change has been viewed negatively by the CoA.

The interpretation of the number of postdoctoral residents required for adequate socialization into the profession has also been questioned. Residencies argued that the requirement for two psychology trainees is not appropriate when socialization can be adequately accomplished through interaction with trainees of other disciplines and through collegial relationships among residents and faculty. The APA CoA has recently revised guidelines related to this criterion to reflect such a broadened interpretation (APA, 2002).

Changes in the health care system also have implications for the accreditation of training programs in terms of both curriculum and administrative support. Many managed health care organizations will not reimburse for services provided by psychology interns or unlicensed postdoctoral residents; in fact, a growing number of internship sites are finding it more difficult to fund their training programs (Constantine & Gloria, 1998; Spruill & Pruitt, 2000). This difficulty may lead to problems paying salaries commensurate with experience, or even funding positions, both of which raise red flags for accreditation. In addition, staff and faculty in settings with high managed care penetration often have less time available to devote to training as their jobs (or salaries) demand more direct service. Such a trend has been noted in VA Medical Centers, where psychologists have been required to assume more direct service responsibilities in accord with the shift to product line organization (Zeiss, 2000). Decreased availability of faculty has negative implications for meeting accreditation guidelines concerning supervision. In addition, faculty and staff have less time available to complete the accreditation self-study and have more limited resources, including funds, available to aid in this endeavor.

In this time of rapid change, how well training programs prepare their trainees for dealing with current marketplace issues and future roles and functions is also an accreditation issue, as this is integrally related to the self-study process and the assessment of outcomes. Although it is likely that internship programs embedded in managed care markets would have training in managed care as part of their goals, some programs never include such training despite purporting to train psychologists for practice.

Another issue concerns the relationship between generalist and specialist training. Although postdoctoral training is clearly accredited as advanced training in a formally recognized specialty, which can either be a specialty in general practice or a more focused specialty, internship training is accredited as generalist in nature. However, more and more specialty groups are advocating for the accreditation of specialty internship training programs in such areas as clinical neuropsychology, clinical health psychology, clinical child psychology, and family psychology. Several programs have models for specialty training in these areas (e.g., Black, 1986; Middleman & Ebner, 2000), and analyses have been conducted for specialty training at the internship level (e.g., LaGreca, Stone, & Swales, 1989). There is clear tension in the field regarding the taxonomy of specialties and which of them are broad and general in nature and thus appropriate for accreditation at the doctoral level.

As of this writing, a task force is conducting a required review of the composition of the CoA with respect to its allocated seats for professional education and training organizations. APPIC has expressed the desire to expand its number of seats given the number of internship programs accredited. In addition, the Association of Counseling Center Training Agencies, the VA psychologists, the Council of Specialties, and various other groups have voiced concerns about their nonrepresentation on the CoA and the subsequent impact this nonrepresentation might have on the accreditation of internships and postdoctoral residencies. Clearly there is no turning back from the interorganizational approach to accreditation that APA began in 1991, but any changes are likely to be fraught with turmoil.

There are no data that can demonstrate exactly how accreditation of internships and postdoctoral residencies has affected the quality of training. Clearly the accreditation process is time consuming and not inexpensive. Yet it also provides an opportunity for thoughtful analysis of goals and objectives, resource allocation, and practices in training. The self-study approach also promotes a shared identity as a training faculty, which in many internship and postdoctoral sites is the major cohesive force in the setting for psychologists.

It is also noted that APA accreditation of internships and postdoctoral residencies appears to be increasing in value. Many regulatory bodies give preference to individuals from APA-accredited internship programs; for example, some state licensing boards require less documentation regarding the internship experience if the applicant has completed an APA-accredited internship. Further, graduation from an APA-accredited internship is often specified as a prerequisite for employment (e.g., VA). Moreover, APA accreditation for postdoctoral programs will be required for those VA sites that wish to maintain their funding for postdoctoral fellows. Most recently, with the creation of the new Graduate Psychology Education program in the Bureau of Health Professions, APA accreditation has become a criterion for eligibility for federal funding of education and training in professional psychology. Therefore, it seems likely that accreditation activities in internship and postdoctoral training programs will continue to grow, and creating solutions for the problems and tensions detailed in this chapter will remain a high priority for psychology.

REFERENCES

American Psychological Association. (1956). Internships for doctoral training in clinical psychology approved by the American Psychological Association. *American Psychologist, 11*, 710–711.

American Psychological Association. (1958). Criteria for evaluating training programs in clinical or in counseling psychology. *American Psychologist, 13*, 59–60.

American Psychological Association. (1973). *Accreditation procedures and criteria.* Washington DC: Author.

American Psychological Association. (1979). *Criteria for accreditation: Doctoral training programs and internships in professional psychology.* Washington, DC: Author.

American Psychological Association. (1996a). *Book 1: Guidelines and principles for accreditation of programs in professional psychology.* Washington, DC: Author.

American Psychological Association. (1996b). *Book 2: Accreditation operating procedures of the Committee on Accreditation.* Washington, DC: Author.

American Psychological Association. (2000). *Guidelines and principles for accreditation of programs in professional psychology.* Washington, DC: Author.

American Psychological Association. (2002). *Guidelines and principles for accreditation of programs in professional psychology.* Washington, DC: Author.

American Psychological Association, Committee on Accreditation. (1999). *APA Committee on Accreditation 1998 annual report.* Washington, DC: Author.

American Psychological Association, Committee on Accreditation. (2002). *APA Committee on Accreditation 2001 annual report.* Washington, DC: Author.

American Psychological Association, Committee on Counselor Training, Division of Counseling and Guidance. (1952). The practicum training of counseling psychologists. *American Psychologist, 7*, 182–188.

American Psychological Association, Committee on Training in Clinical Psychology. (1947). Recommended graduate training program in clinical psychology. *American Psychologist, 2*, 537–558.

American Psychological Association, Committee on Training in Clinical Psychology. (1950). Standards for practicum training in clinical psychology: Tentative recommendations. *American Psychologist, 5,* 594–609.

Association of Psychology Postdoctoral and Internship Centers. (2000). *APPIC Directory, 29th Edition (2000–2001): Internship and postdoctoral programs in professional psychology.* Washington DC: Author.

Belar, C. D., Bieliauskas, L. A., Klepac, R. K., Larsen, K. G., Stigall, T. T., & Zimet, C. N. (1993). National Conference on Postdoctoral Training in Professional Psychology. *American Psychologist, 48,* 1284–1289.

Belar, C. D., Bieliauskas, L. A., Larsen, K. G., Mensh, I. N., Poey, K., & Roehlke, H. J. (1989). The National Conference on Internship Training in Professional Psychology. *American Psychologist, 44,* 60–65.

Black, F. W. (1986). Internship training in clinical neuropsychology: One model. *Professional Psychology: Research and Practice, 17,* 308–312.

Boggs, K. R., & Douce, L. A. (2000). Current status and anticipated changes in psychology internships: Effects on counseling psychology training. *The Counseling Psychologist, 28,* 672–686.

Constantine, M. G., & Gloria, A. M. (1998). The impact of managed health care on predoctoral internship sites: A national survey. *Professional Psychology: Research and Practice, 29,* 195–199.

Gray, S.W. (Ed.). (1963). *The internship in school psychology: Proceedings of the Peabody Conference.* Nashville, TN: George Peabody College for Teachers Department of Psychology.

Hoch, E. L., Ross, A. O., & Winder, C. L. (1966). Conference on the professional preparation of clinical psychologists: A summary. *American Psychologist, 24,* 42–51.

INS–Division 40 Task Force on Education, Accreditation, and Credentialing. (1987). Report of the INS–Division 40 Task Force on Education, Accreditation, and Credentialing. *Clinical Neuropsychologist, 1,* 29–34.

Keilin, W. G., Thorn, B. E., Rodolfa, E. R., Constantine, M. G., & Kaslow, N. J. (2000). Examining the balance of internship supply and demand: 1999 Association of Psychology Postdoctoral and Internship Centers' match implications. *Professional Psychology: Research and Practice, 31,* 288–294.

Korman, M. (1974). National Conference on Levels and Patterns of Professional Training in Psychology: The major themes. *American Psychologist, 29,* 441–449.

LaGreca, A. M., Stone, W. L., & Swales, T. (1989). Pediatric psychology training: An analysis of graduate, internship, and postdoctoral programs. *Journal of Pediatric Psychology, 14,* 103–116.

Middleman, A. B., & Ebner, D. L. (2000). Adolescent health care training in predoctoral psychology internship programs: A model of interdisciplinary training needs in health care. *Journal of Clinical Psychology in Medical Settings, 7,* 185–187.

Oehlert, M. E., & Lopez, S. J. (1998). APA-accredited internships: An examination of the supply and demand. *Professional Psychology: Research and Practice, 29,* 189–194.

Raimy, V. C. (1950). *Training in clinical psychology.* Englewood Cliffs, NJ: Prentice-Hall.

Sheridan, E. P., Matarazzo, J. D., Boll, T. J., Perry, N. W., Weiss, S. M., & Belar, C. D. (1988). Postdoctoral education and training for clinical service providers in health psychology. *Health Psychology, 7,* 1–17.

Spruill, J., & Pruitt, S. D. (2000). Preparing psychologists for managed care settings: Enhancing internship training programs. *Professional Psychology: Research and Practice, 31,* 305–309.

Stigall, T., Bourg, E., Bricklin, P., Kovacs, A., Larsen, K., Lorion, R., et al. (Eds.). (1990). *Report of the Joint Council on Professional Education in Psychology.* Washington, DC: Joint Council on Professional Education in Psychology.

Stone, G. (Ed.). (1983). National Working Conference on Education and Training in Health Psychology. *Health Psychology, 2*(Suppl. 5), 1–150.

Tuma, J. M. (Ed.). (1985). *Proceedings: Conference on Training Clinical Child Psychologists.* Washington, DC: American Psychological Association, Division of Clinical Psychology.

Weiner, I. B. (Ed.). (1973). *Postdoctoral education in clinical psychology.* Topeka, KS: Menninger Foundation.

Zeiss, A.M. (2000). Reinvisioning internship training in clinical and counseling psychology: Developments in the Department of Veterans Affairs System. *Professional Psychology: Research and Practice, 31,* 310–314.

4

THE IMPACT OF ACCREDITATION ON THE PRACTICE OF PROFESSIONAL PSYCHOLOGY

TOMMY T. STIGALL

Accreditation of professional training programs in psychology constitutes one important component of a larger system of professional regulation and standard-setting that is intended to benefit the public. It is assumed that programs meeting accreditation standards do a better job of professional training and that graduates of such programs are better qualified to provide services to the public following licensure and entry into practice. As Box 4.1 suggests, accreditation provides a means of anticipating and intervening when problems occur in training that are likely to reoccur in the career of a practitioner.

Although it is difficult to demonstrate a direct relationship between program accreditation and the later performance of practitioners, there is some indirect evidence bearing on this question. Kupfersmid and Fiala (1991) found that graduates of accredited doctoral programs in clinical and counseling psychology scored higher on the Examination for Professional Practice of Psychology (EPPP) than graduates of nonaccredited programs, but this finding did not extend to programs in school psychology. Other studies (McGaha & Minder, 1993; Ross, Holzman, Handal, & Gilner, 1991; Yu et al., 1997)

BOX 4.1
Issues of Student–Trainee Impairment

*Douglas H. Lamb, PhD, Department of Psychology,
Illinois State University, Normal*

It was during the early to mid-1980s that psychology began to acknowledge the interplay of two professional realities: First, that doing clinical work can take its personal toll, resulting in various degrees of psychic distress, professional vulnerability, and professional burnout, and second, that such professional vulnerability can significantly affect the quality of our professional work. During the 1990s, the profession spent considerable time defining *impairment*; assessing the professional, administrative, and legal implications associated with identifying professionals or student–trainees as *impaired*; and developing remediation strategies ("colleague assistance"). In this abbreviated discussion, I focus on three aspects of *impairment dilemma* (IDs): (a) our professional sophistication in understanding IDs, (b) the evolving status of accreditation guidelines as they relate to IDs, and (c) some suggested refinements of and extensions to current guidelines as they relate to IDs.

Our Sophistication. We have expanded the term *impairment* from referring only to alcoholism, other drug abuse, and mental illness to including domains such as unethical behavior, academic deficiencies, emotional limitations, and dysfunctional interactional patterns. In fact, survey research tells us that the most perplexing IDs faced by faculty and trainers are not academic in nature but relate more to the personality characteristics and interactional patterns of student–trainees. Likewise, faculty–trainers continue to struggle with how, when, and with whom to address suspected impairment in students or trainees. Other perplexing dimensions of IDs faced by both academic programs and internships include translating impairment concepts to specific behaviors, identifying due process procedures, balancing professional responsibilities with concerns about liability issues, and involving all relevant groups (academic programs, practica placements, internships) when impairment issues arise. An encouraging observation relates to the increased specificity, seen in both academic and internship programs, of articulating outcome expectations of student–trainees as they enter the program as well as providing reasonable opportunities for them to meet these competency requirements.

Accreditation Guidelines as They Relate to IDs. The accreditation criteria since 1979 have made explicit reference to the necessity of providing regular evaluations of all students. In addition, the guidelines have evolved in ways that reflect the growing knowledge we have about IDs, with an acknowledgment that serious interpersonal or personality difficulties are the major reasons students have been discontinued in their training. Finally, there have been stronger efforts in current guidelines to delineate grievance and due process procedures, reaffirm the importance of programs articulating their expectations, and require outcome measures. There has also been a modest shift from a more passive stance toward remediation ("counseled early," "made aware of career alternatives," as these phrases appeared in the 1979 *Accreditation Guidelines*) to a greater explicitness regarding remediation possibilities and dismissal considerations.

Suggested Refinements to Accreditation Guidelines as They Relate to IDs. The *Accreditation Guidelines* have been, overall, responsive to the evolving issues related to IDs. I am optimistic that the Committee on Accreditation (CoA) work will continue to reflect current thinking regarding impairment and generate responsive guidelines to be meaningfully integrated into the accreditation policies. Here are several thoughts regarding how such guidelines might be more responsive to IDs.

The *Accreditation Guidelines* clearly focus on student–trainee impairment issues. But what about the problem of impaired faculty–trainers? Again, there is evidence that such problems exist, but virtually nothing is noted in the guidelines that provides guidance on how to proceed when site visitors observe such impairment possibilities.

The *Accreditation Guidelines* might not require extensive reference to the matters identified above, but perhaps the committee should consider adding an appendix with selected references on these topics for concerned individuals.

The importance of communication between academic programs and field sites (on internships, practica) cannot be overemphasized. The CoA has reaffirmed that the responsibilities of the academic program do not cease when students move to their clinical placements. Yet the CoA could more actively develop ways to enhance such communication: For example, the articulation of more specific requirements for communications among all parties concerned with the training of students and sponsoring regional meetings specifically for academic programs and internship directors.

Organizations more intimately involved in the training of students (e.g., Association of Psychology and Postdoctoral Intern-

continues

> BOX 4.1 (continued)
>
> ship Centers [APPIC]) are often more aware of new impairment issues as they emerge in the field. Frequent and formalized updates to the CoA from parent organizations (e.g., APPIC, Councils of Clinical, School, and Counseling Psychology Academic Programs) may assist the CoA in crafting more meaningful impairment criteria.
>
> In summary, the growing appreciation of impairment issues compels us to pay close attention to how to address such issues among emerging professionals. The accreditation process is a critical vehicle that monitors and better ensures that we continue our professional obligation to be responsive to such issues. I hope the *Accreditation Guidelines* can serve as a reference document for how the profession responds to the reality of impaired students and trainees.

also have shown a positive relationship between program accreditation status and scores on the EPPP, a test validated on the basis of job analysis data and widely used by psychology licensing boards. But interpretation of these data is complicated by the correlation between EPPP scores and scores on the Graduate Record Examination (McGaha & Minder, 1993). Higher scores on the EPPP may be, at least in part, an artifact of more stringent admissions requirements associated with accredited programs. To appreciate the impact of accreditation on professional practice, it is necessary to look beyond the limited empirical data from the EPPP studies.

ACCREDITATION, CREDENTIALING, AND PUBLIC POLICY

Generally speaking, program accreditation has the potential to affect professional practice in all venues in which the individual practitioner's education and training credentials may be under review. But the most immediate and obvious impact is in the licensing and credentialing of psychologists.

In carrying out their statutory responsibilities to license practitioners and regulate the practice of psychology, state licensing boards must consider the education and training credentials of applicants for licensure. Even if graduation from an accredited program is not an explicit requirement for licensure, it may nevertheless facilitate the credentials review process. Accreditation thus exerts a direct influence on professional training programs and on the program graduates seeking a license for practice. It can be shown to exert an indirect, but important, effect on public opinion and public policy as well.

Licensing laws commonly require applicants to have completed a doctoral degree in psychology from a regionally accredited institution of higher education. An additional requirement may be graduation from a program accredited by the American Psychological Association (APA) or the Canadian Psychological Association (CPA) or from a program meeting criteria judged by the licensing board to be equivalent (Association of State and Provincial Psychology Boards [ASPPB], 2002). Frequently the educational criteria reference the listing of designated doctoral psychology programs maintained jointly by the ASPPB and the National Register of Health Service Providers in Psychology (National Register, 2001). Internship and postdoctoral residency training programs also are eligible for accreditation by APA (2002). Licensing board rules in some states specify that an accredited predoctoral internship or postdoctoral residency will count toward meeting the supervised experience requirements for licensure.

Because of the implications for licensure of their graduates, training programs have an incentive to achieve accredited or designated status. Students anticipating a career in professional practice are more likely to seek out an accredited or designated program in which to enroll, and graduates of such programs can expect to face fewer obstacles on their career pathway. Programs that are accredited by the APA or by the CPA are automatically eligible for listing as a doctoral psychology program meeting the ASPPB/National Register designation guidelines. Other programs must satisfy more specific designation criteria that were developed as a result of two national conferences on Education and Credentialing in Psychology (Wellner, 1976, 1977). A major concern of the conference participants at the time was to address the problem created for licensing and credentialing bodies by ambiguous language in state licensing laws referring to a doctoral degree "primarily psychological" in nature. Because eligibility for licensure was not limited to graduates of accredited professional training programs, more objective and explicit criteria defining a doctoral degree in psychology were needed. The designation guidelines assert that "the criteria for accreditation serve as a model for professional psychology training" (National Register, 2001, paragraph 1).

Beyond the influence that accreditation exerts on professional training programs and the licensing process, it has the potential to impact other aspects of practitioner credentialing as well. Two of the most notable ones are privileging for institutional practice and managed care contracting. Hospitals and other health care facilities typically require medical doctors, psychologists, and other health care practitioners to undergo a credentials review in the course of granting privileges to practice in the institution. Such clinical privileges are quite specific and, although training program accreditation alone would not be sufficient to justify privileges, it may be one of the criteria for privileging. For example, an accredited clinical internship could be a reasonable requirement for practice on a psychiatric inpatient unit, whereas it may not be required for a generic license to practice psychology.

Specialized health care facilities or programs such as nursing homes, rehabilitation units, or substance abuse treatment centers may have even more circumscribed privileging standards. In such instances, evidence of completion of an accredited specialized training program would be most relevant. As chapter 3 suggests, only within the past few years has organized psychology begun to address the need for accreditation of advanced specialty training programs at the postdoctoral level (Smith, 2001).

With the increasingly dominant marketplace influence of managed care, practitioners must contract with managed care organizations to receive referrals. Eligibility to participate on a provider panel is determined, in part, by a credentials review. Although graduation from an accredited doctoral program or completion of an accredited internship could be a requirement for participation, neither is mandated in the current guidelines promulgated by the National Committee for Quality Assurance (NCQA).

NCQA is an industry-recognized accrediting body for managed behavioral health organizations (MBHOs). Purchasers of group health insurance plans look to NCQA accreditation as a mark of quality in the management of mental health benefits for plan members. Compliance with NCQA standards requires the MBHO to document its credentialing and recredentialing mechanisms for psychologists and other health care practitioners and to verify state licensure for independent practice at the highest level recognized by the state. Also required is "graduation from an accredited professional school or highest training program applicable to the academic degree, discipline and licensure of the behavioral healthcare practitioner"[1] (NCQA, 1999, p. 207). Verification of this information is not required of the MBHO, however, if the state licensing agency conducts primary source verification in the course of issuing a license to practice. The practical effect of this exception may be to look no further than state licensure in considering credentials of applicants for MBHO panels. But managed care companies may also impose additional credentialing requirements for specific privileges. One leading national MBHO's recredentialing standards require completion of an APA-approved training program in child psychology, adolescent psychology, or geriatric psychology for a panel member to be privileged in the corresponding areas of specialty practice. Recognizing the marketplace influence of NCQA as a standard-setting body, the APA has been seeking fuller participation in the shaping of MBHO accreditation policies in general (Rabasca, 1999). The potential for training program accreditation to have an impact

---

[1] Quoted with permission of the National Committee for Quality Assurance.

on professional practice through this venue should not be overlooked by organized psychology.

Public opinion about psychologists and the perceived value of psychology as a profession is reflected in public policy. In addition to the licensing laws that define the scope of psychological practice and who is qualified to practice, other statutes and regulations affect practice and the ability of psychologists to serve the public. Organized psychology worked for many years to get psychologists recognized in federal law as eligible to provide services to the Medicare population. More recent efforts have been directed toward establishing the principle of mental health parity in health plan benefits and advocating for a federal patients' bill of rights. In framing such laws and regulations, public policymakers must take into account the education, training, and credentialing standards of the profession.

Often working in partnership with the APA, state and provincial psychological associations (SPPAs) play a significant role in influencing public policy and public opinion about psychology. Each time a bill is introduced in a state legislature affecting the practice of psychology, psychologists must be prepared to defend the education and training standards of the profession. The credibility and societal value of the profession is enhanced to the extent that SPPA leaders can point to relevant and meaningful standards. Simply knowing that program accreditation exists is probably of greater interest to public officials than the accreditation criteria themselves, but both are always potentially on trial in the court of public opinion. The profession itself should be able to demonstrate that accreditation criteria are appropriate and that accreditation ultimately benefits the public.

TWO CULTURES

The relationship between accreditation and practice is a dynamic one that reflects not only the impact of accreditation on practice but also the influence (or lack of it) exerted by practitioners on accreditation. Whereas practitioners and public officials tend to see advantages in uniform and well-defined standards for professional education and training, academic psychologists may resist what they regard as stultifying rigidity and a possible erosion of academic freedom. As Box 4.2 reveals, two cultures can be seen in these countervailing positions. After reviewing 20 years of experience of practitioner training in psychology, Peterson (1985) called attention to the distinctively different cultures of research and practice:

> A research culture is created by a group of investigators who share the values of science, probe into the questions that intrigue them, dig out the facts, frame ideas and findings into coherent conceptions, talk with each other, and work with each other to find out what is going on in the world—all in an environment that encourages inquiry....

BOX 4.2
The Impact of Differing Educational Cultures

Ronald E. Fox, PhD, The Consulting Group, A Division of Human Resources Consultants, Chapel Hill, North Carolina

Much of my career as an educator has unfolded against a backdrop of controversy regarding the role and meaning of accreditation within our discipline and profession. When American Psychological Association accreditation was first initiated almost 50 years ago, all of the eligible training programs were operated by academic departments housed in graduate schools within regionally accredited universities. These programs were committed to producing graduates with both research and practice skills and were controlled by faculty whose views of accreditation were formed by the arts and sciences graduate faculty culture. When explicitly professional-model programs housed in regionally accredited institutions appeared 30 years later, the same accreditation criteria were used to evaluate them, despite important conceptual differences between the two types of programs. The new programs were committed to producing informed, skilled practitioners rather than scientist–practitioners, and their faculty were motivated by a professional school rather than a graduate school culture. Both cultural traditions are found in most modern universities today, and each hold very different views of the purpose, role, and value of accreditation. In my view, the wonder of our accreditation process is not that it does not work well but that it works at all! We are using the same criteria and process to evaluate widely divergent programs, with different values, aims, responsibilities, and cultures.

Consider the different cultures in which graduate and professional school faculties operate. Graduate faculties eschew facile applications of knowledge and are likely to proceed cautiously when exploring new issues or new situations. Professional faculties, on the other hand, constantly look for newer, better, more cost-effective practices to address the problems presented by clients. The needs of clients rather than the dictates of science shape their behavior. Their imperative is to treat a patient's needs now rather than after all the research data are in.

Nowhere do the differences between the two cultures loom larger than with respect to curriculum and program requirements. Graduate faculties fiercely guard their absolute right to determine what is taught and to certify the competence of graduates. They resist all efforts by external bodies to do so. They favor curriculum changes only after careful review rather than in response to outside pressures. Consequently, they eschew the notion of a common curriculum. The primary allegiance of graduate faculties is to the needs of science. Free and unfettered inquiry, they believe, is ultimately in the best interests of society at large and therefore preferable to changing courses and research interests in response to what may be only a temporary shift in the social climate or professional customs.

Professional school faculties are compelled by different realities. They are training professionals who are granted special privileges by society and who are allowed to set and police their own standards of professional care and conduct. They are committed to graduating students who will be eligible for licensure and who have the knowledge, attitude, and skills necessary to practice their profession. Consequently, professional school faculties tend to favor core curricula because they help ensure the eligibility of graduates for licensure in all state jurisdictions, provide a public record of the knowledge members of the profession have mastered, and assure students that their education is sanctioned by both the profession and state licensing agencies.

These are not minor differences. They are the logical outgrowths of two different subcultures within the larger academic community. Both are legitimate and serve equally important purposes. Neither is superior to the other. However, I do not believe that it will be possible to develop the more stringent accreditation requirements that many think will be needed as the profession matures without some greater rapprochement between them. In my opinion, an important piece of that resolution will involve criteria that assess the core competencies of graduates rather than the courses that are required.

The competencies I favor are quite similar, if not identical, to those identified by the National Council of Schools of Professional Psychology several years ago:

- Competency in establishing various types of professional relationships
- Competency to assess individual, group, and organizational problem areas
- Competency to design and use interventions on the basis of the above
- Competency to identify and apply useful research to current practices

continues

> BOX 4.2 (continued)
>
> - Competency in consultation and education
> - Competency in the management and supervision of cases
>
> Evaluating these or similar competencies would not be easy, but what profession is better prepared than psychology to make the effort?

> The culture of practice is different. There a group of professionals are doing their best to provide services to the public. They are engaged in working out the puzzles of the individual case, talking these over with colleagues, despairing over their failures, enjoying their successes, exulting now and then when particularly stubborn problems yield to the solutions they have engineered, designing new programs together, working these into the community, and helping people right now with the best professional service they can offer. (p. 448)

Peterson (1991) contended that "scientific research and professional service are different in important ways, and that different forms of education are required to prepare people for careers of research, in the one case, or careers of professional service, in the other case" (p. 422).

Tensions between the two cultures give rise to important, and sometimes contentious, questions concerning accreditation. What role should practitioners play in the accreditation process? And how specific should the accreditation criteria be? Definitive answers to these questions are beyond the scope of this chapter, but it is not difficult to see that the needs and goals of psychologists engaged primarily in practice might lead to answers divergent from those of nonpractitioners.

For psychologists employed in academic institutions, whose careers are centered in teaching, research, and scholarship, a paramount consideration is academic freedom and the accompanying flexibility to design programs and develop curricula consistent with the faculty's philosophy of training and areas of scholarly interest and scientific inquiry. Broad accreditation guidelines that do not dictate specific courses or a particular model of professional education and training best serve the career goals and aspirations of psychologists working in these settings. On the other hand, psychologists engaged in practice must be able to demonstrate that their education and training adequately prepares them to engage in the professional activities they are licensed, certified, or otherwise credentialed to perform. For practitioners, more content-specific accreditation criteria are seen as desirable because of their usefulness in professional advocacy and career enhancement.

One line of reasoning is that program accreditation is needed only because "the academic discipline of psychology turns out health care practitioners..." and that it "would not be necessary (and some would argue it would be intolerable) if psychology only turned out scientists, scholars, or educators none of whom were engaged in the public practice of psychology as a health care profession" (K. deS. Hamsher, personal communication, October 25, 1999).

As is discussed in chapter 1, guidelines for recognition of specialized accrediting bodies in the professions promulgated by the U.S. Secretary of Education and the Council of Higher Education Accreditation anticipate that both practitioners and educators are to be involved in the accreditation review and decision-making process. Former director of the APA Office of Program Consultation and Accreditation Paul Nelson reported that, with some notable exceptions, "it has been difficult, despite attempts to recruit more private practitioners, to obtain the private practitioners' commitment to accreditation work." He concluded that "private practitioners of psychology are probably underrepresented in the accreditation site visitor pool" (P. D. Nelson, personal communication, July 2, 2002). Because of the way that the APA Committee on Accreditation (CoA) is constituted with a specified number of seats designated for various constituencies, practitioners are also in the minority on this body relative to those representing education and training. Two seats are reserved for independent practice and two for institutional practice on the 21-member CoA, which has responsibility both for developing accreditation policy and criteria and for accrediting professional training programs. Nelson noted that the two members appointed to represent independent practice are just as likely as not to be "'academic practitioners' who have private practices on the side."

If one accepts that accreditation is needed principally (or exclusively) for practitioner training and to benefit the public, why then have practitioners been so little involved in accreditation? Lack of interest by practitioners due to practice responsibilities and limited contact with educational institutions and training programs may be partly responsible. Private practitioners could have difficulty justifying the substantial time commitment required to serve on the CoA or as site reviewers. Another factor may be resistance from the academic community to have practitioners participate in the site review process or other aspects of accreditation.

In spite of barriers such as these, there is reason to hope for a growing rapprochement, founded on improved communication and interaction between the two cultures that could lead to greater involvement of practitioners in the accreditation process (see Box 4.3 in this chapter). Consensus-building, empathy, and collaboration between the two cultures might improve if SPPAs were more effective in recruiting members from the academic community and if academic departments of psychology were more open to utilizing the services of local practitioners as adjunct faculty and student supervisors for practicum students. A more unified position on the part of organized psychology concerning the need for accreditation and its purpose should benefit both practitioners and educators.

BOX 4.3
Science and Practice: Finding Common Ground
Stanley Moldawsky, PhD, Private Practice, Chatham, New Jersey, and Institute for Psychoanalysis and Psychotherapy of New Jersey, South Orange

The Council of the American Psychological Association (APA) created a 21-person Committee on Accreditation (CoA) in 1990, and the Committee for the Advancement of Professional Practice and the Board of Professional Affairs appointed Norine Johnson and me to represent the domain of private practice. I had already spent 2 years working with a dedicated group of practitioners and academicians to create a manifesto stating what graduate education for practice should look like. This manifesto was the product of the Joint Council on Professional Education in Psychology (JCPEP) chaired by Tommy Stigall. Armed with this document, I approached our task of writing a new set of guidelines as if it were a piece of cake. All we had to do was simply incorporate all the JCPEP ideas into the guidelines and get on with the business of accrediting programs and internships.

It turned out that it wasn't so simple. Other constituencies had quite different ideas as to what the guidelines should look like. Members of the committee's subgroup working on criteria revisions were mainly from the Council of Graduate Departments of Psychology and had crafted a preliminary draft of criteria that suited that council. When I read it, I was stunned. The group had written criteria for accreditation that rested on a research knowledge base. The importance of an experiential knowledge base was omitted. I suggested we needed more discussion coming from the following positions:

- The program should emphasize core competencies rather than a required core curriculum.
- Program faculty should ensure acquisition by its graduates of the following knowledge domains: theories of individual and systems functioning and change, life span development, dysfunctional behavior or psychopathology, professional ethics and standards, psychological measurement, and history and systems of psychology.
- Program faculty should require acquisition of knowledge in the following bases of behavior: biological, cognitive–affective, social, and cultural.

- Research competence should be stressed.
- Practice competencies, including interpersonal skills, assessment, intervention, consultation and teaching, application of research, administration, and supervision, should be gained.
- Plenty of practica should be held in many settings with lots of supervision.
- Three full-time academic years, 2 in one institution and at least 1 in full-time residence, would allow for socialization.
- Diversity should be an ideal in courses, faculty hiring, and student admissions.

The CoA had agreed that we needed to resist a checklist mentality and give programs freedom to demonstrate how they met the various criteria. When the chair of the criteria subgroup invited me to go over my letter with them, I was stunned again—this time because they found my points compatible—and we incorporated the changes to expand the knowledge base to experiential learning.

I realize this process was an amazing experience. We had started on opposite poles and developed some respect for the position of the other. We ended up with compromises that did not leave us feeling we'd lost. A state senator in New Jersey once said, "You want it all." But when there are several constituencies working together on one product, you can't have it all. We often said, "Back to the drawing board" and wrestled with our differences.

One area that did not find us bickering was diversity. We all agreed that this be one of the main criteria for a program to meet in the hiring of faculty, the admission of students, and the incorporation of content throughout the curriculum.

It was reassuring to me that, after we completed writing the new guidelines and started applying them, we seemed always to be in strong agreement about a particular program's accreditation status. To me, this was awesome.

Of the many APA boards and committees on which I have served, I found CoA to be the hardest working. A month before each meeting, a huge box of materials would arrive to be read and evaluated before we met. It would be too much to carry on the airplane, so it had to be read early enough so that the box could be shipped back to APA. I often wondered how I had gotten myself into this amount of stuff to do.

continues

> BOX 4.3 (continued)
>
> When it came time to discuss standards for professional schools, I learned a lesson in how democracy really works. I had had a hand in creating the Rutgers University Graduate School of Applied and Professional Psychology, so I was sensitive to the fact that many traditional clinical programs had been influenced by the professional school movement and had moved in the direction of experiential learning. One of my pet issues was how much actual hands-on supervision was going on in a program. Setting a high number of hours was a priority of mine, but we had to respect our checklist mentality modus operandi. Folks didn't want to list a required number. I did, and I wanted it high! We compromised and determined that a level of competency had to be achieved.
>
> In conclusion, my 4 years on CoA was an awesome experience in democracy at work. When I think about the experience now, I think about the friends I made. The struggles fade, and the pleasure in accomplishment remains.

SPECIALTY PRACTICE, POSTDOCTORAL TRAINING, AND ACCREDITATION

The continuous expansion of knowledge in psychology and related disciplines and the increasing differentiation of psychological practice provide an impetus for postdoctoral specialty training and accreditation of postdoctoral programs. The challenge for organized psychology has been the need for an orderly system linking educational preparation for specialty practice, specialty credentialing, and accreditation of specialty training programs.

The movement to expand the scope of practice of licensed psychologists to authorize prescribing of medications serves as an example of the increased demand for specialized postdoctoral training. In 1995, the APA Council of Representatives adopted as policy a position in favor of seeking statutory authority for properly qualified psychologists to prescribe psychotropic medication (DeLeon, 1996, p. 841). Since that time, APA guidelines for psychopharmacology training have been put forward, a national examination in psychopharmacology has been developed for psychologists, and postdoctoral psychopharmacology training programs are underway. Some of these programs are affiliated with universities or professional schools, whereas others are freestanding. All of them aspire to comply with the APA guidelines. But, in the absence of a formal accreditation mechanism, there is no objective way to judge the quality of any of them.

New Mexico holds the distinction of being the first state to enact legislation authorizing psychologists to prescribe medication (Daw, 2002). With prescriptive authority bills being introduced rapidly in legislatures across the nation, it is only a matter of time before other states follow suit. As state laws are changed, the demand for postdoctoral psychopharmacology training can be expected to escalate. Increasingly, state licensing boards will need appropriate standards by which to evaluate the educational qualifications of practitioners seeking to become certified as prescribing psychologists.

In 1990, the Joint Council on Professional Education in Psychology (JCPEP) issued a report (Stigall et al., 1990) calling for the expansion of postdoctoral residency training that could meet the needs of doctoral program graduates seeking to satisfy the postdoctoral, supervised work experience required for licensure or prepare for advanced specialty practice. Established in response to a perceived need from the practice community to study critical issues and develop recommendations intended to enhance professional education and training, the JCPEP was constituted as an interorganizational body with representatives appointed by APA practice divisions and other national organizations concerned with education and training in psychology.

The JCPEP report (see Appendix H, this volume) included specific recommendations concerning postdoctoral training and specialization, as well as two general resolutions relevant to this topic:

> The JCPEP endorses the establishment within the APA of a mechanism for the official recognition and definition of professional practice specialties and skill proficiencies, based upon a systematic taxonomy and set of definitional criteria....
>
> The JCPEP urges the APA to approve accreditation criteria for postdoctoral residency training that, in addition to providing advanced specialty training, could satisfy the statutory requirements in most jurisdictions for the supervised experience prerequisite to licensure. The JCPEP further calls upon the APA Education Directorate, the Council of Graduate Departments of Psychology, the various councils of training directors in psychology, the Association of Psychology Internship Centers, and the National Council of Schools of Professional Psychology to promote the development of residency training opportunities at the postdoctoral level. JCPEP encourages U.S. and Canadian licensing authorities to look to residency training standards for evaluating the adequacy of postdoctoral experience needed for licensure as a psychologist. (Stigall et al., 1990, p. 25)

The consensus position of this body, composed of both practitioners and academics, was to recognize the great potential of postdoctoral education and training for the future development of practice and the related need for access to postdoctoral accreditation (see also chapter 3, this volume).

Within the past decade, two national conferences have addressed issues of postdoctoral education and training in psychology. A conference in

1992, held in Ann Arbor, Michigan, and sponsored by the Association of Psychology Postdoctoral and Internship Centers (APPIC), was designed to answer several specific questions regarding postdoctoral training in professional psychology. A policy statement endorsed by the 52 conferees included various recommendations aimed at promoting excellence and innovation in postdoctoral education and training. The first of these asserted that "appropriate agencies and mechanisms must be established for the review and accreditation of postdoctoral residency programs. In the accreditation process, provisions are made for programs in newly emerging specialties" (Belar et al., 1993, p. 1288). Thus, the conference participants both anticipated a growing demand for postdoctoral specialty training and expressed their conviction about the need to accredit postdoctoral residency programs.

Two years later, the APA convened in Norman, Oklahoma, a more broadly conceived National Conference on Postdoctoral Education and Training in Psychology. The purpose of this conference was to "study postdoctoral education and training extant across different areas of psychology and identify postdoctoral education models, directions, and mechanisms for quality assurance which may be needed by individuals entering the discipline of psychology in the 21st century" (as cited in Reich, Sands, & Wiens, 1995, Preface). Some 100 psychologists representing teaching, research, and practice were chosen to participate. The format of this conference allowed for multiple subgroup discussions focused separately on teaching, research, practice, and the integration of these activities.

In a synthesis of the five subgroup reports on practice (Bourg & McNamara, 1995), recommendations can be found that reflect the conference participants' recognition of the importance of postdoctoral specialization and accreditation. One recommendation endorses efforts within APA to formally recognize specialties and proficiencies in professional psychology. Another calls for the development of guidelines "for certifying psychologists in assessment and treatment in the specialty and proficiency areas." A third recommendation states that "postdoctoral programs which educate and train psychologists for specialty areas should be accredited by APA" (pp. 75–76). The final summary recommendations prepared by the conference steering committee echo these sentiments: "Accreditation is necessary for those postdoctoral programs which are designed to develop competency for the professional practice of psychology or for advanced expertise in a recognized specialty in professional psychology" (Reich, Sands, & Wiens, 1995, p. 15).

CoA guidelines and procedures for the accreditation of postdoctoral programs have existed since 1997 but, as is true with doctoral program accreditation, the guidelines are generic rather than specialty-specific (APA, 2000, January 1). As of December 2002, 11 postdoctoral-residency training programs had been accredited, 2 of which were identified by specialty area (clinical health psychology; APA, 2002). Meanwhile, 74 postdoctoral programs were listed in a recent directory (Hsu & Simoneau, 2001) published by

APPIC. Listing in the directory indicates only that a program has met the membership requirements of APPIC. The impact of accreditation on professional practice will be multiplied as increasing numbers of practitioners seek advanced specialty training and more postdoctoral programs achieve accredited status.

Accreditation of postdoctoral training programs should be facilitated by a systematic means of recognizing specialties and proficiencies in psychology. Both the profession and the public stand to gain by a clearer understanding of the defined scope of practice of psychology, including areas of specialized service delivery. The Commission for the Recognition of Specialties and Proficiencies in Professional Psychology (CRSPPP) was created in 1995 by the APA Council of Representatives. Its purpose is to review evidence submitted by petitioning organizations of psychologists seeking recognition of a new specialty or proficiency and to make recommendations to the Council concerning such formal recognition (Stigall, 1998). In carrying out its delegated function, CRSPPP relies on explicit criteria and procedures developed for this purpose. An archival definition for each specialty and proficiency becomes a part of the official record.

As of February 2002, four proficiencies[2] and the following 11 specialties had been recognized by the APA (n.d.):

- Clinical neuropsychology
- Clinical health psychology
- Psychoanalytic psychology
- School psychology
- Clinical psychology
- Clinical child psychology
- Counseling psychology
- Industrial/organizational psychology
- Behavioral psychology
- Forensic psychology
- Family psychology.

Postdoctoral training programs in any of these areas of specialty practice would be eligible to apply for APA accreditation, but only under the generic accreditation criteria. Whereas certain of the criteria may be applicable to all specialties, the addition of accreditation content relevant to each specialty would be consistent with the common understanding of specialties as differentiated domains of knowledge and practice. It also would lend credibility to the accreditation process for both practitioners and consumers of psychological services. It remains to be seen how soon specialty-specific criteria will be forthcoming, but the increasing interest and involvement of other bodies

---

[2]Biofeedback: Applied Psychophysiology; Clinical Geropsychology; Psychopharmacology; Treatment of Alcohol and Other Psychoactive Substance Use Disorders.

external to the APA, such as the Council of Credentialing Organizations in Professional Psychology (Stigall, 1998, p. 227) and the newly formed Council of Specialties (Murray, 1999), suggests that change may not be far off. With the recognition of new and emerging specialties in professional psychology and the increased demand for postdoctoral specialty training has come a realization of the need for a more robust and responsive accreditation system, one that will best serve the interests of the profession and the public.

CONCLUSION

Accreditation should be a process that contributes not only to excellence in professional education and training but also to the quality of psychological service delivery. Accreditation criteria, therefore, should be relevant to professional practice and credible from the standpoint of public policy. Research data are lacking to show that completion of an accredited professional training program makes one a better practitioner. Data showing a positive correlation between accreditation and scores on the EPPP appear to be specialty specific and may be confounded by program admissions criteria. It remains to be demonstrated whether modification of the accreditation criteria to make them more job-related and specialty-specific would lead to more persuasive outcome studies. Yet, accreditation continues to be widely regarded as an important indicator of quality in professional education and training, and it does affect practitioners in significant ways.

Whereas the impact of accreditation on the education and training enterprise has been obvious and direct, the impact on practice has been somewhat indirect and perhaps less apparent but nonetheless significant. Licensing for entry-level practice, specialty recognition and credentialing, privileging for institutional practice, managed care provider contracting, and professional advocacy with public officials and lawmakers are aspects of professional practice affected by accreditation of professional training programs.

As a voluntary process of self-regulation, accreditation of professional training programs principally affects two communities of interest within psychology: education and practice. In the past, the process of accreditation has been managed and influenced more by psychologists involved in education, training, and higher education administration than by practitioners. It has been difficult to get practitioners involved as accreditation site reviewers or in other roles, such as training program faculty. This may be due, in part, to the traditional "town and gown" separation. Or, it may be the result of general indifference on the part of practitioners.

Another reason for the relatively limited influence of practitioners has been the composition of the CoA, which currently has only 4 of its 21 seats allocated to professional practice, 2 for institutional practice and 2 for independent practice. The remainder of the seats are reserved for those representing graduate departments of psychology (4 seats), professional schools and training programs (10 seats), the general public (2 seats), and graduate students (1 seat; APA, 2000, January 3). More balanced representation on the committee could result in a greater sense of ownership and involvement in the accreditation process on the part of practitioners. By the same token, practitioners need to keep in mind that any workable system of accreditation must be one that is acceptable to the education and training community whose programs are subject to evaluation by these standards.

Societal and technological changes present challenges to be faced and thoughtfully addressed within the existing accreditation system. Nontraditional models of organizing and delivering information more efficiently and more conveniently appeal to both prospective doctoral students and midcareer professionals seeking postdoctoral specialty training. As discussed also in chapter 2, new technology raises difficult questions. Should training programs that rely heavily or exclusively on distance learning and electronic dissemination of knowledge be eligible for professional accreditation? What about programs designed as a series of continuing education modules? Is it necessary for a training program to have a physical presence, or will a virtual campus suffice? How essential is a resident faculty, an assembled body of students, and ready access to library and clinical or research facilities? What is a meaningful residency requirement for professional education and training? How are opportunities for supervised practice provided, and how are practice skills acquired? Answers to questions such as these will need to be found as societal needs, practice patterns, and new models of education and training emerge in an era of rapidly advancing information technology (Jerome et al., 2000).

Accreditation will continue to exert an influence on professional practice through practitioner education, training, and credentialing. The impact of accreditation on the job performance of practitioners and the quality of psychological service delivery is yet to be demonstrated. Issues of proper venue, oversight, scope, and criteria for the accreditation process are matters about which there is ongoing debate within organized psychology. A satisfactory resolution of these issues depends upon participation by all of the principal stakeholders in shaping policy and sharing responsibility for implementing sound accreditation practices. An overarching goal should be to achieve an integrated system of professional education, training, and credentialing standards that is both durable and useful and that can be shown to serve the public interest.

REFERENCES

American Psychological Association. (2000, January 1). *Guidelines and principles for accreditation of programs in professional psychology.* Retrieved May 4, 2000, from http://www.apa.org/ed/gp2000.html

American Psychological Association. (2000, January 3). *2000 Committee on accreditation membership profile.* Retrieved February 10, 2000, from http://www.apa.org/ed/coalist.html

American Psychological Association. (2002). Accredited internship and postdoctoral programs for training in psychology: 2002. *American Psychologist, 57,* 1074–1095.

American Psychological Association. (n.d.). *Specialties and proficiencies in professional psychology.* Retrieved July 1, 2002, from http://www.apa.org/crsppp/rsp.html

Association of State and Provincial Psychology Boards. (2002). *2002 handbook of licensing and certification requirements for psychologists in the U.S. and Canada.* Montgomery, AL: Author.

Belar, C. D., Bieliauskas, L. A., Klepac, R. K., Larsen, K. G., Stigall, T. T., & Zimet, C. N. (1993). National conference on postdoctoral training in professional psychology. *American Psychologist, 48,* 1284–1289.

Bourg, E. F., & McNamara, K. M. (1995). Practice. In Education Directorate, American Psychological Association (Ed.), *Education and training beyond the doctoral degree: Proceedings of the American Psychological Association National Conference on Postdoctoral Education and Training in Psychology* (pp. 71–81). Madison, CT: International Universities Press.

Daw, J. (2002, April). New Mexico becomes first state to gain Rx privileges. *Monitor on Psychology, 33,* 24–25.

DeLeon, P. H. (1996). Proceedings of the American Psychological Association, incorporated for the year 1995: Minutes of the annual meeting of the council of representatives, August 10 and 13, 1995, New York, NY, and February 16–18, 1996, Washington, DC. *American Psychologist, 51,* 805–848.

Hsu, J., & Simoneau, T. (Eds.). (2001). *APPIC Directory 2001–2002* (30th ed.). Washington, DC: Association of Psychology Postdoctoral and Internship Centers.

Jerome, L. W., DeLeon, P. H., James, L. C., Folen, R., Earles, J., & Gedney, J. J. (2000). The coming age of telecommunications in psychological research and practice. *American Psychologist, 55,* 407–426.

Kupfersmid, J., & Fiala, M. (1991). Comparison of EPPP scores among graduates of varying psychology programs. *American Psychologist, 46,* 534–535.

McGaha, S., & Minder, C. (1993). Factors influencing performance on the Examination for Professional Practice in Psychology (EPPP). *Professional Psychology: Research and Practice, 24,* 107–109.

Murray, B. (1999, March). Group offers muscle and a voice to psychology's specialties. *APA Monitor Online.* Retrieved February 10, 2000, from http://www.apa.org/monitor/mar99/muscle.html

National Committee for Quality Assurance. (1999). *Standards and surveyor guidelines for the accreditation of MBHOs.* Washington, DC: Author.

National Register of Health Service Providers in Psychology. (2001). *Doctoral Psychology Programs Meeting Designation Criteria.* Retrieved July 26, 2002, from http://www.nationalregister.org/doctoraldegrees.html

Peterson, D. R. (1985). Twenty years of practitioner training in psychology. *American Psychologist, 40,* 441–451.

Peterson, D. R. (1991). Connection and disconnection of research and practice in the education of professional psychologists. *American Psychologist, 46,* 422–429.

Rabasca, L. (1999, April). Greater involvement with NCQA may help psychology shape the future of health care, APA officials say. *APA Monitor Online.* Retrieved February 10, 2000, from http://www.apa.org/monitor/apr99/dog.html

Reich, J. N., Sands, H., & Wiens, A. N. (Eds.). (1995). *Education and training beyond the doctoral degree: Proceedings of the American Psychological Association National Conference on Postdoctoral Education and Training in Psychology.* Madison, CT: International Universities Press.

Ross, M. J., Holzman, L. A., Handal, P. J., & Gilner, F. H. (1991). Performance on the Examination for the Professional Practice of Psychology as a function of specialty, degree, administrative housing, and accreditation status. *Professional Psychology: Research and Practice, 5,* 347–350.

Smith, D. (2001, July/August). Making the grade. *Monitor on Psychology, 32,* 80–82.

Stigall, T. T., Bourg, E. F., Bricklin, P. M., Kovacs, A. L., Larsen, K. G., Lorion, R. P., et al. (Eds.). (1990). *Report of the Joint Council on Professional Education in Psychology.* Baton Rouge, LA: Joint Council on Professional Education in Psychology.

Stigall, T. T. (1998). Commission for the Recognition of Specialties and Proficiencies in Professional Psychology. In A. S. Bellack & M. Hersen (Series Eds.) & A. N. Wiens (Vol. Ed.), *Comprehensive clinical psychology: Vol. 2. Professional issues* (pp. 221–230). New York: Pergamon.

Wellner, A. M. (Ed.). (1976). *Education and credentialing in psychology: Preliminary report of a meeting.* Washington, DC: Author.

Wellner, A. M. (Ed.). (1977). *Education and credentialing in psychology II: Report of a meeting.* Washington, DC: Author.

Yu, L. M., Rinaldi, S. A., Templer, D. I., Colbert, L., Siscoe, K., & Van Patten, K. (1997). Score on the examination for professional practice in psychology as a function of attributes of clinical psychology graduate programs. *Psychological Science, 8,* 347–350.

5

THE FUTURE OF ACCREDITATION

DEBORAH C. BEIDEL, SUSAN D. PHILLIPS, AND SUSAN ZLOTLOW

The history of specialized accreditation resembles closely the history of psychology as a profession. As noted by Matarazzo (1977), psychology, like other professions, evolved from a loose guild of practitioners into a highly organized membership that develops ideas about a formalized training curriculum and implements a system for the evaluation (accreditation) of training programs and the licensure or certification of program graduates. According to the preamble of the *Guidelines and Principles* (American Psychological Association [APA], Committee on Accreditation, 2000), psychology's accreditation procedures are designed to ensure the highest standards of training for the profession and the public. Despite what sounds like a lofty and worthy goal (who can argue against quality standards?), accreditation is seldom without controversy, often encompassing both its substance and process. In particular, as noted in several previous chapters, the past decade has been marked by continued concern within psychology and across other professions that the promise of accreditation—that is, quality education—has not been fulfilled (Dill, Massey, Williams, & Cook, 1996). In this chapter, we address several challenges facing the future of specialized professional accreditation in psychology. However, it is important to note that many of these challenges are not unique to psychology but are being voiced by other professions and by academic institutions in general.

THE VOLUNTARY NATURE OF ACCREDITATION

In psychology, as for many other professions, accreditation is usually defined as a voluntary process of quality assurance. Few involved in the process really see it this way. For example, without regional accreditation by one of the six regional accrediting bodies, students enrolled at an educational institution are not eligible for various types of federal financial assistance. Additionally, lack of accreditation can limit the opportunities to practice for graduates (e.g., practicing law; Mangan, 1998), thus limiting the number and type of students who matriculate from nonaccredited programs. With this type of constraint, it is easy to see why schools view accreditation as essential rather than as optional.

Reflecting the national landscape, nonaccredited doctoral programs in psychology are at a similar disadvantage in comparison with accredited programs. First, students often are reluctant to attend a nonaccredited program. To do so could present difficulty in obtaining a license to practice, achieving advanced recognition (e.g., certification), or listing in various registers of health service providers (chapter 4 provides greater detail on why this difficulty occurs). Students from nonaccredited doctoral programs have great difficulty getting positions in accredited internship programs. Graduating from a nonaccredited doctoral program (or perhaps a nonaccredited internship program) could limit the psychologist's professional prestige. Further, many employers require graduation from both accredited doctoral programs and internships. In turn, programs that are not accredited feel that they cannot compete for the most qualified students. Thus, although accreditation of doctoral programs in psychology may be defined as voluntary, the reality is somewhat different. Some states have recently considered proposals that licensure be limited solely to graduates of accredited doctoral programs. If such modifications of state laws are successful, the voluntary nature of accreditation will no longer exist.

Some professional associations have already put forth proposals to make accreditation a requirement, citing the need to raise the prestige of their profession or ensure the highest training standards. For example, in 1995, the American Association of Colleges for Teacher Education proposed that all teacher-training programs be nationally accredited (Nicklin, 1995). Although this proposal was defeated, a resolution was later passed encouraging programs to seek accreditation voluntarily. The original resolution was defeated not because the members considered accreditation to be an inappropriate aspirational goal. Rather, the concern was the costly and time-consuming nature of the process and the fact that the accreditation standards might not be the best measure of educational quality. Four years earlier, some deans of library and information science schools threatened to forgo accreditation rather than continue their participation in the process (Leatherman, 1991). Calling the process burdensome and a waste of time and money, they described their accreditation requirements as excessive and providing little benefit to well-established schools. Law school deans have voiced similar concerns, calling accreditation standards for law schools that force all schools to adhere to one model of legal education overly prescriptive and rigid (Leatherman, 1994).

Interestingly, arguments about time and cost often are heard among doctoral programs in professional psychology. In some cases, however, these concerns do not appear to be valid. For example, psychology training programs that for various reasons have been precluded from seeking accreditation through the APA often set up alternative accreditation procedures. For example, the Consortium of Diversified Psychology Programs accredits master's and PhD programs in humanistic psychology, and the North American Association of Masters in Psychology participates in an accreditation process for programs offering a master's degree in psychology. Some doctoral training programs in clinical psychology, although still participating in the recognized APA accreditation process, have set up additional recognition programs: Several university-based PhD programs have elected to seek membership in the Academy of Clinical Science, which has training guidelines that are more restrictive than the *Guidelines and Principles* of APA. If programs are willing to engage in alternative or additional recognition programs, this fact mitigates complaints about expense or time and suggests that the need for accreditation remains strong. Despite what are viewed as cumbersome procedures, it appears almost certain that the process of accreditation will continue. However, just continuing the process does not address the issue of whether accreditation standards are the best measure of quality.

ACCREDITATION AS QUALITY ASSURANCE

As is described in chapter 2, the most recent revision of the accreditation standards for doctoral programs in psychology attempted to address quality through an outcomes-based assessment strategy rather than through documenting the provision of courses. The decision to move to an outcomes-based strategy is not exclusive to psychology. Across many professions, adopting outcomes-based accreditation standards reflects dissatisfaction with the previous system. In the late 1990s, engineering educators, for example, protested that accreditation standards did not allow for innovation (Schachterle, 1999). Further, they noted that as their knowledge base expanded, there were more required courses to fit into the curriculum. Library deans raised similar concerns, describing accreditation as limiting and denying training potential opportunities in a changing field (Leatherman, 1991). In response to these concerns, which could just as well have come from graduate training directors in professional psychology, engineering accreditors moved to a system that enumerated a set of student outcomes. In addition, institutions had to identify a specific mission, general curriculum requirements, methods by which students achieve specified outcomes, and faculty evaluation of student achievement (Schachterle, 1999).

For psychology, the Committee on Accreditation (CoA) implemented a virtually identical outcomes-based assessment strategy in 1996. The new *Guidelines and Principles for Accreditation of Programs in Professional Psychology* (APA, 1996) reflects an outcomes-based model that requires programs to articulate their philosophy of training, goals and objectives, and desired competencies. A strategy for assessing the extent to which goals had been achieved by the program is also required. As is detailed in chapter 2, this model was intended to promote innovation and protect the program's right to be evaluated in light of its own particular philosophy of training and also to ensure that all accredited programs include attention to foundational principles for quality preparation in professional psychology.

Initially, it was difficult for many programs to adapt to this new conceptualization. Internships in particular struggled with how to conceptualize their programs and how to present their outcomes assessment. However, others viewed the self-study procedure as a learning experience and were pleased with the process. In this regard, the CoA has expanded, and will continue to expand, its consultative functions by making available training opportunities regarding self-study preparation, particularly concerning the establishment of coherent goals, objectives, and outcomes. The CoA expects that, as programs progress through a second or third review under the *Guidelines and Principles*, they will find that the outcomes-based model will help them respond quickly to needed changes in the substance of their training and also to remain active in ensuring the quality of their training. Therefore, it is likely that this consultative function will be time limited.

Given that the outcomes-based model is intended to promote both quality training and opportunities for innovation, one consequence of this new system is a proliferation of new training philosophies and unique training strategies. As might be expected, these innovations are greeted by the profession with some controversy as they deviate from the traditional models of professional psychology training. Because every program must demonstrate the achievement of appropriate outcomes and also must conform to the foundational principles for quality preparation, the effectiveness of innovative approaches theoretically is continually monitored by actual program outcomes and student competencies. However, "letting a thousand flowers bloom" may have limitations that could occupy the CoA for the next decade. First, the proliferation of models may result in a loss of a distinctive identity for psychology and psychological services. Without a common core and set of skills, it will be difficult to say exactly what psychologists do and what differentiates us from other helping professions. Second, the CoA ultimately will be forced to consider whether there is a finite set of acceptable training models. Particularly as the provision of services becomes increasingly specialized, it is possible that the CoA will have to become more specific regarding acceptable doctoral training models.

INCREASING SPECIALIZATION AT THE DOCTORAL LEVEL

As psychology continues to mature, there is increasing pressure to create specialties and subspecialties within the discipline. In addition to the traditionally accredited professional specialties of clinical, counseling, and school psychology, the Commission for the Recognition of Specialties and Proficiencies in Professional Psychology (CRSPPP) has recently recognized clinical health psychology, clinical child psychology, and clinical neuropsychology, among others. Currently, many of these specialties exist as training tracks within a broader based accredited program in clinical psychology. However, the current *Guidelines and Principles* make provisions for the accreditation of emerging substantive areas. Thus, it is likely that as these specialties continue to mature, they will seek independent accreditation status at either the doctoral or postdoctoral level. The challenge for accreditation will be to consistently and fairly evaluate the increasing variety of programs that will seek accredited status. This challenge most likely will involve changes to the process and structure of the CoA and a fresh look at the substantive nature of training.

First, with respect to changes in substance, the CoA will be faced with the necessity of expanding the sets of competencies required for the various specialties. Most likely, this process will entail seeking outside assistance from specialty groups themselves, some of whom have independently promulgated guidelines for training. However, if these specialties seek accreditation at the doctoral level, there still will be the necessity of evaluating the program's overall ability to produce individuals broadly trained for professional practice. This criterion means that programs will have to address a broader range of training outcomes.

In addition to necessary changes in the substance of training programs and thus the criteria for accreditation, the wider array of programs seeking accreditation will require alterations in the accreditation process. First, there will need to be a recruitment of a larger and broader pool of potential site visitors, some of whom must have specialized expertise in the specialty areas seeking accreditation. This addition will further complicate an already complicated process of site visitor selection. Second, new specialty programs might call for specialized expertise at the level of CoA program review. One potential review structure that the CoA might use is the addition of ad hoc external reviewers, a format currently used by the National Institute of Mental Health. Ad hoc reviewers would not be members of the CoA but might review a particular program with respect to the success of the program's specialized training outcomes. Alternatively, the actual structure of CoA could change such that certain specialties are represented on the committee itself. Given that the current CoA consists of 21 members, simply enlarging the existing membership is not feasible. Therefore, one alternative is to establish separate Committees on Accreditation for doctoral training programs, internship training programs, and postdoctoral training programs. In addition to providing the needed expertise, this change would distribute the workload of the committee, which is currently quite extensive.

With respect to the CoA's evolution, the policies governing the structure and function of the CoA stipulate that the composition of Domain II (Association of Postdoctoral and Psychology Internship Centers, Council of University Directors of Clinical Psychology, Council of Counseling Psychology Training Programs, Council of Directors of School Psychology Programs, and National Council of Schools and Programs in Professional Psychology) be reevaluated every 3 years. However, this reevaluation has not occurred since the original inception of the 21-person committee in 1991. A reevaluation currently is underway, and it is very likely that during it the committee will address the question of how to incorporate specialties at the doctoral and postdoctoral levels.

THE SCOPE OF ACCREDITATION

As noted above, specialized programs at the doctoral level have, to date, been excluded from the eligibility for accreditation. However, a provision in the current *Guidelines and Principles* for the accreditation of programs in emerging substantive areas provides a possible avenue. Critical to this possibility, however, is the development of a common understanding across the profession and its various recognition units (e.g., CRSPP, CoA, American Board of Professional Psychology) of the desired preparation for entry-level practice. Currently, the accreditation principles endorse broad and general training at the doctoral level, an emphasis that would appear to preclude an exclusively specialized program and to raise further questions about what constitutes a "substantive area." An alternative view is that specialized training should occur at the doctoral level and be further realized through specialized internships and postdoctoral residencies. It is unclear, however, that doctoral specialization would be consistent with the goal of a broadly educated psychologist. Some fear that specialization at the doctoral level will result in doctoral level psychologists who are merely technicians rather than professionals who can apply a range of scientific and problem-solving skills to deal with a broad array of problems.

As noted above, some emerging specialties may be accredited at the postdoctoral level rather than at the doctoral. Clinical neuropsychology is the clearest example of such a specialty. In 1994, the CoA voted to expand accreditation to the postdoctoral level. The first programs were accredited as general postdoctoral programs in professional psychology. To date, 11 programs have been accredited, and 2 are specifically in a specialty area. In addition, several of the generalist programs have specific tracks.

The low number of postdoctoral programs seeking accreditation suggests that there does not appear to be an excessive demand for postdoctoral accreditation, at least as promulgated by the CoA. There may be several reasons for this limited interest. First, licensure requirements are not tied to matriculation from an accredited postdoctoral training program. The postdoctoral supervised clinical experience, required for licensure and necessary in every state, can be satisfied in many different ways: employment, training programs, or one-on-one supervision. Because a formalized postdoctoral training experience is not required for licensure, it is unlikely that many psychologists will insist on an accredited postdoctoral program. Similarly, most current postdoctoral programs may not feel the need to seek accredited status to attract high-quality fellows.

Second, many postdoctoral positions follow a mentorship model rather than a program model. This emphasis is particularly true for multidisciplinary training programs, such as clinical neuropsychology. That is, many postdoctoral positions are tied to a particular person rather than a broad program of study. The process of accreditation is the evaluation of a training program, not the certification of a particular individual, which is what would be done if the program consisted of training by a particular person.

Third and related to the above point, postdoctoral positions are often research-based rather than solely advanced clinical training. Thus, although most provide enough clinical hours for the individual to qualify for the licensure exam, they often do not have advanced training for professional practice as their main goal. Therefore, most training programs have goals that are not entirely consistent with the guidelines for accreditation of postdoctoral training.

The current situation may change in the near future, however, because the Veterans Administration (VA) recently instituted a training initiative for postdoctoral training. Approximately 30 programs have received funding from the VA to institute and seek accreditation for postdoctoral training. From their initiation, programs have 2 years until they must seek accreditation. Thus, over the next several years, the CoA expects to receive an increased number of applications for accreditation of postdoctoral training programs.

The most contentious issue in accreditation is accreditation of programs that train students at the master's level. The profession continues to affirm the doctoral degree as the entry degree for independent practice (APA, 1987). However, numerous master's degrees are issued every year by psychology programs, even as leaders of the profession continue to deny independent status to these graduates. Lately, associations representing master's-level psychologists have developed their own accreditation system for programs offering a master's degree in psychology. Currently, the Masters in Psychology Accreditation Council, which consists of representatives from the Council of Applied Masters Programs in Psychology and the North American Association of Masters in Psychology (NAMP), accredits several master's programs in psychology.

Furthermore, the Professional Psychologist Certification Board, a subsidiary of NAMP, now offers certification as a Nationally Certified Psychologist for those with a master's *or* doctoral degree in psychology. Many psychologists with a master's degree have been licensed independently using titles such as "licensed professional counselor." These organizations and the individuals who support them have not given up their quest, however, to become licensed using the term *psychologist,* and whether or not these efforts will lead to licensure using the term at the master's-degree level remains unresolved.

Should psychology continue to train psychologists at the master's level and then deny them the opportunity to practice independently? If it is sincerely believed that doctoral-level training is necessary for independent practice, why continue to admit students into terminal master's programs? The changing landscape of health care suggests that psychology has not done a very good job of educating the general public or providing managed care programs with data that support the need for doctoral training for health care provision. With its new model of outcomes-based assessment, the accreditation process may have crucial data to address this issue, if the profession desires to seriously examine it.

WHAT CONSTITUTES AN ADEQUATE DOCTORAL TRAINING PROGRAM?

When the CoA expanded from 10 to 21 persons, there was concern that a group so large would never agree on what constituted a good training program. However, what became clear very early in the process was that, despite different theoretical orientations among different types of psychologists, it often was possible to agree on quality training. However, the revised *Guidelines and Principles* allowed programs new latitude in the definition of their training mission, goals, and outcomes. Although most programs still define themselves in terms of the traditional dichotomy, scientist–practitioner versus practitioner–scholar, it remains unclear if these different philosophies produce equivalent outcomes.

An important aspect of any doctoral program is its faculty. A recent report examined research-oriented and professional-applied PhD doctoral programs in terms of faculty resources, attributes, and activities (Maher, 1999). The study used National Research Council ratings to evaluate the scholarly quality of program faculty. Results revealed that ratings of faculty at professional-applied programs were lower than at research-oriented programs. Furthermore, over time there has been a substantial increase in the number of PhDs being produced by programs with the lowest ratings of faculty quality. Such reports are disturbing because they call into question whether the goals of accreditation are being fulfilled. The recent evidence of an erosion in psychology's ability to consistently train for science and practice should cause concern for the profession and provide the impetus for a reevaluation of the goals of doctoral training. It is important for the CoA to keep in mind that a variety of training models should not equate to a variety in educational quality.

How many psychologists should the profession be training? One of the most controversial issues of the 1990s was the issue of supply and demand: The number of graduate students seeking internships outstripped the number of available accredited internship training slots. This situation created controversy among various training groups, some of whom demanded that the CoA accredit more internships, allow nonpaid internships, or develop more internships to meet the need. Of course, none of these are the function of the CoA. Some say this bottleneck was reached because of the larger number of students being turned out by programs adhering to a practitioner–scholar model, in which case job market forces would eventually handle the oversupply. Indeed, this rebalance may be starting to happen.

More recently, another bottleneck has been identified: the inability of some graduate students to find the suitable postdoctoral clinical training experiences necessary for licensure. However, instead of viewing this oversupply of trainees (or undersupply of training opportunities) as representing market forces, APA recently established a commission to evaluate the structure of graduate education and training for licensure. After their initial meeting in May 2000, the commission issued a statement that 2 years of supervised clinical experience should be considered necessary for licensure. However, given the extensive predoctoral training now part of some graduate programs, the commission did not endorse the necessity for one of those years to be postdoctoral. It did affirm that a structured predoctoral internship was necessary, but the other year of structured training (i.e., the non-internship year) could actually be pre-internship. In effect, the commission's statement endorses the necessity of 2 years of experience but allows all of the experience to be predoctoral. Although the commission's statement may carry some weight, at the time of this writing, it has not yet been examined or discussed by the general APA membership. Furthermore, even if the profession accepts it, eliminating the postdoctoral requirement will require changes in the licensing laws in 50 different states, which will not be an easy task. The ramifications of this change for the CoA will be substantive in that pre-internship practicum training will become extremely important and require closer monitoring.

As the provision of psychological services continues to undergo a series of changes, some in the professional leadership and also students whose ca-

> **BOX 5.1**
> **Reflections on Accreditation Through the Lens of Evolving Professional Roles**
> *Martha Dennis Christiansen, PhD, Counseling and Consultation, Arizona State University, Tempe*
>
> *1980, Graduate Student in Counseling Psychology, Indiana State University.* As a first-year graduate student, I was not really sure what accreditation meant for me personally. I did grasp that it was important to graduate from an accredited doctoral program and that it would be important for finding internships, getting jobs, and achieving licensure. But at that point I had only a vague notion of the value of "quality assurance" for me as a student–consumer in this doctoral program. Internships, jobs, and licensure seemed very far away.
>
> The tension was high as the faculty prepared the graduate students for the initial site visit. I wondered if this would be like the comps exam that was also on my horizon. I studied hard to be able to talk lucidly about the Boulder Model and the finer points of the history of the various conferences. I wondered what else we students were going to say to ensure our evaluators that we were being trained as the proper scientists that accredited doctoral programs in psychology were supposed to produce. I was particularly nervous because I was invited to have lunch with the site visitors—the "expert psychologists" from the American Psychological Association (APA). The site visit was held, the team was friendly and easy to speak with, and the experts were just real people. The final outcome was positive—"full and five" (as they said in those days). Now, I was a doctoral student in an accredited counseling psychology program, and not surprisingly, this new status of my program gradually became more and more important to me.
>
> *1983, Predoctoral Intern in Professional Psychology, University of Iowa Counseling Service.* I was a predoctoral psychology intern at my first choice, the APA-accredited internship training program at the University of Iowa Counseling Service. During my internship year, the agency director, Ursula Delworth, had assumed the responsibility for this internship by also serving as director of training. As a doctoral student, I had benefited by being selected to be trained at a highly sought after accredited internship, a program that had met the threshold of quality. Our training experience was predictable, organized, and both broad and intensive.

My training director had served on the Committee on Accreditation (CoA) from 1977 to 1979, so our intern class and trainers received good direction as we prepared for the internship's next site visit. We wore our best clothes, cleaned and straightened the offices, set out our work samples for review, and knew how our program met the criteria for accreditation. This site visit was not a first for any of us, and we were ready to show our quality and eager to hear the feedback about how our program could improve. We closely observed our site visitors. They were our professional role models. Another "full and five"—the words we were waiting for—came in the letter to the president. We smiled, celebrated, and went back to work and to being trained as psychologists in a *quality* internship program.

1986–1997, Director of Training, University of Iowa Counseling Service Internship Training Program. Leading an accredited internship training program was both an exciting and awesome responsibility. By now I certainly knew what accreditation meant for me. Managing a quality program was always a balancing act: meeting accreditation criteria and responding to agency needs, standardizing training and being responsive to individual trainee differences, building consensus and taking stands, preserving traditional curriculum and creating new training activities, and undergoing intense emotional experiences of mentoring trainees and then letting trainees go—all under the umbrella of the standards of accreditation. I kept records, led retreats, wrote reports and letters, provided supervision and consultation, made up forms, created self-studies, and tried to find time to think about the quality of the training we provided. Those darn site visitors always seemed to be on their way to evaluate us.

Through two site visits during these years, our program, staffed by dedicated and excellent trainers, received the CoA stamp of approval. I do think the process of accreditation, which we took very seriously, encouraged us and guided us to also take very seriously the training we provided. In particular we used the criteria of accreditation standards to maintain a scientific approach to training and to ensure our attention to valuing and training about diversity.

1989–2000, Professional Roles in Psychology. Through my involvement in several professional organizations, including the Association of Psychology Postdoctoral and Internship Centers, the APA Site Visitor Pool, and the CoA, I began to see psychol-

continues

> **BOX 5.1 (continued)**
>
> ogy training and accreditation through a much wider lens. I noted more clearly outside of my home program how politics, competing agendas, market pressures, and responsibilities to a broad range of constituencies all potentially influence the content and process of accreditation. Serving as a site visitor, representing organizations who interacted with the CoA, and, ultimately, serving as a member of the CoA have helped to demystify what accreditation is all about.
>
> I have a great appreciation for the very human and humane committee members who have served before me or who serve with me now. The work of CoA and of assuring quality training in the profession of psychology is complex, grueling, and humbling. My colleagues and I try to listen sensitively, work long hours, deliberate carefully, and attempt to serve the best interests of the profession. In that the issues typically involving accreditation reflect the dilemmas of the profession of psychology at-large, our work will continue to bring us many challenges and, I hope, rewards in the form of results of quality training—increasing the numbers of strong and effective psychology professionals in our ranks.
>
> *A Final Reflection.* The history of accreditation is full of stories both told and untold with more yet to come. Stories have always been an important way for me to learn. In my psychology training I credit much of my growth from hearing the stories of my mentors, Jerry Stone and the late Ursula Delworth. I hope that my stories will provide a window into the experience and meaning of accreditation from various professional perspectives.

reer goal is the provision of psychological services have lobbied for the addition of courses that more clearly address the profession's evolving nature. Such courses would include accounting, business management, or subjects that many see as representing emerging specialty areas, such as psychopharmacology. Currently, there are at least 11 training programs in psychopharmacology, most of which have started in the past 2 years (APA, 2000). The APA College of Professional Psychology has introduced a standardized test for use by state licensing boards to assess knowledge in psychopharmacology, and the Association of State and Provincial Psychology Boards is currently drafting a set of suggested guidelines for psychopharmacology education and licensing. New Mexico is currently the only state to grant prescription privileges to psychologists. If psychologists do acquire prescription privileges on a wider basis and decide to prescribe medication as part of their professional services, it will be only a matter of time before there is pressure on the profession to come up with a consistent set of training standards. However, how much additional training can be included in an already strained doctoral curriculum is unclear. One alternative to lengthening doctoral training may be to eliminate part of the current curriculum. This change would require a consensus among doctoral training programs, graduate departments of psychology, and the CoA, a process that would be long and difficult.

DISTANCE EDUCATION

An even newer model of graduate training is distance education. This issue, which will continue to challenge accreditation, addresses whether a student needs to be in residence at a university to receive the advanced and intensive training considered appropriate for doctoral psychology education. Some universities, including some that are regionally accredited, interpret the residency requirement via a combination of on-line classes, small-group regional meetings, and university-wide functions. In these instances, the regionally accredited universities have a physical address with administrative offices.

Most recently, the Internet has caused a technological revolution, which now is further influencing the accessibility of education to the general public. In this light, the definition of distance education has expanded. For example, the North Central Association of Colleges and Schools (NCACS) recently accredited Jones International University, one of the first virtual institutions. This university, with 2 full-time and 54 adjunct faculty, has been described by the American Association of University Professors (AAUP) to be deficient in learning resources such as libraries and research laboratories (McCollum, 1999). Despite the AAUP's concerns, NCACS stated that the university met the accreditation requirements. Whether or not such facilities will begin to offer advanced training programs in psychology remains unknown. However, virtual universities are changing the definition of a college education and, as they continue to expand, the likelihood of offering programs in psychology, an always popular career choice, will increase. Unless psychology as a discipline can provide evidence, rather than opinion, that physical residency, on-site libraries, and face-to-face contact with full-time faculty are necessary for quality education, it is possible that in the near future the CoA will see applications for accreditation from an increasing variety of distance-based educational programs, including virtual universities.

RECIPROCITY

The APA and the Canadian Psychological Association (CPA) have had a long-standing policy of conducting joint site visits for those programs

BOX 5.2
A Mirror to Our Profession

Kenneth M. Adams, PhD, Ann Arbor Veterans Affairs Health System, Ann Arbor, Michigan

Accreditation is an activity of the American Psychological Association (APA) that touches sensitivities in all those involved in the enterprise. Although the reasons for the touchiness seem to vary, others outside our professional tribe doubtless are entertained by the ways in which we, who consider ourselves to be experts on emotion, get emotional. Accreditation shows our best and worst attributes. It challenges us to demonstrate that what we *say* we are doing in training corresponds to a rough reality of what we *are* doing. In my experience over many roles in the accreditation process, the response to that analysis of intention, action, and outcome tells much about the pedagogic and professional maturity of a program. Most program directors and even department chairs (whose blood pressure has normalized) would allow today that the accreditation process holds up a mirror to what we are doing and offers constructive and consultative ways to make it better.

When accreditation gets cast in the role of intruder, ogre, or bean counter, one can reliably predict the presence of ignorance, the current politics of APA, or a training institution culture that is inimical to the education of professional psychologists in the first place. With respect to the first influence, it is my observation that the certainty of opinions about what the accreditation process *should* be (or whether it should exist at all) are highly negatively correlated with any substantial experience in the process of accreditation outside one's own backyard. It also reliably predicts little to no knowledge about the inside workings of APA accreditation.

With respect to the second influence, every APA entity takes its lumps from psychologist crusaders set on having their one issue or their version of social justice wrapped around everything the association does—or else! We haven't quite gotten a requirement mandating training programs to certify (for example) that they won't manufacture weapons of mass destruction or that they must teach the psychology of global warming just yet. But it is not for lack of trying by some.

With respect to the third influence, some psychologists find themselves working in institutions that don't quite understand or subscribe to the scientific or human bases that represent our core identity. In some of these settings, students would encounter attitudes or practices that demean the helping professions as a whole. Training here is an activity that is not rooted in a culture that would grow it. Experienced site visitors can feel the tension at such thankfully rare sites.

On the occasion of 50 years of accreditation, one can't help but marvel at what growth has been achieved. An early, standard-setting, and learning childhood took place wherein the Committee on Accreditation (CoA) did everything. This gave way to a prolonged adolescence in which accreditation infrastructure and political overseers had to learn to move the process to another order of magnitude and to trust their own site visitors and programs to do the right thing. Finally, we have come to a more adult version of the process wherein the term *program consultation* has become the lead identity in the moniker of the APA office directing the CoA's daily operations. This progression to maturity and the emphasis on collegiality and attention to outcomes has had many participants, but there is no doubt that Paul Nelson's vision and gentle insistence led the way.

Yet it bears repeating that accreditation shows us as well at our best. Year after year, new appointees to the CoA arrive at spring training to find that the politics that may have resulted in their nomination to the CoA have no relation or value to the work at hand. The mutual respect of committee members and the respect with which APA programs are handled by both staff and CoA appointees is remarkable and rather heart-warming, particularly for anyone used to research review panels in which levels of criticism are contaminated with overtones of scientific competition and fiscal survival.

There is now an expectation that applicant programs with sufficient preparation, planning, and forward consultation will succeed in the accreditation process. The range of settings for training programs has also expanded, although in this regard forgetting totally the standard-setting function of accreditation will not be a good thing where "sites" no longer exist for training. New ideas and ways of doing things should excite rather than concern us if we keep in mind our scientific roots and professional purposes in training. At the level of the student–consumer, training settings, and faculty, the net effect of the accreditation process now affirms the standing of these programs. Approval indicates to our colleagues and the public that we have passed a test of national credibility and even excellence in a way that no amount of internal campaigning and persuasion might do.

continues

> **BOX 5.2 (continued)**
>
> Because psychologists are so hard on themselves in so many review activities, we should rejoice when we have one like accreditation that has been rigorous but also fair and constructive. It is a process of self-scrutiny of which we can be proud.

wishing to seek accreditation from both associations. At one time, this was a fairly simple procedure, as both associations had virtually identical criteria. However, the adoption of the *Guidelines and Principles* resulted in a very different format and procedure, making the preparation of documents for joint accreditation overly difficult. Specifically, the *Guidelines and Principles* hinge more on the evaluation of training outcomes that are consistent with the stated training model, whereas the CPA accreditation criteria are similar to the old APA criteria. Using two disparate sets of guidelines has sometimes resulted in different accreditation decisions by the two agencies, creating controversy and confusion.

There have been some recent attempts to resolve these issues by proposing several possible concepts. One of these is reciprocity, whereby any program accredited by one association would automatically be accredited by the other. In other words, the CPA would accredit programs in Canada, and in the U.S. this accreditation would be accepted as the equivalent of accreditation by the APA. Another avenue for consideration has been mutual recognition, whereby each association acknowledges that the process of accreditation engaged in by the other is comparable to its own. A third concept is to restrict accreditation activities to those programs within the respective nation's borders. A fourth option has been suggested to entertain accreditation applications from a program in the other country only after that country has made an accreditation decision about that particular program.

Although there is much to redeem these proposals, there also are several roadblocks. Specifically, antitrust laws prohibit any movement toward allocation of markets. Further, a portion of Canadian programs do not want to relinquish the possibility of receiving U.S. accreditation. Finally, questions about multiple decision-making bodies have been raised in the recent review and recognition process by the U.S. Department of Education (DoE). In this recognition process, it became apparent that, to retain its recognized status, the CoA needs to ensure that it does not delegate its decision-making authority to any other body. Thus, recognition of decisions made by another body, such as the CPA accreditation panel, would be necessarily excluded. Canadian and U.S. accreditation bodies continue to discuss the challenges of the concurrent accreditation process with an eye toward cooperative and collaborative options that would ease the burdens of dual accreditation processes for individual programs and also respect the right of each accrediting body to promulgate the accrediting standards and guidelines that it has developed.

CONFLICT OF INTEREST WHEN ACCREDITATION IS RUN BY THE PROFESSION

Schools whose applications for accreditation are denied often levy accusations of conflict of interest and antitrust violations. The schools who are the subject of the denial accuse the accrediting body of being under the influence of the profession that, in turn, is attempting to limit the number of practitioners in a certain field to keep the demand for services high. This is an issue faced not only by psychology but also by other specialized accreditors, such as the American Bar Association (ABA), which has been a defendant in several antitrust suits (Leatherman, 1994). The basis for these suits was a charge that the ABA's accrediting arm violated antitrust laws. In 1998, the DoE threatened to revoke the ABA's accrediting authority unless it changed methods that unfairly excluded certain schools (Mangan, 1998). Similarly, the Congress on Professional Education recommended in the late 1990s that the accrediting body of the American Library Association become an independent accrediting agency (Berry, Blumenstein, & DiMattia, 1999).

Psychology's CoA has, and continues to face, similar issues of autonomy. When the new committee was formed in 1992, issues of autonomy were at the forefront. Many groups, not all in agreement with the ideas of the APA, were invited to send representatives to the new committee. Although there was official oversight from the Board of Educational Affairs, the committee enjoyed substantial autonomy with respect to the development of the new system of accreditation. Initially, all parties respected the CoA's need for autonomy. However, more recently and apparently not in response to any specific action by the CoA, members of the APA Board of Directors perceived a need to exert more oversight. Now there is a board member liaison who attends all meetings of the CoA, even those devoted to program review. How this new oversight by the Board of Directors might affect the autonomy of the CoA or exert an influence on its decision-making capabilities remains to be seen. The constituent groups that make up the CoA are watching the new Board of Director's liaison arrangement closely and are also watching to see how the Council of Representatives handles petitions from the field about matters of accreditation. Although CoA governance documents specifically reserve the right of CoA to be the sole initiator of accreditation policy, that does not preclude other groups from feeling as though they ought to have a voice in these matters. In this regard, there continues to be concern that the guild issues of APA will overly influence accreditation, and the tension within and among the education community, the science community, and the prac-

BOX 5.3
A Provost's Musings
Edward P. Sheridan, PhD, Division of Academic Affairs,
University of Houston, Houston, Texas

I have had the good or bad fortune, depending on one's perspective, to view psychology accreditation from the perspectives of a student being interviewed by an accreditation site visit team, as director of American Psychological Association (APA) accredited programs, as a member and chair of the APA Committee on Accreditation (CoA), and as a provost at two institutions with APA-accredited programs. In these later roles, I also have been visited by myriad professional accreditation committees. The conclusion I reach from these experiences is that the APA has done a better and more responsible job than most accrediting bodies of academic disciplines. I am especially impressed that, over the 50 years that APA has accredited programs, it has consistently and seriously examined the accreditation process and its value.

The most creative and constructive improvement in accreditation probably occurred in the early 1990s. It seemed to start with a gentle (meaning soft sledgehammer) nudge from Paul Nelson, who surely is psychology's expert on accreditation. At his suggestion, the then-chair of the CoA brought together several disparate groups that proposed a new and expanded membership for the CoA that was eventually adopted. Two consecutive CoA chairs did an extraordinary job in transitioning from the old committee system to the current one. At the same time, they made major changes that have significantly improved APA's system over other academic accreditation policies.

Within psychology, I have found the often-stated position that "great universities do not need accreditation of professional programs" to be a falsehood. Indeed, personal experience has shown me that psychology programs in some of the nation's finest universities and teaching hospitals are woefully lacking in standards. I have witnessed inappropriate curricula, utterly out-of-date courses, and inadequate clinical supervision in accredited programs in our best institutions. At the same time, I have observed student abuse, sexism, racism, and other forms of prejudice that departments have allowed to run rampant. Accreditation has served as a process to improve the quality of instruction, clinical training, and student life in such programs.

At times, accreditation has brought attention to important issues that were neglected. Surely, creating diversity in both student and faculty bodies as well as enhancing cultural awareness in the curriculum occurred in many institutions because of accreditation requirements. Although some would argue that these changes would have evolved without accreditation, a stronger argument can be made that the accreditation process hastened these important innovations by a decade.

Without always declaring it, the CoA, for at least its first 40 years, promoted the scientist–practitioner model in psychology. Many of us are extremely fond of this model and see it as the distinguishing educational characteristic that separates psychology from other practitioner professions. Within the scientist–practitioner model, advocates of one side of the model often indicate that too much emphasis is given to the other side. Actually, such arguments are accurate to a point. With the development of more sophisticated research strategies and increasing knowledge of psychopathology, diagnosis, and treatment, there is not sufficient time to educate students as completely as some would wish. This is also true in many other disciplines.

I believe there is a neglected area in this argument that lies with several programs that use tenure track faculty to teach diagnoses and intervention strategies. Too many of these individuals have either very narrow or no research programs and, at the same time, are dramatically out of touch with the current clinical world. Internship directors and practicum supervisors have been among the few voices to alert the profession to this problem. However, because many of these individuals are dependent on universities to supply students, the issue never has received appropriate attention. Numerous examples exist of how graduate faculty are not current. As drugs have become available that have a significant impact on psychological functioning, many psychology programs resist even teaching courses in this area and hide their ignorance by opposing the idea of psychologists prescribing these drugs. When managed care began to assault the health care world, most psychology programs evidenced no understanding of the impact this would have on the careers their students would pursue. And, although this change affected both research and practice careers, few faculty could give students a sophisticated explanation of this dominant system.

All accreditation systems are flawed. Thus, it is easy to argue that such systems should not exist. Certainly, it is always important to monitor the accreditation process so that it does not interfere with the free exploration of new knowledge that is the hallmark of

continues

> BOX 5.3 (continued)
>
> any fine university. However, on balance, accreditation in psychology has done much to improve the profession. In its current form, we now appear to have the kind of representation on the CoA that can enable psychology to be a national leader in this activity. My experience convinces me that our profession is far ahead of most others in examining our system, trying to make it better, overcoming its weaknesses, and promoting academic excellence.

tice community could return to the level that it was in 1992, when the new CoA was formed.

Finally, the independence of the CoA's accreditation and decision-making processes from influences external to CoA has become a particularly thorny issue with respect to the continued recognition of CoA from the DoE (Patton, 1998). Specifically, to be in compliance with the DoE's criteria for recognition as an accrediting agency, the accreditation process and policy decision-making process must operate without influence from the governing board of the host association. How the CoA will be able to demonstrate that independence when a Board of Directors liaison attends every aspect of the meeting will be a challenge. It is noteworthy, however, that among the CoA's five planned achievements for the next 5 years is to ensure noninterference by APA into accreditation decisions and greater fiscal autonomy (APA, 2000).

SPECIALIZED ACCREDITATION AND THE GOVERNMENT

As chapter 1 described, one of the CoA's planned achievements was to achieve full recognition by the DoE, and this goal was very recently realized. Having undergone recent review, the DoE requested changes in the *Guidelines and Principles for Accreditation* and the *Accreditation Operating Procedures* before it would grant full recognition. As noted above, the DoE has noted some difficulty with the CoA's relationship to the APA. This concern presents an interesting issue: Specifically, what is the role of the government with respect to a profession's ability to establish procedures for the accreditation of its training programs?

For example, the DoE has a far more prescriptive mindset than the CoA. The former would be quite comfortable with the CoA establishing an absolute level of achievement for students in accredited programs (e.g., a student must publish a paper before graduation). In contrast, psychology's system does not permit such specific prescriptions but rather relies on the program to specify its own goals and then also to choose its own indices of achievement. Another concern is that the DoE has definitions of *reliability*, *validity*, and *practitioner* that are different from those of the psychological community. In future reviews, it is possible that the DoE will question the CoA regarding its practice of using academic professors (who also deliver psychological services) as practitioners for the purposes of satisfying a DoE requirement that each site visit team have a practitioner on it. This raises the question of whether the profession of psychology or the DoE gets to define whether teaching and research constitute the practice of the profession of psychology and whether a practitioner must provide health care services and do so on a full-time basis. Although these issues are often areas of conflict within the profession, it is unlikely that psychology would accept an external group providing the final decision.

SUMMARY

In this chapter, we have outlined some of the issues facing the future of accreditation. In addition to issues that are generic to graduate education, there are those specific to psychology. To resolve many of these issues, changes in the structure and function of the CoA would occur. Currently one such review is under way and could very well result in some committee structure changes. This prospect should not be alarming as the structure of the CoA (even the name of the committee) has changed many times over the past 50 years. In general, we have attempted to take a broader perspective and, in doing so, we have discussed many issues that will probably change the landscape of accreditation in the near future. In addition to those discussed above, the CoA will continue to evolve structures and processes, hopefully meeting the needs of the profession and the public. As Boxes 5.1, 5.2, and 5.3 reveal, despite changes in form and function, it is clear that the commitment to quality education remains strong within the activities related to accreditation and among those people charged with carrying out those activities. Furthermore, readers should take heart because, as this chapter illustrates, these challenges are not unique to our profession but affect virtually every type of education and training program. The challenge is to address these issues while continuing to maintain the highest standards of training.

REFERENCES

American Psychological Association. (1987). Model act for state licensure of psychologists. *American Psychologist, 42,* 696–703.

American Psychological Association. (1996). *Guidelines and principles for accreditation of programs in professional psychology.* Washington, DC: Author.

American Psychological Association. (2000). *The 1999 five-year report of the Policy and Planning Board and the Blue Ribbon Panel.* Washington, DC: Author.

American Psychological Association, Committee on Accreditation. (2000). *Guidelines and principles for accreditation of programs in professional psychology.* Washington, DC: Author.

Berry, J., Blumenstein, L., & DiMattia, S. (1999, June 1). Move accreditation apart from ALA? *Library Journal, 124,* 16–20.

Dill, D. A., Massey, W. F., Williams, P. R., & Cook, C. M. (1996). Accreditation and academic quality assurance. *Change, 28,* 16–25.

Leatherman, C. (1991, February 27). Deans say process of library–school accreditation is overly prescriptive and must be changed. *The Chronicle of Higher Education, 36,* A15–A16.

Leatherman, C. (1994, June 1). Rebellion brews in tight-knit world of law accreditation. *Chronicle of Higher Education, 41,* pp. A14, A16.

Maher, B. A. (1999). Changing trends in doctoral training programs in psychology. *Psychological Science, 10,* 475–481.

Mangan, K. S. (1998, September 18). Education department threatens to revoke Bar Association's accreditation authority. *Chronicle of Higher Education, 45,* p. A42.

Matarazzo, J. D. (1977). Higher education, professional accreditation, and licensure. *American Psychologist, 32,* 856–859.

McCollum, K. (1999, April 2). Accreditation of on-line university draws fire. *Chronicle of Higher Education, 45,* p. A33.

Nicklin, J. L. (1995, February 24). Teacher-education colleges reject required accreditation. *Chronicle of Higher Education, 41,* p. A23.

Patton, M. J. (1998). Chair's column. *Committee on Accreditation 1998 annual report* (pp. 2–3). Washington, DC: American Psychological Association.

Schachterle, L. (1999). Outcomes assessment and accreditation in US engineering formation. *European Journal of Engineering Education, 24,* 121–132.

INTRODUCTION TO THE APPENDIXES

JASON KANZ

Accreditation has a relatively short but important history in the field of psychology, as this book demonstrates. During the past 50 years, many psychologists, through their work on the American Psychological Association's (APA's) Committee on Accreditation (CoA) and preceding committees, have sought to improve the educational system through the process of accreditation. Documentation of much of this work is readily available, but there are resources important to the history of accreditation that are not easily accessible. What follows are several of those important resources, excerpted for the purpose of this book. More specifically, these appendixes contain historical articles relevant to accreditation, early curriculum requirements and accreditation criteria, and excerpts from personal correspondence.

Appendix A is excerpted from an article written by Loyal Crane in 1925 regarding the professional training of psychologists. Peterson (1992) pointed out that Crane was the first to suggest a professional degree in psychology. The excerpt from this article is interesting not only because of its early mention of a professional degree in psychology but also because Crane suggests a formal, standardized course of education for psychologists.

In 1945, the subcommittee on graduate internship training came up with recommendations for both personal and academic qualifications for internship programs in professional psychology (Shakow et al.), excerpted in Appendix B. However, the authors address the importance of the entire training program from personal qualifications of the students, to curriculum requirements, and to internship training. Again, although different from current requirements, the stated principles demonstrate a commitment to the standardization and improvement of training at all levels.

Another early reference included "specific qualities experienced observers believe clinical work calls for" (APA Committee on Training in Clinical Psychology, 1947, p. 541), a list of which appears in Appendix C. Current accreditation criteria take the student body's collective characteristics into consideration as well. Although qualities such as "sense of humor" no longer appear in the criteria, "superior intellectual ability and judgment" and "a regard for the integrity of other persons" are clearly part of current desired student characteristics.

In 1958, the Education and Training Board published criteria for program evaluation in the *American Psychologist* (Moore, 1958), an excerpt of which appears in Appendix D. Comparing these criteria to Crane's (1925) suggested curriculum shows how far the field had advanced during those 30 years. The curriculum content suggested by the board much more closely represents the curricula of today's professional training programs.

Appendix E features a series of letters that contain some of the earliest documented occurrences of accreditation. The move toward accreditation in psychology was set in motion by requests first from the Veterans Administration (VA; January 1946) and later from the U.S. Public Health Service (PHS). However, these requests were apparently made informally, and no written record of the requests is available. The first letter in this appendix is from Donald Marquis (1945) to the directors of graduate study at training universities requesting information about their programs. In this letter, he mentions requests he has received regarding the selection of universities. The second letter, from Dael Wolfle (1946) to Robert Sears, details the requests from the VA and the PHS. Wolfle also notes that it was Robert Sears who began the work of accreditation of training universities and that he was named the director of the Committee on Graduate and Professional Training. This letter also briefly delineates some of the goals set by the committee regarding accreditation. The third letter is from Sears (1946) to the committee regarding the letter to him from Wolfle. In this letter, Sears more clearly delineates the goals and early work of accreditation necessary for the committee. He outlines the goals of the committee with regard to accreditation to decide on accreditation criteria, processes by which to secure that information, and processes by which to evaluate those criteria. He also briefly addresses the development of a psychology curriculum and the selection of clinical psychology graduate students.

Along with the mention of the VA and PHS requests for a listing of qualified training programs, one of the most significant references in the history of accreditation is a chapter by Raimy (1950) in the Boulder Conference report. In this chapter, excerpted in Appendix F, Raimy acknowledges many of the arguments forwarded against accreditation, yet goes on to discuss why accreditation of training institutions was essential at that point in history and why it was considered during the Boulder Conference.

Appendix G contains the accreditation procedures adopted in 1970 by the APA's Council of Representatives, some 25 years after the earliest discussions of accreditation had taken place (APA Education and Training Board, 1970). By this point, the standardization of the accreditation process had become more explicit.

The Joint Council on Professional Education in Psychology was established in 1988 to "articulate and integrate the domains of professional education and training (including field training experience), entry level credentialing, accreditation and specialization" and, more specifically, "the education and training for the delivery of psychological services" (Stigall et al., 1990, p. 2). In their 1990 report, featured in Appendix H, they make recommendations regarding accreditation "in the spirit of strengthening the present accreditation process" (Stigall et al., 1990, p. 20). That information, minus their recommendations, is included in the appendix.

In the history of accreditation in psychology, more than 200 psychologists and public members have been involved with developing and refining the criteria and procedures. Everyone who has ever served on the CoA or its preceding committee through 2000 is mentioned in Appendix I, along with their service and whether they chaired the committee.

There have been many conferences that have focused all or in part on important questions related to accreditation, beginning with the historic Boulder Conference in 1949. In the half-century since that conference, there have been many other conferences, each of which had an important contribution to extending accreditation in psychology. Those conferences are listed in Appendix J.

Officially beginning with a request from the VA and later from the PHS, the accreditation of psychology training programs has an interesting history. The early work of people such as Robert Sears, David Shakow, and Victor Raimy and the later work of Paul Nelson and others have brought accreditation to the point that it is at today. What has been presented in these appendixes is a glimpse of the history of accreditation within psychology. Certainly, there will be many changes in accreditation as future committees consider how to best accredit training programs. However, with continued service from people like those who have already been involved, the accreditation process will continue to serve psychology in better ways over the next 50 years.

It seems only fitting to end this book with a year retrospect on the field of psychology written by James McKeen Cattell in 1937 (Appendix K). As one reads this selection, it becomes apparent that Cattell's retrospect also has a great deal to offer to understanding accreditation. His foresight in seeing both a science and a profession of psychology was in fact realized, and there are now hundreds of training programs for professional psychologists accredited by the APA.

REFERENCES

American Psychological Association, Committee on Training in Clinical Psychology. (1947). Recommended graduate training program in clinical psychology. *American Psychologist, 2,* 539–558.

American Psychological Association, Education and Training Board. (1970). Accrediting procedures of the American Psychological Association. *American Psychologist, 25,* 100–102.

Cattell, J. M. (1937). Retrospect: Psychology as a profession. *Journal of Consulting Psychology, 1,* 1–3.

Crane, L. (1925). A plea for the training of psychologists. *Journal of Abnormal and Social Psychology, 20,* 225–233.

Marquis, D. G. (1945, August 31). [Letter to directors of graduate study]. Archived at Box 470, American Psychological Association, Library of Congress, 101 Independence Avenue, SE, Washington, DC 20540.

Moore, B. V. (1958). Criteria for evaluating progress in clinical or in counseling psychology. *American Psychologist, 13,* 59–60.

Peterson, D. R. (1992). The doctor of psychology degree. In D. K. Freedheim, H. J. Freudenberger, D. R. Peterson, J. W. Kessler, H. H. Strupp, S. B. Messer, & P. L. Wachtel (Eds.), *History of psychotherapy: A century of change* (pp. 829–849). Washington, DC: American Psychological Association.

Raimy, V. C. (1950). Accreditation of training universities. In V. C. Raimy (Ed.), *Training in clinical psychology* (pp. 170–179). London: Prentice-Hall.

Sears, R. R. (1946, October 21). [Letter to Graduate and Professional Training Committee]. Archived at Box 470, American Psychological Association, Library of Congress, 101 Independence Avenue, SE, Washington, DC 20540.

Shakow, D., Brotemarkle, R. A., Doll, E. A., Kinder, E. F., Moore, B. V., & Smith, S. (1945). Graduate internship training in psychology: Report by the subcommittee on graduate internship training to the committees on graduate and professional training of the American Psychological Association and the American Association for Applied Psychology. *Journal of Consulting Psychology, 9,* 243–266.

Stigall, T. T., Bourg, E. F., Bricklin, P. M., Kovacs, A. L., Larsen, K. G., Lorion, R. P., et. al. (1990). *Report of the Joint Council on Professional Education in Psychology.* Baton Rouge, LA: Joint Council on Professional Education in Psychology.

Wolfle, D. (1946, September 25). [Personal communication with Robert Sears]. Archived at Box 470, American Psychological Association, Library of Congress, 101 Independence Avenue, SE, Washington, DC 20540.

APPENDIX A:
EXCERPT FROM LOYAL CRANE'S *PLEA FOR THE TRAINING OF PSYCHOLOGISTS*, 1925

And the first step, it would seem, should be taken by our great universities in the organization of a definite four years' course of study leading to the degree of Ps.D. Admission to this course should be restricted to students who have completed three years of regular college work including at least one major course in physics, biology, chemistry, sociology, economics, mathematics and psychology.

In the first two years of the psychological course, emphasis should be placed upon the fundamental medical sciences; in the last two, upon the more strictly technical psychological subjects. In outlining the course as a whole, recognition should be given the general principle that there are many aspects of the classical medical education such as surgery and obstetrics in which the psychologist will require merely what we may term "familiarization courses" instead of "training courses," just as there are aspects of the classical medical curriculum such as neurology and psychiatry in which the candidate for the Ps.D. should be trained even more intensively than the medical student. Other of the standard medical courses, such as gynecology, laryngology, otology, etc., may be omitted in toto.

Our suggestion, which we would submit for criticism, would provide for a course of the following general character [see table, next page]:

Doubtless many criticisms of this program will immediately occur to every psychologist who peruses it. That is as it should be. The ideal course can obviously result only from the free submission of other and better plans by a large number of interested persons. But such changes and refinements

Subject	Percent of Student's Time
First Year	
*Anatomy, including dissection	40
*Physiology, including laboratory exercises	20
Experimental Psychology, including lectures on behavior	20
Embryology and Histology	10
Physiological Chemistry	10
Second Year	
*Pathology	20
Neurology, elementary clinical	15
Physiological Psychology	15
Pharmacology	15
†Physical Diagnosis	10
†Medicine	10
†Bacteriology, including lectures on immunology and public health	5
†Surgery	5
Social Psychology lectures	5
Third Year	
Mental Testing, including lectures on the theory and social problems of mental deficiency	20
Statistics, including introductory mathematical review	15
Abnormal Psychology	15
Child Psychology	10
Educational Psychology, including psychoeducational problems	10
Industrial Psychology and Vocational Guidance, including the psychology of advertising and selling	10
Neurology	10
†Pediatrics	5
†Therapeutics	5
Fourth Year	
Theory and technique of psychoanalysis	25
Clinical mental testing, including lectures on problem children and delinquency	20
Neurology, advanced clinical	15
Psychiatry, special problems in second term	15
Endocrinology	5
†Obstetrics	5
†Syphilology	5
Elective	10‡

*These courses should emphasize neuroanatomy, neurophysiology, and neuropathology, respectively.
†Familiarization courses, including both lectures and laboratory or ward demonstrations.
‡These figures may roughly be interpreted on the basis of 5 = 1 hr. a week for a year or 2 hrs. a week for a term, 2 lab hrs. being equal to 1 lecture hour.

can only serve to strengthen the general plan of organizing a well integrated four year course leading to the Ps.D. degree.

From "A Plea for the Training of Psychologists," by L. Crane, 1925, *Journal of Abnormal Psychology, 20*, pp. 225–233. In the public domain.

APPENDIX B: EXCERPT FROM "GRADUATE INTERNSHIP TRAINING IN PSYCHOLOGY," 1945

QUALIFICATIONS—PERSONAL AND ACADEMIC

Personal qualifications

Although the need for a reasonably well-adjusted and attractive personality as the foundation upon which to build an adequately prepared clinical psychologist is generally recognized, it cannot sufficiently be emphasized since it is so frequently forgotten in practice. A more specific enumeration of the requirements in this respect would include the following:

> 1. Superior intellectual ability and judgment, 2. Demonstrated industry, originality and resourcefulness, 3. Breadth of cultural background and versatility, 4. Integrity, tact, self-control and discriminating sense of ethical values, 5. Deep interest in psychology, with special interest in clinical psychology; promise of being able to make a worthwhile contribution to its advancement, 6. Demonstrated interest in persons as individuals and not merely as material for manipulation, 7. Insight into one's own personality characteristics and sensitivity to the complexities of motivation, 8. Genuine aptitude for clinical psychology; ability to adopt a "therapeutic" attitude.

At first reading these personal requirements may seem formidable but second thought will indicate their reasonableness for practice in a field which places such heavy demands upon the person's maturity, sensitivity, and knowledge.

From undergraduate days on, students should be encouraged to use their summer holidays and other spare time for the acquisition of experience in fields which bring them into close contact with both ordinary and unusual persons, whether it be in the factory, field, institution or laboratory. Underlying this suggestion is the recognition of the principle that the broader the base of human experience possessed by the clinical psychologist, the greater the value he will derive from his formal preparation and the more adequate his practice.

Academic course

General Principles:—With respect to the academic program the following general principles appear to us important:

1. The program should be organized and planned in such a manner that there is direction towards a fairly definite goal from the beginning of graduate work and, to some extent, even from undergraduate days on. Although clinical psychology is not so well known and defined as some other fields and, therefore, cannot expect prospective students to be aware of their interest in it early in the undergraduate period, there is good reason for setting up some standards of preparation of this period at least as a rough guide. This should help to lay the ground for increased control of professional preparation in the future.
2. The program should be organized around an integrated combination of academic and field work in which representatives of both groups will have had an opportunity to determine the content of each.
3. The program should not be too rigidly organized since considerable experimentation with respect to persons, background and content is essential for the development of the most adequate program. The considerable progress which stems from such an elastic attitude can be gauged from an examination of the development of the medical and social work professions. The former, particularly, has found that the necessity for establishing rigid detailed requirements in order to enforce proper standards resulted in an inelasticity and uniformity which was quite handicapping in a field going through rapid growth. It should be the aim of psychology to attempt to establish standards in a setting of flexibility and reasonable freedom. In addition to the general grounds for such an approach there must be some latitude to fit the specific needs of the

individual and to meet local university requirements and regulations.

4. A process of careful discrimination in the choice of content is essential if the program is not to become impossibly broad and dilute. It may be anticipated that considerable pressure will be brought to bear on those organizing programs to include a great variety of subjects and content; almost everything remotely related to the field will undoubtedly be argued for as indispensable. It must constantly be kept in mind that the available time is limited and that to familiarize the student with all the facts and methods of every aspect of clinical psychology, let alone psychology, is impossible. To meet this situation the emphasis of the program should be on principles rather than on technical aspects.

5. The preparation should be basic, that is, directed to the preparation of *clinical* psychologists, rather than specialized towards a particular type of clinical psychologist, for example, the *school* psychologist, *reformatory* psychologist, *hospital* psychologist.

6. Except at the level of elementary courses and such highly standardized courses as physics and chemistry, the philosophy and manner of teaching, as well as the content, are most important. Little of significance, obviously can be surmised from the mere title of a course. Until there is some supervision and evaluation of instructors and instruction as well as of course titles, considerable liberality will have to be shown in this respect. In general, the trend already developing in the direction of the individualization of instruction should be encouraged. As far as possible the formal lecture system should be replaced by small teaching sections, personal conferences between students and instructors and the multiplication of opportunities for independent work.

7. The program of education should be at least as rigorous and extensive as that for the Ph.D. It should include the equivalent of the requirements for the Ph.D. with an additional year of internship.

The academic program will be discussed from the standpoint of three different levels of professional operation: *senior*, *junior*, and *postgraduate*. Main consideration will be given to the first, with some discussion of the latter two as they relate to the senior level preparation.

There are several forms of field work which are frequently incorrectly subsumed under the heading of "internship." For our purposes it will help to clarify the issues if we think of field work (and this does not include practicums or clinical clerkships) as falling into four types:

Internships (residence appointments): Full-time and part-time.
Externships (nonresidence appointments): Full-time and part-time.

In the discussion thus far the assumption has been that the internship would come in the third year of training and would consist of a full year block (consecutive plan) devoted solely to the internship. There are advocates of another system who would have the internship run concurrently with the second and third years of graduate work, part of the time being spent in courses at the university and part of the time being spent at the internship center. (There are, of course, externships of the same two kinds.) Each has its conveniences, inconveniences, advantages and disadvantages. A full consideration of these leaves the Committee with the judgment that the block system, especially that involving residence, is to be preferred. Its relative advantages may be summarized as follows:

1. It offers an opportunity for *real* acquaintance with the aims, principles, and techniques of clinical psychology, an opportunity to get not only the "feel" and the "know" of psychology, but the "feel" of other fields, as well, through both professional and personal contacts.
2. It is unsurpassable trying-ground for intellectual and personality fitness for clinical work. (The special strains which institutional work and living place on the person offer both the supervisor and the student an unusual opportunity for the evaluation of interest and fitness for this work.)
3. It offers the student an opportunity to get away from the academic atmosphere for an extended period, usually a very desirable and much appreciated opportunity after some eighteen successive years of academic work.
4. It affords experience in carrying a full-time position which has many similarities to that in which the intern is likely to work after completion of the full course.
5. It encourages the development of resourcefulness and independence of thinking in integrating his own experiences with his academic background.
6. It offers an opportunity for consistent and full-time occupation with the clinical field. There is not, in contrast with part-time internships and externships, the confusion and strain which come with shifting back and forth from the clinical to the academic settings. The gain in wholeheartedness of occupation would appear to more than balance whatever may be gained from continued contact with the university.
7. The choice of institution is not limited by accessibility, as it is in a part-time program. This permits the use of desirable institutions at some distance from the universities.

8. It permits (as against short-term internships or externships) the more detailed study of the unfolding and development of a case—the kind of opportunity which psychologists in ordinary settings generally do not have.
9. It permits twenty-four hour residence in an atmosphere permeated with a psychology of a living kind and appears to have more potentiality for the maturation of the personality than almost any other experience ordinarily available to the psychologist.

From "Graduate Internship Training in Psychology: Report by the Subcommittee on Graduate Internship Training to the Committees on Graduate and Professional Training of the American Psychological Association and the American Association for Applied Psychology," by D. Shakow, R. A. Brotemarkle, E. A. Doll, E. F. Kinder, B. V. Moore, & S. Smith, 1945. In the public domain.

APPENDIX C:
EXCERPT FROM "RECOMMENDED GRADUATE TRAINING PROGRAM IN CLINICAL PSYCHOLOGY," 1947

1. Superior intellectual ability and judgment.
2. Originality, resourcefulness, and versatility.
3. "Fresh and insatiable" curiosity; "self-learner."
4. Interest in persons as individuals rather than as material for manipulation—a regard for the integrity of other persons.
5. Insight into own personality characteristics; sense of humor.
6. Sensitivity to the complexities of motivation.
7. Tolerance; "unarrogance."
8. Ability to adopt a "therapeutic" attitude: ability to establish warm and effective relationships with others.
9. Industry; methodical work habits; ability to tolerate pressure.
10. Acceptance of responsibility.
11. Tact and cooperativeness.
12. Integrity, self-control, and stability.
13. Discriminating sense of ethical values.
14. Breadth of cultural background—"educated man."
15. Deep interest in psychology, especially in its clinical aspects.

From "Recommended Graduate Training Program in Clinical Psychology," by the American Psychological Association, Committee on Training in Clinical Psychology, 1947, *American Psychologist, 2*, p. 541.

APPENDIX D: EXCERPT FROM "CRITERIA FOR EVALUATING PROGRESS IN CLINICAL OR IN COUNSELING PSYCHOLOGY," 1958

CONTENT AREAS

This is not a list of courses, and it is liberally interpreted when applying it in an evaluation of a program.

1. General psychology (a. General, physiological, and comparative, b. History and systems or theory, c. Developmental or child psychology, d. Social psychology)
2. Psychodynamics of behavior (a. Theory of personality and motivation, b. Psychopathology)
3. Diagnostic methods
4. Psychotherapy and counseling (a. Psychotherapeutic theory and methods, *or* b. Techniques of guidance and counseling)
5. Research methods (a. Experimental psychology, b. Advanced statistics and quantitative methods, c. Research in dynamic psychology, d. Dissertation, preceded by master's thesis or a research project)
6. Related disciplines. Not all of the following are necessary, but it is expected that the graduate program in psychology will be a part of a strong graduate school with graduate studies in

supporting areas, such as: a. Physiological sciences, b. Study of social and economic environment, including occupational information. This is important for counseling psychologists, c. Cultural anthropology, d. Philosophy of science.

From "Criteria for Evaluating Progress in Clinical or in Counseling Psychology," by B. V. Moore, 1958, *American Psychologist, 13*, pp. 59–60. In the public domain.

APPENDIX E:
LETTERS FROM DONALD MARQUIS TO DIRECTORS OF GRADUATE STUDY AT THE OFFICE OF PSYCHOLOGICAL PERSONNEL, 1945; DAVID WOLFLE TO ROBERT SEARS, 1946; AND ROBERT SEARS TO THE COMMITTEE ON GRADUATE AND PROFESSIONAL TRAINING, 1946

OFFICE OF PSYCHOLOGICAL PERSONNEL
National Research Council
2101 Constitution Avenue, Washington 25, D.C.

31 August 1945

To Directors of Graduate Study:

During the next twelve or eighteen months some 500 or 600 individuals will be seriously considering enrolling for graduate study in psychology and allied fields. Some of them had started graduate work before the demands of war service interrupted it; others had just completed or nearly completed their undergraduate work; still others (and this is a surprisingly large number) had not considered graduate study in psychology until their contact with psychologists in the Armed Forces, in the ASTP, and in OSRD research.

Most of these potential students have not decided what university they want to attend; many of them have no adequate information about possible graduate departments. This Office has received numerous requests for guidance in selecting a university, and officers in the Army and Navy report similar requests from their men. Such guidance should not be given in an offhand manner—at least it seems to me that objective factual information about the several departments should be available to all prospective students.

The OPP has a reasonably complete file of the addresses of psychologists in national service, and we propose to send to each of them a summary of factual information about graduate departments. Those who have completed their graduate work will be asked to make the information available in their units to younger men who are planning to undertake graduate study.

The Department of Psychology in your University has already filled out the questionnaire with respect to its program and has suggested that you be asked to describe the graduate training programs in your school or department which are related to the field of psychology.

Not all of the items of information requested here will be included in the collation to be distributed. Other items have been included at the request of the APA Committee on Graduate and Professional Training. This committee is carrying out an extensive study of the fields of professional employment of psychologists and of the training facilities available. On the basis of these findings the committee will prepare a number of reports, including recommendations for optimal training programs for the several fields of professional specialization. The data of the questionnaire will furnish a picture of present training programs on which such recommendations may be based.

Your cooperation in this study is earnestly invited for the eventual development of better and more uniform standards of graduate training. Your comments on the general problem and on specific items of the questionnaire will also be welcome.

You will of course be sent preliminary copies of any reports or publications in which the information is used.

Donald G. Marquis, Director
Office of Psychological Personnel

AMERICAN PSYCHOLOGICAL ASSOCIATION
1515 Massachusetts Avenue, N.W.
Washington 5, D.C.

25 September 1946

Dr. Robert R. Sears
Child Welfare Research Station
University of Iowa
Iowa City, Iowa

Dear Bob:

The Council of Representatives of the APA took advantage of your absence to name you as chairman of the *Committee on Graduate and Professional Training*. I am sure this makes the whole Council unpopular with you, but it was very generally agreed that the committee's work has been of extreme value, that it had to continue, and that you were the proper person to take charge of it. The other members for the coming year are John G. Darley, Lowell Kelly, Elaine Kender, Jean Mcfarlane, Donald Marquis, Bruce C. Moore, Sidney L. Pressey, Marion Richardson, and Carroll Shartle.

There are several things which the Association hopes the committee can accomplish during the coming year. First is to continue the work started by you on accreditation of graduate training facilities. As a long range basis for handling that problem a new Committee of University Department Chairmen was appointed. It consists of the chairmen or their representatives of the 33 departments of psychology which conferred 10 or more doctoral degrees in psychology during the years, 1934 to 1942 inclusive. The committee was instructed to study its field of activity and to consider plans for establishing a permanent APA committee or an independent Association of Graduate Departments of Psychology. However, that committee is just getting organized. It will undoubtedly take some time before it can begin to function. In the meantime the need continues to be pressing for evaluation and listing of graduate training facilities. The Committee on Graduate and Professional Training is asked to continue to be responsible for this work until the new Committee of University Department Chairmen can take it over in a year or two.

I have already sent you the request from Michael J. Shortley asking for a list of schools qualified for training to the MA or PhD level. An answer to that request should be one of the topics on your committee's program. Enclosed with this letter is a catalogue from the Catholic University and a letter from Thomas V. Moore. I have written to Dr. Moore informing him of the committee structure and that the letter has been forwarded to you. A copy of my note to him is enclosed. Some time within the next six months you can anticipate a request from the United States Public Health Service for a list of schools with which they can make arrangements for a cooperative training program preparing clinical psychologists with the PhD degree. The list will probably be essentially the same as the one given to the Veterans Administration. The request, however, provides a good excuse for reconsidering the whole VA list.

The U.S. Public Health Service program has raised another question for your committee to consider. They have asked the APA to prepare and transmit to them the outline of a four-year curriculum leading to the PhD degree in clinical psychology. The situation seems to be as follows. The 1933 report to the AAAP of the committee of which Bruce Moore was chairman was approved by AAAP. The 1945 report on internship training by the committee of which David Shakow was chairman has never been given any formal approval either by the APA or the AAAP. As a statement of principle perhaps it should be formally approved, but as the outline of a four-year course of instruction approval would be questionable. Does it for example include as much instruction in basic general psychological theory and methods as we would care to endorse? At any rate the Board of Directors asked me to transmit the Public Health Service request to you in order that the committee can consider it and can if possible prepare a curriculum which the APA can endorse and transmit to the Public Health Service.

The third major item which the Board of Directors wishes the committee to consider is the problem of the selection of graduate students in psychology. Because the Veterans Administration has written a contract with the University of Michigan and because Lowell Kelly will be responsible for that contract there, he was placed on the Graduate and Professional Training Committee with the expectation that you might wish to appoint him as chairman of a sub-committee to work on problems of selection of graduate students. Marion Richardson was placed on the committee to have his critical abilities available to you in working out methods on graduate student selection.

You may also wish to have explanations for the presence of two other members on the committee. Jack Darley has been more familiar with the work of the Federal Security Agency and the Retaining and Reemployment Administration than anyone I know. I believe that he can be of great usefulness to you in answering Shortley's request. Jean Mcfarlane was placed on the committee because of the very active interest she has been taking in problems of graduate training in the field of clinical psychology. She has outlined a course of instruction for California which you will probably be interested in examining if you have not already seen it.

I am very sorry that you did not get to the APA meeting. There was a crowd of approximately 2000. They all seemed to have a good time. We missed you in the lengthy two-day session of the Board of Directors.

Dael Wolfle

AMERICAN PSYCHOLOGICAL ASSOCIATION
Committee on Graduate and Professional Training

October 21, 1946

TO: Members of the Graduate and Professional Training Committee, APA
FROM: Robert R. Sears, Chairman
SUBJECT: Committee problems and work for 1946–47

According to a letter from Dr. Wolfle, the Committee on Graduate and Professional Training has been appointed by the Council, for this coming year, with the following membership:

John G. Darley, Dept. of Psychology, University of Minnesota, Minneapolis
Lowell Kelly, Dept. of Psychology, University of Michigan, Ann Arbor
Elaine Kinder, Rockland State Hospital, Orangeburg, N.Y.
Jean Macfarlane, Dept. of Psychology, University of California, Berkeley
Donald G. Marquis, Dept. of Psychology, Pennsylvania State College, State College
Sidney L. Pressey, Dept. of Psychology, Ohio State University, Columbus
Robert R. Sears, Child Welfare, University of Iowa, Iowa City, Chairman

Please inform me at once if any of the above addresses is not the most expeditious way to get mail to you in a hurry.

In his letter, Dr. Wolfle informs me that the Council of Representatives has charged the Committee with three main tasks for this year.

1. *Accreditation.* In January, 1946, the Veterans Administration requested the APA to provide a list of institutions which were adequately prepared to offer training to the PhD degree in clinical psychology. The purpose of this was to have a basis on which the VA might select institutions in which to place its training program. Since no such list existed at that time, Dr. Wolfle turned this request over to the Committee on Graduate and Professional Training, and the Committee agreed to prepare such a list on the basis of data that had been secured through a survey undertaken late in 1945. A report of that survey material was presented in the May number of the AMERICAN PSYCHOLOGIST. Crude criteria of "comprehensiveness of facilities" were then set up, and the institutions were analyzed and catalogued according to these criteria. This provided a list of top-ranking institutions. A copy of the interim Committee report which described this process is enclosed. By September 1st, a total of 24 institutions had been accredited. A list of these is also enclosed.

Four matters require that an accreditation procedure be continued and that the work on it be undertaken at once. First, the VA wishes to have a 1947 list by February. Second, several institutions have modified their personnel and training facilities to such an extent that they now wish to be considered for accreditation. Third, the U.S. Public Health Service anticipates the development of a similar clinical psychology training program and will probably request an up-to-date list of institutions by next spring. Fourth, the Federal Security Agency's Office of Vocational Rehabilitation has requested a list of institutions that are prepared to train counselors in that field.

The Committee's first step appears to be to decide on what criteria to use in accrediting institutions for (a) PhD training in clinical psychology, and (b) MA and PhD training in vocational rehabilitation counseling. Those used for clinical psychology last year were not altogether satisfactory; the definitions of practicum facilities and specialized training personnel were quite inadequate. Furthermore, no consideration was given to basic (non-clinical) doctoral training; this was not a serious matter with the larger institutions, but for certain of the smaller ones, there was reason for considerable doubt as to whether the facilities for training in general, experimental, and child psychology were adequate, even though there might be technical fulfillment of the requirements for specialized clinical personnel.

The second step appears to be to devise a method for securing adequate information with which to determine whether a given institution meets the criteria. Enclosed are the verification blanks that were used last year; they were mailed to department chairmen (see procedure described on pp. 135–136 of the enclosed reprint). This procedure has been criticized on the grounds that it permitted department chairmen too wide latitude in their judgment about both the people and the areas of training that were covered, but this criticism is really directed at the inadequacy of the blanks rather than at the questionnaire method involved, I think.

The third step will require an evaluation of information obtained. In all likelihood there should be informal visits, by members of the Committee, to doubtful institutions. There should be a final physical meeting of the Committee to make a decision as to which institutions are to be accredited.

Because of the VA's need for a list in February, this whole task should be completed by the end of January. This means a physical meeting of the Committee sometime around the middle of January. I believe it is safe to predict that there will be funds available for the travel expenses, at least in large part. Such a proposed schedule means that the questionnaire material will have to be secured very soon. Tentatively I would suggest the following time schedule:

By November 4th   Committee members reply to this memo with detailed proposals concerning *criteria* and *methods of securing data*.

By November 11th	Chairman abstracts and collates these replies, and prepares a rough draft of the questionnaire; mailed to the Committee.
By November 20th	Suggested modifications of the questionnaire returned to the chairman.
By November 28th	Final draft of questionnaire mailed to the Committee for modification or approval.
By December 5th	Questionnaire mailed to institutions with request for immediate reply.
During December	Mimeographing of returns from individual institutions and forwarding of this material to members of the Committee for their evaluation.
About January 15th	Physical meeting of Committee (Is Chicago a central place?)

This kind of a schedule is set up on the supposition that we will seek our information by means of a questionnaire to be sent to departmental chairmen. This is the first question for the Committee to decide. If this is satisfactory, then I would urge you to give very immediate and serious consideration to the nature of the criteria which we should establish as being satisfactory for an accredited institution which proposes to present the PhD degree in clinical psychology. I suggest that you keep in mind not only the problem of training facilities for the clinical psychology itself, but also the problem of measuring other aspects of the training program such as experimental psychology, statistics, and the general basic ground work for the PhD degree. Darley is thoroughly familiar with the Federal Security Agency's needs for a list, and will provide some special information and suggestions relating to the kinds of criteria that are needed for accrediting to that agency.

2. *Curriculum for clinical psychology PhD.* The following paragraph is quoted from Dr. Wolfle's letter:

"The U.S. Public Health Service program has raised another question for your committee to consider. They have asked the APA to prepare and transmit to them the outline of a four-year curriculum leading to the Ph.D. degree in clinical psychology. The situation seems to be as follows. The 1933 report to the AAAP of the committee of which Bruce Moore was chairman was approved by AAAP. The 1945 report on internship training by the committee of which David Shakow was chairman has never been given any formal approval either by the APA or the AAAP. As a statement of principle perhaps it should be formally approved, but as the outline of a four-year course of instruction approval would be questionable. Does it for example include as much instruction in basic general psychological theory and methods as we would care to endorse? At any rate the Board of Directors asked me to transmit the Public Health Service request to you in order that the committee can consider it and can if possible prepare a curriculum which the APA can endorse and transmit to the Public Health Service."

So far as I know, this request is not urgent and I propose that we postpone action until we can have an informal discussion of it at our physical meeting in January. If anyone feels that there is reason for preparing some materials and discussion before that meeting, let me know now and I will inform the rest of the Committee when the next memo on accreditation goes out.

3. *Selection of graduate students in psychology.* During the last three years the Committee has considered from time to time the problem of the selection of the graduate students in psychology. With the growing demand for psychologists, and the increasing salaries being paid to them, it is natural to expect a larger number of applicants for psychological training in our graduate schools. The Council of Representatives has urged the Committee to take a more active approach to the development of selection devices. I have therefore asked Lowell Kelly to serve as chairman of a Sub-committee on Selection. He has accepted this appointment and the following have been invited to serve as members: Marion Richardson, John G. Darley, Dewey Stuit and Robert H. Seashore (to serve as liaison member for the Committee of Departmental Chairmen). Dr. Kelly is already engaged in an extensive project on contract with the VA; this will be largely directed toward the selection of clinical psychologists, but by providing some minor additional funds the APA can have the advantage of the groundwork laid by this large project and can also secure data on selection devices for other branches of psychology.

Since I did not get to Philadelphia, my chief sources of information have been a letter from Dr. Wolfle and a single telephone call from Dr. Marquis. If there were other matters which the Committee, in discussion at Philadelphia, decided should be taken up this year, I would be very happy to have you send me information about them at your earliest convenience. In any case, please be sure to get me a reply to the queries concerning the accreditation program at once.

APPENDIX F:
EXCERPT FROM V. C. RAIMY'S "ACCREDITATION OF TRAINING UNIVERSITIES" IN *TRAINING IN CLINICAL PSYCHOLOGY*, 1950

ACCREDITATION OF TRAINING UNIVERSITIES

Any profession that attempts to organize its practices and policies is sooner or later faced with the problem of determining the procedures appropriate for training new members. This, in essence, was the broad task faced by the members of the Conference. Their agreements and disagreements are the basis for the present report. When a group of fundamental policies finds general acceptance, the profession inevitably is called upon to make public its program for safeguarding the interests of society and to aspirants hoping to qualify as members of the profession. Licensing and certification are methods for providing such safeguards, since they entail a public statement of the qualifications necessary to become a member of the professional group. In addition, these methods also control the use of professional status in a given state or locality.

Another method adopted by some professions is that of publicly certifying to the adequacy of training programs in particular training centers. This published approval is a highly limited type of professional recognition that it certifies only to the adequacy of training facilities and makes no claim for the individual graduates of the accredited institution. Since the accrediting procedure must publicly endorse some training centers and, either explicitly or by simple failure to mention, exclude other training centers, accreditation at its inception normally may produce anxiety and resistance; for those centers excluded may suffer loss of status, of students, and of financial support. Few psychologists are likely to be concerned over protests from institutions proposing to undertake the training of clinical psychologists with obviously inadequate staffs and training facilities. Everyone recognizes, however, that honest differences of opinion are bound to occur in regard to the borderline institutions that may form a sizeable proportion of the training centers being evaluated. The frictions that arise from such differences of opinion are intensified on both sides by the knowledge that lasting injustices may be perpetrated by a group sincerely training to complete a necessary but largely thankless task.

One of the great dangers commonly recognized by those concerned with accreditation lies in the possibility of failing to provide channels whereby new training centers can establish themselves in the face of the inevitable handicap of not already being accredited. Instructors and students alike are justifiably reluctant to commit themselves to university programs that may not be accredited. Obtaining financial support for an "unrecognized" training program, whether from university or outside sources, requires a degree of salesmanship and pedagogical collateral that is, to say the least, rare.

An additional hazard of the accrediting procedure lies in the possibility that it may be used to safeguard, not the public and would-be candidates, but the accumulated privileges of dominant groups within the profession or among the already approved training centers. Competition for good candidates and deliberate restrictions on the number of new members entering a given occupation are not unknown. These are not necessarily reprehensible tactics in professional training; but when used for the benefit of entrenched interests and against the public welfare, such tactics must be condemned. Of more importance than condemnation, however, is the establishment of policies for preventing the occurrence of such abuses of accreditation.

In considering accreditation for university departments engaged in training clinical psychologists, an additional danger of considerable magnitude is encountered. Without exception, the training of clinical psychologists is only one part of the graduate training program of psychology departments. Graduate degrees are also awarded for concentration in research or in general psychology, industrial psychology, physiological psychology, social psychology, educational psychology, and so on. There is no necessary relation between the department's adequacy in training for clinical psychology and its facilities for training in other areas of psychology. In fact, certain universities well recognized for their graduate training have preferred to concentrate their energies in nonclinical fields and have no program for clinical psychology. These facts of academic organization are well known to psychologists, but are likely to be unknown to members of related professional groups and may not even be clearly recognized by university administrators, now that universities have enrollments up to forty thousand students. How can one insure that approval of one portion of a university psychology department, clinical psychology, is not misinterpreted as approval of the whole department? The question, phrased in terms of clinical training programs that are not accredited, arouses even more possibilities of manifest injustice.

These major hazards of a program for accreditation were frankly faced at the Boulder Conference. To most participants it was (and is) a very serious problem, one that almost makes the accreditation question a choice between two evils, particularly when special circumstances surrounding the present training of clinical psychologists are considered. There has been a marked if not desperate shortage of qualified instructors in the field ever since the end of the war. To a large extent, most training programs in clinical psychology have been initiated or have been forced to undergo reorganization within the last three years. Add to these difficulties what was thought to be a lack of generally accepted goals and training methods, and the prospect for accreditation becomes even more bleak.

In spite of the very serious arguments against immediate accreditation, there seemed to be no real opposition at the Conference to the acceptance of accreditation in the future. What were some of the factors behind this acceptance?

In the first place, accreditation of training programs in clinical psychology had been going on for two years and was preceded by several years of preliminary investigation. The needs of the Veterans Administration and of the Public Health Service played a part in the start of this program. In 1946, the Veterans Administration requested the American Psychological Association to provide a list of universities approved for the training of clinical psychologists. Also in 1946 the Public Health Service requested the American Psychological Association to recommend a suitable program of training for clinical psychologists. The *1947 Report of the APA Committee on Training in Clinical Psychology* was a result, in part, of this request. The needs of the Veterans Administration for lists of approved training centers, and of the Public Health Service for all relevant information to assist staff and consultants in making the most effective allocation of training grant and stipend funds, have continued to emphasize the importance of the work of this APA Committee. The government agencies could not do for themselves what the American Psychological Association could do for them. Accordingly, the American Psychological Association, through the work of the Committee, evaluated university training programs in 1947, 1948, and 1949. Parts of the 1947 evaluations were published; the 1948 results were not published, because of actions taken by the APA Board of Directors, the Council of Representatives, and votes of university department chairmen. The 1949 results also were left unpublished.

It is thus apparent that self-evaluation by psychologists themselves became a necessity at a time thought by many to be inopportune. Yet at the same time still other forces were acting in the same direction to force consideration of accreditation.

Members of the American Psychological Association set up the American Board of Examiners in Professional Psychology in September, 1946, as a means of public certification for clinical psychologists, industrial psychologists, and counseling and guidance psychologists at the diplomate level. While ABEPP has no direct relationship to an accreditation program for training universities, the establishment of certification procedures by the psychological profession necessarily involves the problem of discriminating among certain institutions capable of engaging in the training of professional persons. Since clinical psychology is a profession that attracts many persons without adequate educational and personal qualifications, the problem of evaluating doctoral training programs is perhaps more acute in the clinical area than in industrial or counseling and guidance psychology. Although ABEPP's establishment was one of the forces pushing toward accreditation, it should be noted that certification by ABEPP does not necessarily depend upon the awarding of the PhD by one of the currently accredited universities.

Another impelling force toward accreditation stems from the very great influx of new students into the field of clinical psychology immediately after the second World War. The Conference believed that the profession of psychology has an ethical responsibility to answer as honestly as possible inquiries from students about centers where adequate training in clinical psychology can be obtained. To some extent, such requests for information may have resulted from the steps that had already been taken in accrediting. Nonetheless, the responsibility for providing such guidance is not dodged ordinarily even by those universities that have not been accredited.

A certain amount of hindsight was also available at the Conference, since accrediting had been in effect for two years. Each of the four sub-groups that considered accreditation problems reported favorably on the desirability of the procedure. One of the sub-groups voted unanimously that "the general effects of the APA Committee on Training in Clinical Psychology appear to have been salutary." Standards have been raised; departments have scrutinized their programs and incorporated many improvements; and university administrations have become more aware of the problems of training clinical psychologists. Irritation at specific procedures and doubts of the omniscience of the Committee were freely expressed, but no sentiment to halt the accrediting of training programs in clinical psychology was discernible.

Publication of Ratings. Although accreditation has been under way for two years and was endorsed by the Conference, the problem of publication of the results remains an unsolved issue. This problem was discussed from all angles and over several sessions of the Conference. Suggested publication times ranged from "immediately" to "after 1952." Suggested forms of accreditation ranged from the publication of a list with multiple categories, such as A, B, and C schools, to one list of approved schools only.

The discussion finally boiled down to two major principles with which the majority seemed to agree. First, the Conference should recommend that publication should *not* occur until the Committee on Training in clinical Psychology feels confident that its ratings are adequate. Secondly, although the Committee was then in its third year of evaluating departments and sufficient confidence in its rating could be expected in the near future, the date of publication should be left for the Committee to decide. As a result of these decisions, the Conference framed a resolution that was submitted to the American Psychological Association and approved by the APA council at the Denver meeting. The recommendation was as follows:

> Not earlier than 1950 and not later than 1952, two lists should be published: an alphabetical list of accredited departments without differentiation or classification; and a similar list of departments visited and regarded as in a promising stage of development.

Accrediting Policies. Earlier sections of this discussion reviewed many of the hazards in the evaluation of professional training programs. The Conference considered various methods for safeguarding the general development of professional training, and also individual universities, against the possible disadvantages arising from the evaluating procedure.

That accrediting is likely to crystallize the profession itself has been widely recognized by both friendly and unfriendly critics of recent accrediting moves. It is often pointed out that clinical psychology is a rapidly developing field that has sought real professional stature only in the postwar years. If formal and public approval is given too early to a particular type of training program, progress is very likely to be impeded, particularly if either the schools or the evaluating Committee hold slavishly to set principles of training. Conference members were very outspoken in recommending both to universities and to the Committee that university departments should feel free to experiment resolutely and to follow their own convictions without adherence to either established objectives or published criteria. Although such public endorsement of the right of university departments to experiment with their programs is likely to increase the difficulties of any accrediting body, there can be little disagreement with the conviction that one of the major reasons for accrediting is to implement the desire of the profession to raise training standards as new and better methods of training become available. New and better methods are unlikely to be developed if the training universities do not feel free to engage in thoughtfully-worked-out programs that aim at better training, even if they depart from those conventionally approved. Conference participants who had served or were serving on the evaluating Committee felt that this policy has been explicitly accepted by the Committee during its deliberations.

The Conference also suggested that the Committee should routinely adopt two further procedures that might be difficult to administer, but that would help to insure objectivity in the rating process. The first procedure would make it incumbent upon the Committee to publish as explicitly as possible the criteria used in evaluating training departments. While no one suggested that matters pertaining to individual schools should be made public, the general policies upon which the Committee acts should be made available.

The second procedure suggested was that a discussion of the results of the evaluation made by visitors of the Committee on Training in Clinical Psychology should be made at the time of the visit when requested by department chairmen. This latter procedure is already being followed to a large extent, and letters to department chairmen from the Committee contain the final conclusions of the Committee in regard to the individual department.

Since the present evaluating Committee is a creature of the American Psychological Association rather than of the training universities, the appeal from Committee ratings can be made to the Board of Directors of the Association itself. Nonetheless, many participants were concerned over the three-fold functions now entrusted to the Committee. It decides on standards to be followed in the accrediting process; it visits the training centers and decides on the ratings to be made for individual schools; and it provides advice to departments of psychology. To a large extent it acts as both judge and jury with only the right of appeal to the American Psychological Association and the influence of professional opinion as checks on its broad powers. While there was little criticism expressed of the way in which the Committee had exercised its powers to date, the problem of setting up policies that would help to insure the objectivity of its operations was discussed at considerable length.

The obvious solution to the problem would involve the creation of two committees with separate functions. One committee would set up standards for approving universities; the other committee would carry out the directions of the first. Experience has shown, however, that proliferation of committees is not the most efficient or the most workable method, nor does it necessarily insure objectivity. Communication between widely scattered members of a single committee is none too good even under the best conditions. Two groups with divided responsibilities might create more difficulties than would be solved. The problem is obviously one that requires considerable deliberation by psychologists in addition to those who were in attendance at the Conference. As a result of the discussion, the following resolution was decided upon:

> The APA Conference recommends that the APA consider the possible advantages of separating the two functions of establishing objectives and standards for training in psychology, on the one hand, and accreditation, on the other.

While the Conference felt that the question of separation of functions in accrediting schools was a matter to be decided by the American Psychological Association, there was general agreement that accreditation might well be given too much consideration at the expense of the even more important task of encouraging the profession in its efforts to review constantly its present educational procedures and to develop new and better ones. Accrediting committees almost always become engaged in practical matters that are likely to limit their vision and focus their energies upon their immediate duties. Furthermore, the present Committee on Training in Clinical Psychology has no authority to accredit in fields of graduate training other than clinical, although its actions indirectly affect training programs outside of clinical psychology. Conference participants felt that the American Psychological Association should have a committee concerned primarily with *educational* policies, a committee that is not limited to the problems of *clinical* psychology but is in a position to evaluate the actions of accrediting committees as they relate to desirable educational principles. The following resolution, directed to the American Psychological Association, aims at the establishment of such a committee:

> We urge the creation of a committee with broad powers to examine and review educational philosophy, methods, and standards beyond those serving as the foundation for accrediting in any one field of applied psychology, and with the power to review accreditation policies and practices.

Many of the difficulties inherent in accrediting schools in clinical psychology remain for future decision. The especially irksome problem of having psychology departments as a whole known on the basis of their rating in clinical psychology alone found no ready solution at the Conference. One suggestion made was that the American Psychological Association again publish an up-to-date description of the areas of interest of each psychology department training graduate students. The interests and training facilities should be furnished by the departments themselves as was done in the 1947 report of the Sears Committee.[*]

One other matter that related to general policies of training was considered by a sub-group that discussed a medical orientation in regard to accreditation. This group felt that although in the past training in clinical psychology seems to have been particularly good in medically oriented schools, accreditation is not, and should not be, withheld because a school has another basic orientation.

In summary, the Conference viewed accreditation in clinical psychology as a somewhat mixed blessing. Its establishment as a general policy seems to be an accepted fact. The procedural details are still in the process of development and will require thoughtful consideration by psychologists other than

---

[*] Sears, R. R. (1947). Clinical training facilities. *The American Psychologist, 2,* 199–205.

those on the Committee on Training in Clinical Psychology. There are many possible obstacles to be overcome, but frank recognition of the dangers, coupled with the development of reasonable safeguards, can avoid most of the anticipated problems.

From "Accreditation of Training Universities" (pp. 170–179) by V. C. Raimy, 1950, in V. C. Raimy (Ed.), *Training in Clinical Psychology*, London: Prentice Hall. Copyright 1950 by Prentice Hall. Reprinted with permission.

APPENDIX G:
ACCREDITING PROCEDURES OF THE AMERICAN PSYCHOLOGICAL ASSOCIATION, 1970

ACCREDITING PROCEDURES OF THE AMERICAN PSYCHOLOGICAL ASSOCIATION, EDUCATION AND TRAINING BOARD[1]

At its fall 1969 meeting the Council of Representatives voted to adopt the following procedures, which describe the methods to be employed in carrying out the accreditation function of the Association. They were formulated in consultation with APA's legal counsel and are extensions of the practices developed by the Committee on Evaluation in its many years of activity. As such they reflect the concern with fair play and due process that has always been paramount in the approach of the Association to accreditation. Specifically, they make provision for a formal appeal mechanism. These procedures are in keeping with the Code of Good Practice promulgated by the National Commission on Accrediting for the guidance of the accrediting bodies which it recognizes. They will go into effect immediately.

1. *Purpose*—The American Psychological Association (hereafter referred to as the "Association") accredits university programs in certain professional areas of psychology and approves programs in institutions offering internship training in those areas. The purpose of accreditation and approval is to pro-

---

[1] Requests for reprints should be sent to the Educational Affairs Office, American Psychological Association, 1200 Seventeenth Street, NW, Washington, DC 20036.

mote excellence in psychological training programs, and to provide a professional and objective evaluation of these programs.

2. *Standards for Accreditation and Approval*—All actions with respect to accreditation and approval taken by the Association shall be governed by the Guidelines for Accreditation and Approval (hereafter "Guidelines") in force at the time an accrediting decision is made. The Guidelines shall be established and promulgated by the Association's Education and Training Board and published in the *American Psychologist*.[2]

The following criteria were established in 1979 for programs to be considered eligible for accreditation. By clearly delineating these criteria, it became easier for programs to be able to quickly identify what was required for accreditation.

Programs must meet the following criteria to be eligible for accreditation by the APA:

A. Training in professional psychology is doctoral training offered in an institution of higher education accredited by one of the six regional accrediting bodies recognized by the Council on Postsecondary Accreditation (COPA).

B. The program, wherever it may be administratively housed, must be clearly and publicly identified and labeled as a professional psychology program.

C. A recognizable, coherent organizational entity must be responsible for the program.

D. The faculty of the program must have clear authority and primary responsibility for all aspects of the program (even if the program cuts across institutional administrative lines).

E. The program must include an integrated, organized plan of study and must ensure a breadth of exposure to the field of psychology.

F. The program must include supervised practicum, internship, field, or laboratory training appropriate to the practice of psychology.

G. There must be an identifiable psychology faculty and a psychologist responsible for the program.

H. The program must have an identifiable body of students who are matriculated in that program for a degree.

I. The institution must demonstrate its commitment to the program by appropriate financial support.

---

[2]The Guidelines in force at the time these Accrediting Procedures were adopted are in the *American Psychologist* (1967, 22, 153–155).

From "Accrediting Procedures of the American Psychological Association," by American Psychological Association, Education and Training Board, 1970, *American Psychologist, 25*, pp. 100–102.

APPENDIX H:
REPORT OF THE JOINT COUNCIL ON PROFESSIONAL EDUCATION IN PSYCHOLOGY, 1990

PROGRAM ACCREDITATION

In its public document of policies, the Council on Postsecondary Accreditation (COPA) states:

> Accreditation is a system for recognizing educational institutions and professional programs affiliated with those institutions for a level of performance, integrity, and quality which entitles them to the confidence of the educational community and the public they serve. In the United States this recognition is extended primarily through nongovernmental, voluntary institutional or professional associations. These groups establish criteria for accreditation, arrange site visits, evaluate those institutions and professional programs which desire accredited status, and publicly designate those which meet their criteria....

Throughout the evolution of its procedures, the aims of postsecondary accreditation have been and are to:

- Foster excellence in postsecondary education through the development of criteria and guidelines for assessing educational effectiveness
- Encourage improvement through continuous self-study and review
- Assure the educational community, the general public, and other agencies or organizations that an institution or program has clearly defined and appropriate objectives, maintains con-

ditions under which their achievement can reasonably be expected, is in fact accomplishing them substantially, and can be expected to continue to do so
- Provide counsel and assistance to established and developing institutions and programs
- Endeavor to protect institutions against encroachments which might jeopardize their educational effectiveness or academic freedom. (1990, pp. 3–4)

The APA has been engaged in the accreditation of professional training programs since the 1940's. Accreditation policies, procedures, and activities always involve a dynamic tension between two conflicting and extremely vital values. On the one hand, upholding the critical academic freedom necessary to support innovation, optimize the skills of a particular faculty, maintain unfettered inquiry, and protect program autonomy is essential to the evolution of the discipline. On the other hand, there are the equally vital needs of regulatory bodies, employers of professional psychologists, and the public to expect some uniformity, minimal levels of competency, and standards for the manner in which professional psychologists are educated and trained (APA Task Force on Education and Credentialing, 1985; "National Conference on Clinical Training Policy in Psychology," 1988; Stigall, 1977, 1983; Wellner, 1976, 1978).

Thus, accreditation is to serve the public as a quality assurance process, while also affording educational institutions and programs the autonomy they require in teaching, research, and service. In this context, it is generally assumed to be the responsibility of the profession to establish minimal standards of competency required for the entry level of practice, while it is the right and responsibility of educational institutions and programs to determine how those standards will be met.

In other sections of this report, the JCPEP recommends standards appropriate to predoctoral and postdoctoral levels of education and training for the practice of psychology. In this section, the JCPEP identifies issues and sets forth recommendations pertaining to the structure and procedures for program accreditation.

The recommendations are offered in the spirit of strengthening the present accreditation process in psychology relative to the purposes of accreditation (APA Task Force on Review of the Scope and Criteria for Accreditation, 1989). In some instances this is done by recommending policy statements that reinforce current practices; in other instances recommendations call for new or more rigorous procedures.

Issue 27: Candidacy Status in Accreditation

It is the interest of students, the profession, and the public that all programs engaged in education and training for the professional practice of psychology be accredited. It is a natural extension of this policy that a formal accreditation review process be instituted for new programs and previously existing programs that choose to engage the process of accreditation. The purpose of establishing a candidacy status category is to provide guidance to faculty and administrators in the process of planning and developing programs and to assure students, the profession, and the public that a program in candidacy status is seeking to conform to accreditation standards and criteria.

Issue 28: Site Team Composition

It is a requirement of COPA (1990, pp. 40–41) that the nationally recognized accrediting body for a profession provide in its site visit evaluation process "an appropriate balance between educators and practitioners." Thus, the APA must ensure that the visiting teams sent to evaluate doctoral programs, internships, and residencies are comprised of persons who represent balance between education and practice and diversity with respect to ethnicity, gender, and age. It is essential that site visitors have sufficient experience to conduct a thorough, searching, and meaningful evaluation of the program being visited.

Issue 29: Conduct of Site Team Visits

In order to ensure compliance with accreditation criteria, outcome measures should be assessed by site visitors. Relevant information from students, graduates, practicum supervisors, internship supervisors, residency supervisors, and employers of graduates should be sought and considered whenever feasible.

Suggested revisions in the current system of program review are to ensure that site visits are sufficiently comprehensive to assess program quality, with intervals between site visits sufficient for program development to occur. The accrediting body must rely heavily on program self-study reports focused on major issues of program development in periods between site visits.

Issue 30: Public Disclosure

It is essential that programs be clear in public documents about their education and training goals and objectives. Clarity is necessary to avoid confusion on the part of prospective students and also for the accrediting body to evaluate a program's effectiveness in terms of achieving its goals and objectives. If accreditation is to serve the public interest, full disclosure of the process and outcome of accreditation evaluation is necessary, albeit within the limits set forth by COPA (1990, pp. 145–148) in its policies on public disclosure and confidentiality.

Issue 31: Program Self-Monitoring

Professional education and training programs, whether doctoral, internship, or postdoctoral programs, have a responsibility to engage in self-study and outcome monitoring so that corrective feedback can be achieved based upon a review of the education and training process.

Issue 32: Accreditation Structure

It is a requirement of COPA (1990) that the nationally recognized accrediting body for a profession provide in its policy and decision making processes "an appropriate balance between educators and practitioners" (pp. 40–41), as well as "impartial and objective public representation" (p. 39). The current APA procedures for appointing its Committee on Accreditation should be revised to more fully comply with these provisions.

The following recommendations assume that the duly recognized accrediting body for the profession of psychology will remain within the APA. COPA presently recognized the APA Committee on Accreditation as the accrediting body for the profession of psychology. After some experience in operating under the following procedures, a consortium model could be considered in which the APA would become one member of an independent, separately incorporated board for accreditation in the field of psychology.

From "Report of the Joint Council on Professional Education in Psychology," by T. T. Stigall et al., 1990, Baton Rouge, LA: Joint Council on Professional Education in Psychology. Copyright 1990 by the Joint Council on Professional Education in Psychology. Reprinted with permission.

APPENDIX I: LISTED MEMBERS OF THE COMMITTEE ON ACCREDITATION, PAST AND PRESENT

Abel, Howard (1968–1971)[f]
Acosta, Frank (1977–1979)[g]
Adams, Donald K. (1951–1952)[d]
Adams, Kenneth M. (1989–1991)[g]
Alexander, Irving, chair (1963–1966)[f]
Altmaier, Elizabeth M., chair (1990–1994)[g]
Altman, Irwin, chair (1972–1975)[g]
Anderson, Gordon V. (1964–1967)[f]
Aponte, Joseph F. (1990–1992)[g]
Auld, Frank, Jr. (1962–1965)[f]
Barcelo, Nancy (1985–1987)[g]
Bascuas, Joseph W. (1993–1998)[g]
Basowitz, Harold (1965–1966)[f]
Beidel, Deborah C., chair (1993–1995)[g]
Benbow, Camilla P. (1997–1999)[g]
Bent, Russell J. (1989–1991)[g]
Benton, Arthur L. (1951–1953)[d]
Berdie, Ralph F. (1961–1964)[f]
Berent, Stanley (1986–1988)[g]
Berg, Irwin A., chair (1956–1959)[f]
Biaggo, Maryka (1998–2000)[g]
Bijou, Sidney W. (1958–1961)[f]
Birk, Janice M. (1993–1996)[g]
Blom, Bernhard E. (1993–1998)[g]
Bolton, Earl (1987–1989)[g]
Bordon, Edward S., chair (1951–1954)[d,f]
Brener, Roy, chair (1951–1954)[e], (1956–1957)[f]
Brewer, Joseph E. (1961–1964)[f]
Brown, Judson S. (1954–1957)[f]
Burstein, Alvin G. (1968–1971)[f], (1968–1972)[g]

Callan, Joann E., chair (1984–1986)[g]
Callis, Robert M. (1969–1971)[f]
Carlson, Cindy I. (1996–2001)[g]
Carroll, James, vice-chair (1985–1987)[g]
Carter, Henry Lee (1994–1996)[g]
Challman, Robert C. (1948–1949)[c]
Christiansen, Martha Dennis (1995–2000)[g]
Clement, Paul (1978–1980)[g]
Cohen, Louis D., chair (1961–1964)[f]
Conoley, Jane Close (1995–1998)[g]
Craddick, Ray (1983–1985)[g]
Crutchfield, Richard S. (1951–1954)[d]
Darley, John G. (1946–1947)[b]
David, Henry P. (1960–1963)[f]
Davis-Russell, Elizabeth (1995–2000)[g]
Dawson, Joseph G. (1959–1962)[f]
Dearnley, Marion (1989–1991)[g]
Delworth, Ursula (1977–1979)[g]
Denmark, Florence (1998–2000)[g]
Dilorenza, Thomas M. (1996–1999)[g]
Donchin, Emanuel (1993–1997)[g]
Dorken, Herbert O. (1966–1969)[f]
Duker, Jan D. (1968–1971)[f], chair (1971–1972)[g]
Edwards, Allen L. (1952–1955)[d]
Ehrenfreund, David (1962–1965)[f]
Evans, Dorothy, chair (1978–1980)[g]
Ferguson, Lucy Rau (1993–1997)[g]
Finger, Frank W. (1961–1963)[f]
Fletcher, Frank M. (1959–1962)[f]
Francell, Claire Griffin (1998–2000)[g]
Fredericks, Marilee U. (1972–1975)[g]
French, Joseph (1982–1984)[g]
Gardner, George E. (1951–1952)[e]
Gatz, Margaret (1987–1989)[g]
Goodstein, Leonard, chair (1962–1965)[f]
Gray-Little, Bernadette (1993–1995)[g]
Green, Vicki A. (2000–2001)[g]
Grosslight, Joseph (1976–1978)[g]
Guion, Robert M. (1968–1971)[f]
Hargrove, David Scott (2000–2001)[g]
Harris, Dale B. (1965–1968)[f]
Harris, Robert E. (1951–1952)[d]
Hastorf, Albert H. (1966–1969)[f]
Hefner, Robert (1967–1969)[f]
Heine, Ralph W., chair (1957–1960)[f]
Heiser, Karl F., (1951–1953)[e]
Henry, Edwin R. (1951–1952)[d]
Hilgard, Ernest R. (1947–1948)[c]
Hofer, Randy (1995–1996)[g]
Hollander, Patricia (1982–1984)[g]
Hoyle, Classie (1988–1990)[g]
Hughes, Jan N. (1991–1995)[g]
Hunt, Howard F. (1957–1959)[f]
Hunt, William A. (1945–1947)[a]
Hurst, James C., chair (1983–1985)[g]
Irwin, Francis W. (1948–1949)[c]
Jackson, Thomas L., chair (1996–2001)[g]
Jacobsen, Carlyle (1945–1947)[a]
Jenkins, Adelbert (1974–1976)[g]
Johnson, David F. (1995–1998)[g]
Johnson, Donald M. (1953–1954)[f]
Johnson, Norine G. (1993–1998)[g]
Kamiya, Joe (1967–1970)[f]
Katkin, Edward S. (1993–1997)[g]
Kelly, E. Lowell (1946–1947)[a] (1947–1949)[c]
Kelly, James G. (1968–1971)[f]
Kendig, Isabelle V. (1951–1954)[e]
Kendler, Howard H. (1960–1963)[f]
Kilbey, M. Marlyne, chair (1988–1990)[g]
Kimble, Gregory (1976–1978)[g]
Kinder, Elaine (1945–1947)[b]

Kirk, Barbara (1971–1974)[g]
Klauck, Kenneth A. (1993–1996)[g]
Klepac, Robert (1997–2000)[g]
Kobos, Joseph C. (1996–2001)[g]
Kovacs, Arthur L. (1997)[g]
Kreinik, Phyllis, chair (1981–1983)[g]
Kutash, Samuel (1958–1961)[f]
Laughlin, Philip (1983–1985)[g]
Layton, Wilbur L. (1966–1969)[f]
Lillich, Susan E. (1997)[g]
Lindzey, Gardner (1957–1960)[f]
Littman, Richard A. (1965–1968)[f]
Loganbill, Carol (1983–1986)[g]
Lorion, Raymond P. (1993–1996)[g]
Luckey, Bertha M. (1947–1949)[c]
MacCorquodale, Kenneth (1957–1960)[f]
MacFarlane, Jean W. (1946–1947)[b]
Magaret, Ann (1948–1949)[c]
Marquis, Donald G. (1945–1947)[b]
Martin, Barclay (1967–1968)[f]
Martin, Roy P. (1993–1996)[g]
Martinez, Floyd (1974–1976)[g]
Matarazzo, Ruth G., vice-chair (1980–1982)[g]
McCluskey-Fawcett, Kathleen, chair (1985–1987)[g]
McKinley, Donna (1980–1982)[g]
Melton, Arthur W. (1952–1955)[d]
Meyers, Roger, chair (1980–1982)[g]
Mezey, Michael L. (1999–2001)[g]
Miller, James G. (1946–1947)[a]
Miller, Thomas, chair (1986–1988)[g]
Moldawsky, Stanley (1993–1996)[g]
Moody, Marcia J. (1999)[g]
Moore, Bruce V., chair (1945–1947)[a], (1952–1954)[d]
Mowrer, O. Hobart (1948–1949)[c]
Murphy, Michael J. (1996–2001)[g]
Nagle, Richard J. (1988–1990)[g]
Nagy-Reich, Jill N., chair (1982–1984)[g]
Nickelson, David W. (1994–1995)[g]
Nobel, Merrill (1979–1981)[g]

O'Leary, Virigina E. (1993–1997)[g]
Orgel, Sidney A., chair (1979–1981)[g]
Osipow, Samuel (1975–1977)[g]
Owens, William A. Jr. (1963–1966)[f]
Packard, Ralph E. (Ted) (2000–2002)[g]
Patterson, Marcus D. (2000)[g]
Patterson, Tom W. (1980–1982)[g]
Patton, Michael J., chair (1994–1999)[g]
Penn, Nolan (1981–1983)[g]
Penner, Louis A. (1991–1997)[g]
Pepinsky, Harold B., chair (1954–1957)[f]
Peterson, Donald, chair (1977–1979)[g]
Peterson, Roger L. (1999–2001)[g]
Phillips, Beeman (1971–1974)[g]
Phillips, Leslie (1955–1958)[f]
Phillips, Susan D., chair (1996–2001)[g]
Pooler, Rosemary (1981–1983)[g]
Pomeroy, Donald S. (1967–1970)[f]
Pottharst, Karl E. (1970–1973)[f,g]
Prossey, Sidney L. (1945–1947)[b]
Raimy, Victor C. (1952–1955)[d], (1967–1968)[f]
Ray, William J. (1995–2000)[g]
Richards, Thomas W., chair (1959–1962)[f]
Richardson, M. W. (1946–1947)[b]
Robinson, Donna L. (1996–1997)[g]
Rodnick, Eliot H. (1952–1955)[d,f]
Roe, Anne, chair (1958–1961)[f]
Rosenzweig, Saul (1951–1953)[d]
Ross, Alan O. (1964–1967)[f]
Sanford, R. Nevitt (1947–1949)[c]
Saper, Bernard (1963–1966)[f]
Sarason, Irwin, chair (1966–1970)[f]
Schafer, Robert (1972–1975)[g]
Schlosberg, H. (1951–1954)[d]
Schmidt, Lyle, chair (1987–1989)[g]

Schofield, William, chair (1960–1963)[f]
Scott, Norman, vice-chair (1986–1988)[g]
Sears, Robert R., chair (1945–1947)[b]
Seeman, Julius (1966–1969)[f]
Shaffer, Laurance F., chair (1945–1947)[a], (1947–1949)[c]
Shakow, D., chair (1947–1949)[c]
Shartle, Carroll L. (1945–1947)[b]
Shealy, Craig N. (1993–1994)[g]
Sheridan, Edward P., chair (1989–1991)[g]
Sholl, M. Jeanne (1998–2000)[g]
Silverman, Wade H. (1998–2000)[g]
Simmons, William L., chair (1971–1974)[g]
Sklover, Philip (1976–1978; 1979–1981)[g]
Snyder, William U. (1953 1956)[f]
Solway, Kenneth S. (1990–1992)[g]
Speilberger, Charles D., chair (1967–1970)[f]
Strother, Charles R. (1953–1956)[f]
Super, Donald E. (1951–1953)[e]
Tate, Penfield (1984–1986; 1991–1995)[g]
Teague, Terri L. (1998)[g]
Terrell, David (1984–1986)[g]
Thomas, Charles (1974–1976)[g]
Thompson, Clare W. (1952–1955)[e], (1965–1968)[f]
Thornton, Dozier, chair (1970–1973)[f]
Toomey, Laura (1987–1989)[g]
Tyler, Leona E. (1957–1960)[f]
Ungar, Manya (1993–1998)[g]
Vane, Julia R. (1975–1977)[g]
Vasquez, Carmen I. (1993–1995)[g]
Vasquez-Nuttall, Ena (1998–2000)[g]
Walker, Edward L., chair (1964–1967)[f]
Warren, Neil D. (1951–1952)[d]
Watson, Robert I., chair (1955–1958)[f]
Weinberg, Richard A. (1978–1980)[g]
Wellner, Alfred, chair (1974–1976; 1977–1979)[g]
Whitmer, Caroll A. (1956–1959)[f]
Wickens, Delos D., chair (1951–1953)[d]
Wiens, Arthur, chair (1976–1978)[g]
Wrenn, C. Gilbert (1951–1953)[d], (1965–1968)[f]

---

[a]Committee on Clinical Psychology
[b]Committee on Graduate and Professional Training
[c]Committee on Training in Clinical Psychology
[d]Committee on Doctoral Education
[e]Committee on Practicum Training
[f]Committee of Evaluation
[g]Committee on Accreditation

APPENDIX J: LIST OF CONFERENCES ON ACCREDITATION

Year	Conference	References
2001	Houston Conference on Counseling Psychology	No references yet available.
1997	Houston Conference on Specialty Education and Training in Clinical Neuropsychology	Hannay, H. J., Bieliauskas, L. A., Crosson, B. A., Hammeke, T. A., Hamsher, K. Des., & Koffler, S. P. (1998). Proceedings: The Houston Conference on Specialty Education and Training in Clinical Neuropsychology. *Archives of Clinical Neuropsychology, 13*(2), 154–249.
1992	Ann Arbor Conference	Larsen, K. G., Belar, C. D., Bieliauskas, L. A., Klepac, R. K., Stigall, T. T., & Zimet, C. N. (Eds.). (1993). *Proceedings of the National Conference on Postdoctoral Training in Professional Psychology.* Washington, DC: Association of Psychology Postdoctoral and Internship Centers.
1990	National Conference on Applied Master's Training	Lowe, R. H. (1990). *Executive summary: The national conference on applied master's training in psychology.* Pensacola, FL: University of West Florida.
1990	Gainesville Conference	Belar, C. D., & Perry, N. W. (1992). National conferences on scientist–practitioner education and training for the professional practice of psychology. *American Psychologist, 47,* 71–75.
1987	Atlanta Conference	Gazda, G. M., Rude, S. S., & Weissberg, M. (Section Eds.). (1988). Third National Conference for Counseling Psychology: Planning the future [Major contributions section]. *The Counseling Psychologist, 16.*

continues

(continued)

1987	Utah Conference	Bickman, L. (Ed.). (1987). Proceedings of the National Conference on Graduate Education in Psychology. *American Psychologist, 42*, 1041–1085.
1987	Gainesville Conference	Belar, C. D., Bieliauskas, L. A., Larsen, K. G., Mensh, I. N., Poey, K., & Roehlke, H. J. (Eds.). (1987). *Proceedings: National Conference on Internship Training in Psychology.* Washington, DC: Association of Psychology Postdoctoral and Internship Centers.
1986	Mission Bay Conference	Bourg, E. F., Bent, R. J., McHolland, J. D., & Strichy, G. (1989). Standards and evaluation in the education and training of professional psychologists: The National Council of Schools of Professional Psychology Mission Bay Conference. *American Psychologist, 44*, 66–72.
1983	National Working Conference on Education and Training in Health Psychology	Stone, G. C. (Ed.). (1983). *National working conference on education and training in health psychology.* Baton Rouge, LA: Land and Land.
1981	LaJolla Conference	Callan, J. E., Peterson, D. R., & Stichy, G. (1986). *Quality of professional psychology training: A national conference and self-study.* Norman, OK: Transcript Press.
1978	Virginia Beach Conference	Watson, N., Caddy, G. R., Johnson, J. H., & Rimm, D. C. (1981). Standards in the education of professional psychologists: The resolutions of the Conference at Virginia Beach. *American Psychologist, 36*, 514–519.
1973	Vail Conference	Korman, M. (Ed.). (1976). *Levels and patterns of professional training in psychology.* Washington, DC: American Psychological Association.
1965	Chicago Conference	Hoch, E. L., Ross, A. O., & Winder, C. L. (Eds.). (1966). *Professional preparation of clinical psychologists.* Washington, DC: American Psychological Association.
1964	Greyston Conference	Thompson, A. S., & Super, D. E. (Eds.). (1964). *The professional preparation of counseling psychologists: The report of the 1964 Greyston Conference.* New York: Columbia University Press.
1958	Miami Conference	Roe, A., Gustad, J. W., Moore, B. V., Ross, S., & Skokak, M. (Eds.). (1959). *Graduate education in psychology.* Washington, DC: American Psychological Association.
1955	Stanford Conference	Strother, R. (1956). *Psychology and mental health.* Washington, DC: American Psychological Association.
1954	Thayer Conference on School Psychology	Cutts, N. (1955). *School psychologists at midcentury: A report of the Thayer Conference on the functions, qualification, and training of school psychologists.* Washington, DC: American Psychological Association.

continues

(continued)

1951	Northwestern Conference	American Psychological Association, Committee on Counselor Training, Division of Counseling and Guidance. (1952). The practicum training of counseling psychologists. *American Psychologist, 7,* 182–188. American Psychological Association, Committee on Counselor Training, Division of Counseling and Guidance. (1952). Recommended standards for training counseling psychologists at the doctoral level. *American Psychologist, 7,* 175–181.
1949	Boulder Conference	Raimy, V. C. (Ed.). (1950). *Training in clinical psychology.* New York: Prentice Hall.

APPENDIX K:
JAMES MCKEEN CATTELL'S "RETROSPECT: PSYCHOLOGY AS A PROFESSION," 1937

JOURNAL OF CONSULTING PSYCHOLOGY

Retrospect: Psychology as a Profession

It would be a satisfaction to stand at a place on the bridge of life from which it would be natural to be asked for an article on the future of psychology as a profession rather than for a retrospect. But unfortunately 1937 marks the fiftieth anniversary of my appointment as professor of psychology in the University of Pennsylvania.

Perhaps when a history—modern in point of view as well as in the period covered—comes to be written of these fifty years it will be evident that governments and wars have had less to do with the present condition of the world than the technological developments of science; these have quadrupled the productivity of labor and doubled the length of life. The industrial revolution can be dated from the use of the steam-engine of Watts in the coal mines of Cornwall a little more than a hundred and fifty years ago. The beginnings of a psychological revolution have occurred in the course of the past fifty years; it is possible that the development of psychology as a science and its application to the control of human conduct—may in the course of the coming century be as significant for civilization as has been the industrial revolution.

In an address given in 1917 on the occasion of the twenty-fifth anniversary of the founding of the American Psychological Association, I noted that of 307 members 272 were engaged in teaching, 16 in the applications of psychology. I then remarked that this latter group "now so small may at our fiftieth anniversary surpass in numbers those engaged in teaching." Then came our entrance into the war and the army service of our psychologists put the applications of psychology on the map and on the front page. We now have clinical, educational and industrial psychologists. There will not, however, be a profession of psychology until we have professional schools and professional standards.

The learned professions of medicine, law and theology had prehistoric origins; their professional schools with philosophy formed the medieval universities. Salerno, going back to the ninth century, was a school of medicine. In the first decades of the twelfth century Bologna became a school of civil law, Paris, a school of theology. Oxford, the third of the great medieval universities, like Paris, was primarily a school of theology.

Schools of engineering and of education are of much later origin; their history falls approximately within the past hundred years. In this relatively short time engineering has come to rival theology, law and medicine in its numbers; it probably surpasses them in opportunity for useful service, in adequate rewards, in freedom from external controls. Teaching is the greatest profession in its opportunity, the meanest of all professions in its performance. From the one-room country school to the graduate faculty of the university the teachers are unselected and untrained, without adequate salaries, without freedom. Educational administration is, however, becoming a profession—witness the professional school of the Columbia Teachers College.

There is no real profession of teaching because there has been no adequate science of psychology. Engineering had to wait for the development of the mathematical and physical sciences; medicine was an empirical art until it could be based on these and on the biological sciences. Law and theology, depending on tradition, precedent, words and an obsolete psychology of property rights and souls, of rewards and punishment, of motives, virtue and sin, are at present in the position of medicine and engineering before they had a foundation of science. Like education they must apply the psychology that we have and await the psychology that is to come, before they can attain the position of engineering and medicine.

We have schools of architecture in our universities, recently also schools of government, of journalism and of commerce. In addition there are schools of music and the plastic arts, but they are hardly professional schools. All these schools and professions depend on psychology to the same extent as do theology, law and education. Indeed, while medicine and engineering may rest primarily on the zoological and physical sciences, the place of psychology is not small. This is obvious for medicine; the physician needs psychology as well as drugs. The engineers have placed in their great building in New York City the inscription: "Engineering—the art of organizing and directing men and of controlling the forces and the materials of nature for the benefit of the human race." The selection, training and directing of men are problems of applied psychology; it is also for psychology to determine what does in fact benefit the human race. All the professions need a science of psychology and a profession of psychology.

The situation is appalling in its responsibility, for we are a feeble folk. Still our progress in numbers at least has been notable. When the American Psychological Association was founded in 1892 there were 31 members, about half of whom were not primarily psychologists. When I came to New York in the previous year I found only Henry Rutgers Marshall, M. Allen Starr and Nicholas Murray Butler. Now there are 278 members and associates of the American Psychological Association in the city. The Association had 127 members in 1902, 262 in 1912, 422 in 1922; now there are about 2,000 members and associates. This is a geometrical progression which promises numbers commensurate with those in other sciences and other professions. My prediction that at the fiftieth anniversary of the association the numbers engaged in applied work would equal those engaged in teaching will not be fulfilled—as is likely to be the case with predictions—so I shall repeat it for the seventy-fifth anniversary.

The space limit to which this article must be confined makes it impossible to sketch the history of the emergence of psychology as a profession in the course of the last fifty years. Two efforts in which I was interested failed. In the middle of the nineties when we were making the student tests at Columbia, I asked President Low to let us establish a psychological clinic which would make tests and examinations of the poor without charge and be supported by fees from those who could afford them. President Low, however, decided that it would not do to charge fees in a university laboratory. I was also concerned with the certification of psychologist by the American Psychological Association which finally was found not to be feasible.

Two undertakings in New York City are now proving themselves useful for psychology as a profession. This new *Journal of Consulting Psychology* represents the work of the Association of Consulting Psychologists. The contributors to the first number include four of the seven members of the executive committee of the Psychological Corporation. This organization was chartered in 1921 with twenty of our leading psychologists as directors. They included G. Stanley Hall, G. T. Ladd and E. B. Titchener, who had not until then cared for applied psychology. The stock was held by about 170 psychologists. Its objects and powers are defined in the charter as the "advancement of psychology and the promotion of the useful applications of psychology." It is planned to pay adequately for services of psychologists and to use the profits from professional and industrial work to support research. The corporation had in its early years a success of esteem and accomplished much to interest a large public in the uses of psychology. Now under Dr. Achilles and Dr. Link its work has become of some magnitude. One of its troubles this year has been the need to pay a considerable income tax on its profits.

This statement on psychology as a profession may end with a quotation from an address made at the International Congress of Arts and Science held at St. Louis in 1904 and printed in *The Popular Science Monthly* at the time. It reads:

> The present function of a physician, a lawyer, a clergyman, a teacher or a man of business is to a considerable extent that of an amateur psychologist. In the inevitable specialization of modern society, there will become increasing need of those who can be paid for expert psychological advice. We may have experts who will be trained in schools as large and well-equipped as our present schools of medicine, and their profession may become as useful and as honorable. Such a profession clearly offers an opportunity to the charlatan, but it is not the only profession open to him. For the present the psychological expert should doubtless be a member of one of the recognized professions who has the natural endowments, special training and definite knowledge of the conditions that will make his advice and assistance of a value. But in the end there will be not only a science but also a profession of psychology.[1]

---

[1]Cattell, J. M. (1904). The conceptions and methods of psychology. *The Popular Science Monthly*, 66, 186.
From "Retrospect: Psychology as a Profession," by J. M. Cattell, 1937, *Journal of Consulting Psychology*, 1, pp. 1–3. In the public domain.

INDEX

Academic psychology model, 97–104
    accreditation standards concern, history, 23–24
    culture of, 97–104
    and faculty quality, 120–121
    versus practitioner training models, 8, 23, 44, 97–101, 120–121
    rapprochement with practitioner models, 101–104
    and scientific-practitioner model, 24
Accreditation organizations, recognition of, 21, 23–24, 31–32
Accreditation Handbook (APA), 47
Accrediting Procedures of the American Psychological Association (1970), 16, 167–168
Adequacy standard, 44, 47
Advocacy, accreditation impact on, 97, 108
American Bar Association, 11, 129
American Library Association, 129
American Medical Association, 10
American Psychological Association
    accreditation reciprocity policy, 125, 128–129
    Commission on Accreditation autonomy issue, 54–55, 126, 129, 132
    and school psychology programs, 17–20
Ann Arbor Conference (1992), 81, 106, 177
Association of Psychology Postdoctoral Internship Centers
    function and membership, 70n1
    internship training statement, 71
    postdoctoral specialty training statement, 106
    student–trainee impairment issues, 93–94
Association of Specialized and Professional Accreditors, 30–31
Association of State and Provincial Psychology Boards, 95
Atlanta Conference (1987), 177
Autonomy requirement, challenge of, 27, 129, 132

Boulder Conference (1949), 45, 62, 78, 136, 161, 179

Boulder model. *See* Scientist–practitioner model

California School of Professional Psychology, 45
Canadian Psychological Association
    accreditation reciprocity, 125, 128–129
    and U.S. Department of Education policy, 128
Checklist approach
    abandonment of, 54–55
    and internship programs, 70
    problems with, 48
Chicago Conference (1965), 178
Clerkship standards, 62–63
Clinical internships. *See* Internship programs
Clinical neuropsychology specialty, 118–119
Clinical privileges, accreditation impact on, 95–96
Clinical psychology training. *See* Professional training programs
Coherence of program criterion, 52, 55
Commission for the Recognition of Specialties and Proficiencies in Professional Psychology, 107, 117
Committee on Accreditation
    academic and practitioner model issue, 102–104
    autonomy requirement challenge, 27, 54–55, 126, 129, 132
    burdens on members, 47–48
    criticism of, 21, 23
    current status of, 48–56
    federal government impact on, 17, 132–133
    history, 16–17, 23–24, 45–47
    and internship programs, 72, 74
    outcomes-based model of, 116
    past and present members, 173–176
    and postdoctoral programs, 84–85
    practitioner membership, 101, 108–109
    reformation of, 25–29
    and specialty programs, 118
    and U.S. Department of Education policy, 132

Committee on Training in Clinical Psychology, 42–43
Competency-based assessment. *See* Outcomes-based model
Confidentiality, 16
Conflict of interest issue, 54–55, 129, 132
Core curriculum, 99–100
Council of Graduate Departments of Psychology, 51–54
Council of Higher Education
  areas of service, 31
  formation of, 29–32
  and practitioner accreditation involvement, 101
  recognition of accrediting organizations function, 31–32
Council on Postsecondary Accreditation, 15, 17, 20–21, 23–24, 29–32
Counseling centers, internship programs, 75–78
Counseling internships, 63, 65, 70
Credentialing
  accreditation impact on, 94–97
  prescriptive standards trend, 46
Creedal oath, 48
"Criteria for Evaluating Training Programs . . ." (APA, 1958), 63–65
Curriculum standards, 99–100

Department of Education. *See* U.S. Department of Education
Disclosure policy, 171
Dissertation requirement, internship programs, 72
Distance learning, 57, 109, 125
Diversity, challenge of, 57–58
Due process, accreditation principle, 16

Electronic learning, 57, 109, 125
Ethnic groups
  accreditation issue history, 47
  future challenges, 57–58
Examination for Professional Practice of Psychology scores, 91, 94, 108
Excellence standard, 47
Experiential learning criterion, 103–104

Faculty–trainers, impairment, 93
Fairness principle, 16
Faith-based institutions, 48–50
Federal regulations. *See also* U.S. Department of Education

and accreditation body recognition, 32–33
  accreditation impact of, 12–13
  and self-regulation guideline, 13
Flexner Report, 10–11

Gainesville conferences, 70–72, 78, 81, 177, 178
"Gate-keeping" function, 20
Generalism
  in clinical training, 40–42
  internship programs, 71, 86
  and standards versus principles issue, 43–44, 46
GI Bill, 14–15
Government policy. *See* U.S. Department of Education
"Graduate Internship Training in Psychology" (1945), 62, 141–145
Greystone Conference (1964), 178
Guidelines and Principles for Accreditation of Programs in Professional Psychology (1996)
  faculty self-study orientation of, 58, 75
  internship programs, 72–75
  outcome-based approach in, 52, 55, 74–75, 116
  specialty accreditation broadening in, 50, 52
  training principles emphasis in, 55–56, 72, 74
Guidelines approach, and generalism model, 42
Houston conferences, 177

Impairment dilemma, 92–94
Institutional practice, privileging, 95–96
Internet challenge, 57, 109, 125
Internship programs, 61–89
  accreditation history, 61–89
  accreditation impact on, 86–87
  committee reports (1945, 1947), 61–62, 141–145, 147
  current issues, 85–87
  doctoral programs relationship, 69–70, 75, 77
  Gainesville Conference (1987), 70–72, 78
  generalism versus specialty training, 71, 86
  growth in accredited programs, 75–78
  and managed care, 85–86

practicum hours, 78
    in university counseling centers, 75–78
Interorganizational Council for the Accreditation of Postdoctoral Training Programs, 74, 77, 84

Joint Council on Professional Education in Psychology
    function, 28, 137
    report of, 25, 81, 105, 169–172
Joint ventures, 18–20

Knowledgeable laymen, 17

LaJolla Conference (1981), 178
Law profession, 11
Licensing
    accreditation impact on, 94–98
    and managed care contracts, 96
    professional degree link, 13

Managed care
    accreditation effect on contracting, 96–97
    reimbursement requirements, 85
Master's level accreditation, 53–54, 119–120
Medical education, 10–11
Menninger Clinic Conference (1972), 79
Mentorship model, 119
Miami Conference (1958), 79, 178
Minority populations
    accreditation issue history, 47
    future challenges, 57–58
Mission Bay Conference (1986), 178

National accreditation conferences, 45, 177–179
National Association of School Psychologists, 17–20
National Commission on Accrediting, 13–17
National Conference on Applied Master's Training, 177
National Council on Accreditation in Teacher Education, 17–19
National Register of Health Service Providers in Psychology, 95
Nonaccreditation, consequences of, 114
Norman, Oklahoma conference, 106
North American Association of Masters Psychologists, 120
Northwestern Conference (1951), 179

Outcomes-based model, 115–117
    adoption of, 29, 55
    definitional confusion, history, 43
    and internship programs, 74–75
    proliferation of training strategies consequence, 116–117
    and quality assurance, 115–117

Personality difficulties, student trainees, 92–93
Plea for the Training of Psychologists (Crane), 139–140
Policies of Accreditation Governance (APA), 29
Postdoctoral internship, 75, 77, 79
Postdoctoral residency accreditation, 78–87
    demand for, 119
    current issues, 85–87, 121
    generalist versus specialist issue, 86
    generic accreditation guidelines, 106–107
    history, 52, 78–85
    and managed care, 85–86
    self-study approach, 86
    socialization requirement, 85
    specialty practice preparation, 105
    value of, 86–87
Practicum standards, 43–44, 69, 78
Practitioners. *See also* Professional training programs
    accreditation standards reformation, 25–29
    accreditation work under involvement of, 101, 108–109
    Committee on Accreditation membership, 108–109
    culture of, 97–104
    and standards versus principles issue, 43–44
    training models, 45, 97–100, 120–121
    U.S. Department of Education definition, 133
Prescription privileges, training, 104–105, 124–125
Prescriptive standards, 46, 132–133
Principles versus standards issue, 43–44, 46–47, 55–56
Private practitioners. *See* Practitioners
Privileging, 95–96
Professional degree, first mention of, 135, 139–140
Professional Psychologist Certification Board, 120

Professional training programs
    versus academic programs, models, 23, 97–101, 120–121
        rapprochement, 101–104
    accreditation standards development, 22–29
    culture of, 97–104
    and faculty quality, 120–121
    self-study standard, 22
    specialism versus generalism, 40, 46–47
    taxonomy chaos, 29
Program consultation, 127
Provider panels, 96
Psychopharmacology training, 104–105, 124–125
Public accountability, 7–37
Public disclosure, accreditation outcomes, 33, 171
Public Health Service, 7, 153–154, 156, 161
Public policy, accreditation impact on, 97, 108

Quality standard
    adequacy standard contrast, 44, 47
    models of, 20
    and outcomes-based strategy, 115–117
    self-regulation mechanism, 12–13

Reciprocity, accreditation programs, 125, 128–129
Recognition of accreditation organizations, 21, 24, 31–32
"Recommended Graduate Training Program in Clinical Psychology" (APA, 1947), 62, 147
Recredentialing, and managed care standards, 96
Religion, and accreditation standards, 48–50
Reputation model, 20
Research-oriented programs. *See also* Academic psychology model
    culture of, 97–104
    practice integration value, 40
    versus professional-applied programs, 120–121
Residency training. *See* Postdoctoral residency accreditation

School psychology internships, 69, 70
School psychology programs, 17
Scientist–practitioner model. *See also* Academic psychology model
    and Boulder Conference, 45
    culture of, 97–100
    and faculty quality, 120–121
    future challenges, 58, 120–121, 131
    history, 42, 45
    internship programs, 62, 69
    versus practitioner–scholar model, 97–100, 120–121
Scope of accreditation, 118–120
Self-regulation
    accreditation underlying principle, 12–13, 20–22
    self-study relationship, 21
Self-study
    accreditation cornerstone, 21–22
    postdoctoral accreditation process, 80, 86
Site visit
    checklist mentality problem, 48
    history of guidelines, 43
    internship programs, 64–68
    self-study verification aspect, 21–22
    specialty programs, 117
Specialism
    versus generalism, 40, 46–47
    internship programs, 71, 86
Specialty programs, 104–108
    accreditation, 104–108, 117–119
        specialty-specific criteria need, 107–108
    increases in, 117–118
    and internships, 104–108
    postdoctoral training, 104–108, 118
    in psychopharmacology, 104–105
    taxonomy chaos challenge, 29
Standards
    in credentialing, 46
    versus principles, 43–44, 46–47
    struggle over, 11–13
Stanford Conference (1955), 79, 178
State licensing, accreditation impact on, 94–96
Student loans, and accountability rationale, 32
Student outcomes. *See* Outcomes-based model
Student–trainee impairment, 92–94
Supervision requirements, internships, 64, 69–70

Teaching hospitals concept, 11
Technology, challenges of, 57, 109, 125

Thayer Conference (1954), 178
Trainee impairment, 92–94

Unfunded internships, 85
University counseling centers, internships, 75–78
U.S. Department of Education
    accrediting body recognition, 32–33
    accreditation impact of, 12–13, 32–33
    and accreditation reciprocity, 128–129
    conflict of interest policy, 132
    prescriptive mindset of, 132–133
U.S. Office of Education, 16–17, 21

U.S. Public Health Service, 7, 153–154, 156, 161
Utah Conference (1987), 178

Vail Conference (1973), 23, 45–46, 178
Value orientation, and accreditation standards, 11–13
Veterans Administration
    accreditation impact of, 7, 39–40, 136, 155–156, 161
    postdoctoral training initiative, 119
Virginia Beach Conference (1978), 178
Virtual universities, 125

ABOUT THE EDITOR

Elizabeth M. Altmaier, PhD, is a professor of education and of community and behavioral health at the University of Iowa. She received her PhD in counseling psychology from The Ohio State University in 1977. Her research interests are in health-related quality of life, particularly among cancer patients, and she is principal investigator of the Adult Health Quality of Life substudy of the T Cell Depletion Trial sponsored by the National Heart, Lung, and Blood Institute. She is the current editor of *Clinician's Research Digest*. Dr. Altmaier began site-visiting for the Office of Accreditation in 1981. She was a member of the Committee on Accreditation from 1990 to 1994, serving as chair during the inauguration of the current 21-member format and the development of the revised criteria, procedures, and guidelines. She received the Distinguished Contribution to Education and Training in Psychology award from the American Psychological Association in 1994.